Delictual Liability

In Memoriam

W A W

Delictual Liability

J M Thomson LLB
Regius Professor of Law, University of Glasgow

Edinburgh
Butterworths
1994

United Kingdom	Butterworth & Co (Publishers) Ltd, 4 Hill Street, EDINBURGH EH2 3JZ and Halsbury House, 35 Chancery Lane, LONDON WC2A 1EL
Australia	Butterworths, SYDNEY, MELBOURNE, BRISBANE, ADELAIDE, PERTH, CANBERRA and HOBART
Canada	Butterworths Canada Ltd, TORONTO and VANCOUVER
Ireland	Butterworth (Ireland) Ltd, DUBLIN
Malaysia	Malayan Law Journal Sdn Bhd, KUALA LUMPUR
New Zealand	Butterworths of New Zealand Ltd, WELLINGTON and AUCKLAND
Puerto Rico	Butterworth of Puerto Rico, Inc, SAN JUAN
Singapore	Butterworths Asia, SINGAPORE
South Africa	Butterworth Publishers (Pty) Ltd, DURBAN
USA	Butterworth Legal Publishers, CARLSBAD, California, and SALEM, New Hampshire

A CIP Catalogue record for this book is available from the British Library

ISBN 0 406 02012 4

Typeset by Phoenix Photosetting, Chatham, Kent
Printed by Thomson Litho, East Kilbride

Preface

The purpose of this book is to give a clear account of the principles of delictual liability in modern Scots law. It is primarily intended for law students who require a firm grounding in this very important subject. Unlike W J Stewart's *Delict* (2nd edn, 1993, Greens), I have not attempted to be comprehensive but, instead, have concentrated on those areas of the law which, from experience, students find difficult to grasp. The intentional delicts are treated at length since a knowledge of these is, in my view, essential before the scope of liability for unintentional wrongs can be properly understood. I have then attempted to show how delictual liability operates in specific social and economic situations; here, in particular, a practitioner might also find the book useful. Throughout I have tried to make difficult concepts as simple as possible, without venturing, I trust, on the simplistic: the book has been structured to bring the maximum degree of coherence to the subject. Because I regard it as essential that students should use the primary sources when studying the law of delict, I have deliberately restricted references to the secondary literature.

I am grateful to Desmond Cheyne, Advocate, and Ewan McIntyre, Solicitor, for their invaluable help on the sections on damages and road accidents respectively. My secretary, Mrs Moira Smith, deserves my special thanks for her efficiency and always cheerful manner.

Before he died, Professor Bill Wilson had accepted the dedication of this book. Alas, he did not live to read the text. If he had done so, I am sure that Bill would have been a stern – but constructive – critic. Like so many lawyers in Scotland, I owe an immense debt to Bill, who was an inspirational teacher of delict. This book, however inadequate, is dedicated to him.

J M Thomson
The Law School
Glasgow University
16 May 1994

Contents

PART IV. DAMAGES

APPENDIX

Table of statutes

Table of cases

List of abbreviations

AC	Law Reports, Appeal Cases (House of Lords and Privy Council) 1890–
All ER	All England Law Reports 1936–
App Cas	Law Reports, Appeal Cases (House of Lords) 1875–90
CA	Court of Appeal
Ch	Law Reports, Chancery Division 1890–
D	Dunlop's Session Cases 1838–62
Exch	Exchequer Reports 1847–56
F	Fraser's Session Cases 1898–1906
FC	Faculty Collection (Court of Session) 1752–1825
FSR	Fleet Street Reports 1963–
GWD	Green's Weekly Digest 1986–
HL	House of Lords
Hume	Hume's Decisions (Court of Session) 1781–1822
ICR	Industrial Cases Reports 1972–
IRLR	Industrial Relations Law Reports 1972–
JC	Justiciary Cases 1917–
KB	Law Reports, King's Bench Division 1900–52
LR	Law Reports
M	Macpherson's Session Cases 1862–73
M & W	Meeson & Welsby 1836–47
Macq	Macqueen's House of Lords Reports 1851–65
NY	New York Court of Appeals Reports 1847–1955
PC	Judicial Committee of the Privy Council
QB	Law Reports, Queen's Bench Division 1891–1901, 1952–
QBD	Law Reports, Queen's Bench Division 1875–90
R	Rettie's Session Cases 1873–98
RPC	Reports of Patents, Designs and Trade Marks Cases 1884–
S	P Shaw's Session Cases 1821–38
SC	Session Cases 1907–
SC (HL)	House of Lords Cases in Session Cases 1907–
SCLR	Scottish Civil Law Reports 1987–

SJ	Scottish Jurist 1829–73
SLR	Scottish Law Reporter 1865–1925
SLT (Notes)	Notes of Recent Decisions in Scots Law Times 1946–81
SLT (Sh Ct)	Sheriff Court Reports in Scots Law Times 1893–
SLT	Scots Law Times 1893–1908, and 1909–
Sh App	P Shaw's Scotch Appeals (House of Lords) 1821–26
Sh Ct Rep	Sheriff Court Reports in Scottish Law Review
So Jo	Solicitor's Journal 1856–
TLR	Times Law Reports 1884–1952
WLR	Weekly Law Reports 1953–
WN	Law Reports, Weekly Notes 1866–1952

Introduction

The essence of the modern Scots law of delict is the obligation of a person to compensate another who has suffered loss as a result of the wrongful actions of that person. This obligation to pay compensation is called reparation. The obligation to make reparation when loss has been suffered as a result of a person's wrongful actions is obediential; it arises *ex lege* regardless of the will of the wrongdoer. In this respect, delictual obligations differ from contractual obligations which arise as a result of the agreement of the parties to a contract. However, the delictual obligation is similar to the obligation to make restitution when a person has been unjustifiably enriched by another, since the latter obligation also arises *ex lege*.

But unlike the obligation to make restitution, the delictual obligation to make reparation arises only when the loss has arisen as a result of the wrongful act of the person who caused the harm. It is only when a person has been at fault that the obligation to make reparation arises. In Scots law we use the term *'culpa'* is used to describe fault. *Culpa* covers both intentional and unintentional conduct which causes loss to another, but before there is liability the law must regard the conduct as wrongous. This is encapsulated in the brocard *damnum injuria datum*, viz loss caused by wrongous conduct.

Some examples will make the point clearer. If A intentionally assaults B causing him harm, A is under a delictual obligation to compensate B for his injuries: A is guilty of *culpa* because he deliberately intended to harm B by assaulting him, which the law regards as a wrongous act. If A drives his car carelessly on a public highway, and as a result injures B, a pedestrian, then A is under a delictual obligation to compensate B for his injuries: A is guilty of *culpa* because of his careless driving, which the law regards as a wrongous act. Thus we can say that modern Scots law begins from the premise that there is an obediential obligation on a person to make reparation to another who has sustained harm or loss as a result of the *culpa* or fault of the wrongdoer ie the wrongdoer's intentional or unintentional, but careless, conduct, which caused the harm or loss.

It is, however, not the case that a person who suffers loss as a result of another's intentional or unintentional, but careless, conduct will

1

always be entitled to reparation. The act which causes the harm or loss must be regarded by the law as wrongful (*injuria*). For policy reasons, certain acts are not regarded as wrongful in this sense. So for example, as we shall see,[1] A is free to undercut the prices of his competitor, B, even if B suffers economically; nor does it matter if A deliberately undercuts B's prices with the intention of putting B out of business. The reason for this is that in our society competition is to be encouraged even if persons suffer economically as a result. This is an example of *damnum absque injuria*, viz loss without wrongful conduct.

Before there is an obligation to make reparation, the victim must suffer harm or loss. But, in addition, this harm or loss must arise from an intrusion by the wrongdoer on a right or interest of the victim which is recognised by the law as reparable. One of the fascinating aspects of the law of delict is to see when the courts are prepared to recognise interests as reparable and when they do not.

So, for example, the law has long recognised as reparable a person's right to physical integrity so that if there is an intrusion on that right as a result of culpable conduct, the wrongdoer must make compensation for pain and suffering (*solatium*) and any economic loss arising from the injuries sustained, for example, loss of earning capacity. But the Scots law of delict has, hitherto, not recognised as a reparable interest a person's privacy and protection of that interest is likely to be achieved only by legislation.[2]

An area which has caused controversy is whether the law should recognise as a reparable interest economic loss sustained by a person where the economic loss does not derive from injury to that person's body or damage to his property.[3] So, for example, if A carelessly damages an electric cable owned by B with the result that there is a loss of power to C's factory, should C be able to obtain compensation for his loss of production (pure economic loss) if the power cut did not cause any physical damage to the machinery in his factory? B, of course, can seek reparation from A in respect of the physical damage to B's cable.

Scottish lawyers maintain that Scots law is based on principle rather than remedies. It is probably true to argue that the modern Scots law of delict is based on the general principle of an obediential, *ex lege* obligation to make reparation for loss sustained as a result of conduct which constitutes *culpa*. This, however, was not always the case and

---

1 Page 32 below.
2 See 'Infringment of Liberty' (Lord Chancellor's Dept, Scottish Office, July 1993): see p 221 below.
3 This matter is discussed at length in Chapter 4.

is, indeed, a comparatively recent development. In medieval times, before there was a centralised system for the prosecution of criminal offences, there was a close relationship between what would now be considered delictual actions and the enforcement of the criminal law. What we discover is that there were specific remedies to deal with particular situations which were common in those turbulent times. Stair lists the following:[1]

'besides those of a special name and nature, which are chiefly these, assythment, extortion, circumvention, spuilzie, intrusion, ejection, molestation, breach of arrestment, deforcement, contravention, forgery, which comes in more properly in the process of improbation'.

Three of these deserve further consideration to illustrate the close relationship which existed at that time between delictual or quasi delictual liability and the enforcement of the criminal law.

Assythment was concerned with the regulation of acts which caused death and was an attempt to avoid blood feuds. The remedy of assythment was an action for a sum of money

'to be payit be the committaris of slaughter, to the kin, bairnis and friends of any person that is slane . . . gevin to thame in contentatioun of the hurt, damnage and skeith sustenit be thane throw the wanting of the person who is slane, and for the skaith incurrit be thame thairthrow, and for the pacifying of their rancor'.[2]

Several features of the action should be noted. There had to be a crime which caused death or physical injury to the victim. The action could be brought by any person, however remote, who was a relative of the deceased or injured person. The damages depended on the wrongdoer's means, ie they were not simply compensatory, and, finally, no assythment was due if the wrongdoer was executed. Assythment arose *either* if the wrongdoer was convicted and because of his position received a lesser penalty than was due *or* if there was no conviction and the family of the deceased issued a document known as a letter of slains acknowledging receipt of assythment and petitioning the Crown not to proceed with a prosecution. The latter situation was more important because it short circuited the need for a criminal trial. With the establishment of a centralised system of public prosecution it became contrary to public policy that the victim or his family should be able to circumvent the normal prosecution process by issuing letters of slains. In practice, actions for assythment died out though they were still theoretically possible if the wrongdoer had been

1 *Institutions* IX, 5, 6.
2 Balfour *Practicks* p 516.

prosecuted but had not suffered the due pains of the law. At the same time, the common law developed an action under which the spouse and ascendants and descendants of a person who had been killed as a result of the defender's *culpa* could obtain reparation in respect of the death, ie they could bring an action in delict.

An attempt to revive an action of assythment was made in *McKendrick v Sinclair*.[1] A workman was killed by an electric shock allegedly due to the negligence of his employer. He had financially supported his sister and two brothers. They could not bring an action in delict because at common law brothers and sisters of the deceased had no title to sue.[2] However, the Lord Advocate was not prepared to prosecute the defender or to concur if the relatives had sought a private prosecution. The old practice of letters of slains was inappropriate as the employer denied liability for culpable homicide. Accordingly, assythment would only have been available on the old authorities if there had been a conviction. As this was not the case, the action failed as it did not fall within the recognised parameters of the remedy.[3] Lord Simon of Glaisdale was, however, prepared to dismiss the action on a more radical ground viz that in spite of being a common law remedy assythment had fallen into desuetude, ie had become absolescent:

'This Brunnhilde [assythment] would awake in our uncongenial modern Niebelheim. This Rip van Winkle would find *Eisten*'s case firmly embodied in the law, that private prosecutions are extinct, that capital punishment for homicide has been abolished, and that damages are related to loss to the pursuer and not to the means of the defender. Even if this Sleeping Beauty were so attractive as to tempt your Lordships to favour her with your kisses she could not live happily ever after'.[4]

Asythment was finally laid to rest when it was abolished by section 8 of the Damages (Scotland) Act 1976 which extended title to sue in respect of the death of a relative to include the deceased's brothers and sisters[5] thus closing the lacuna revealed in the *McKendrick* case.

The second old remedy we should consider is contravention of lawburrows. This was a method of primitive law enforcement in the absence of an effective police force and system of public prosecution of criminal offences. If a person had reasonable grounds to believe

1 1972 SC (HL) 25, 1972 SLT 110.
2 *Eisten v North British Railway Co* (1870) 8 M 980.
3 *McKendrick v Sinclair* 1972 SLT 110 at 113 per Lord Reid and at 120 per Lord Kilbrandon, 1972 SC (HL) 25.
4 1972 SLT 110 at 117.
5 For discussion of the right to sue in respect of the death of a relative, see Chapter 13.

that he or his family or their property was in danger from another person, he could apply to a court to have that person find caution (ie to lodge a sum of money in court) not to harm him or his family or their property. This was known as lawburrows. In other words, the defender was ordered not to molest the pursuer or the family or their property on pain of losing caution ie the money lodged in court. If the defender contravened the non-molestation order, he could be sued in an action of contravention of lawburrows for forfeiture of the caution.[1] With the advent of effective law enforcement agencies, the use of lawburrows declined, though it is thought that the action is still technically competent.[2]

Finally there is the action of spuilzie. This action arose when the defender interfered with the possession of another's moveable property, for example, stole cattle or sheep. The pursuer was the owner of the property.[3] The action was to have the property returned, or its value. But the quasi-criminal nature of the action is illustrated by the fact that the pursuer was entitled to violent profits, ie all the profits which the pursuer might have made from the property while in possession of the defender. In many situations, spuilzie has been overtaken by the general principle of liability for *culpa*.[4]

We have seen, then, how these specific remedies had important quasi-criminal aspects. While it is clear that lawburrows and spuilzie remain, theoretically at least, part of Scots law, in practice they have largely been overtaken by the development of effective law enforcement agencies and the general principle of liability to make reparation for loss caused as a result of the defender's *culpa*. Stair laid the basis for the general principle of delictual liability when he recognised that to cause damage by delinquence gave rise to an obediential obligation to make reparation for the damage caused: *damnum injuria datum*. This was a general innominate remedy, based on the defender's *culpa*, which includes deliberate as well as careless conduct. Stair treated the nominate Scottish remedies as simply aspects of the general obligation to make reparation for loss caused by *culpa*.[5] This general obligation was accepted by the later institutional writers.[6] In attempting this synthesis, reliance was, of course, placed on Roman law and in

---

1 Lawburrows Acts 1429 and 1581.
2 On lawburrows generally see 13 *Stair Memorial Encyclopaedia* paras 901–926; *Morrow v Neil* 1975 SLT (Sh Ct) 65.
3 Though there is a dictum of the sheriff in *FC Finance Ltd v Brown & Son* 1969 SLT (Sh Ct) 41 that lawful *possession* of property is sufficient.
4 See pp 22 ff below.
5 *Stair* I, 9, 2.
6 See, for example, Erskine *Institute* III, 1.

particular liability under the Lex Aquilia which included liability for unintentional, but careless, conduct.

While the modern Scots law of delict can be traced back to the institutional writers, nevertheless their treatment is not extensive. Instead, the principles of the law of delict are largely the creation of the courts. The judges have had to develop the law to take account of the increase of potential injury to persons and damage to property created by industrialisation, mass production and distribution of goods, easier access to information, and the motor car. At the same time, they have also appreciated that there must be limits on a person's liability, particularly for unintentional conduct, if that person is to continue to engage in conduct which is socially and economically desirable, even if it is potentially harmful. The traditional Scots law solution has been to restrict liability by insisting that it is only triggered by the defender's fault and by refusing to recognise certain kinds of harm as reparable interests. This book is largely concerned with the rules of common law and statute which have developed to achieve this balance. However, in some areas it has been considered socially and economically desirable that persons should recover compensation for physical injury or damage to property without the need to establish fault on the part of the defender. While the concept of *culpa* has proved flexible enough to create liability where the degree of *moral* blame on the part of the defender is small,[1] nevertheless, some degree of fault is required.[2] Accordingly, legislation has been necessary to introduce into Scots law what is known as strict liability, ie where a person can be liable in delict for breach of duties imposed by a statute without the need for the person who suffers the injury or damage to establish fault. In a modern context, it is therefore important to discuss the principles of strict liability in relation to the breach of statutory duties imposed by some, at least, of the most important statutes.

Nevertheless, it is the author's primary intention to concentrate on the common law principles which underlie delictual liability for *culpa*, ie intentional and unintentional wrongdoing. The book begins with a study of delictual liability for intentionally harmful conduct; the second part contains an analysis of the general principles of liability

---

1 Particularly as the criterion for fault in the context of unintentional conduct is the failure to reach the standards of the reasonable person, as opposed to the standards which the particular defender could morally be expected to reach: see Chapter 3 below.

2 But, for example, where a person has used his property in a potentially very dangerous way, the degree of fault is small: *Kerr v Earl of Orkney* (1857) 20 D 298, 30 SJ 158: see pp 154 ff below.

for unintentional, but careless, conduct; the third part considers delictual liability in the context of some important social and economic relationships. Included in this part is a chapter on defamation and verbal injury where different principles apply. The book ends with a short chapter on damages.

Part I
INTENTIONAL DELICTS

CHAPTER 1

Intentional delicts in respect of persons and property

A. INTRODUCTION

As we have seen,[1] *culpa* includes (a) deliberate conduct intended to harm the victim or the victim's property and (b) unintentional, but careless, conduct, which has harmed the victim or the victim's property. In the case of unintentional conduct, the range of victims is *prima facie* indeterminate, ie it could potentially include any person who has been harmed by the conduct. Because of this, the law has had to invent devices for limiting the number of persons who are entitled to sue in delict if they suffer loss or harm as a result of a person's careless conduct. The most important of these devices[2] is the concept of a duty of care: it is only a person to whom the defender owes a duty of care who can sue in delict for loss arising from the defender's careless conduct.[3]

However, where an act is done deliberately to harm a particular person, there is not the same degree of difficulty as the potential pursuer is normally determinate:[4] the pursuer is the person whom the defender *intended* to harm by his conduct and there is no need to invoke the concept of a duty of care. Intentional delicts in relation to persons and property are discussed in this chapter.

---

1 Page 1 above.
2 There are other devices such as remoteness of injury and causation: see pp 109 ff and Chapter 6 below.
3 The duty of care is discussed at Chapter 3 below.
4 There can be cases where this might not be so: A may intend to harm B by blowing up B's house but injure C instead; while it is thought that A will be liable to C, such cases are rare in practice.

B. INTENTIONAL DELICTS RELATING TO PERSONS

(1) Assault

'Everyone who lives under the protection of the law has an absolute right to the safety of his person; and wherever this right is invaded there is in Civil law a provision for redress of injury, as well as in penal law a punishment for the crime.'[1] A physical assault is a common law crime provided there is the necessary evil intent on the part of the perpetrator (*dolus*).[2] Assault also constitutes a delict. But even though an assault is not criminal because of the absence of *evil* intent, it is still an actionable delict, provided the defender intended to invade the physical integrity of the pursuer. So where A playfully attacked B in order to make B engage in sport, it nevertheless constituted an actionable wrong even although it was done 'for a lark'.[3] If, however, the 'victim' consents to the act, it does not amount to an assault for the purposes of delict,[4] since the essence of the delict is *non-consensual* invasion of bodily integrity.

Where this principle is important is in respect of medical procedures. If a doctor or dentist carries out a medical procedure on an adult[5] without the patient's consent, then the doctor or dentist is liable to make reparation.[6] Although this will usually not be a crime because of the absence of evil intent on the part of the doctor or dentist, it is still a delict. The patient can obtain reparation not only for any resulting patrimonial loss but also for *contumelia* ie, the insult suffered as a result of the non-consensual invasion of bodily integrity. The fact that the procedure was carried out for the patient's benefit is irrelevant.

The question then arises as to when the patient's consent is valid in order that the doctor or dentist concerned can avoid potential

1 Bell *Principles* para 2028.
2 See R A A McCall Smith and D Sheldon *Scots Criminal Law* p 33.
3 *Reid v Mitchell* (1885) 12 R 1129.
4 In criminal law, if there is evil intent on the part of the accused, the consent of the 'victim' is irrelevant: a person cannot consent to a crime: *Smart v Advocate* 1975 SC 30, 1975 SLT 65.
5 A person under the age of 16 will have legal capacity to consent if the doctor or dentist is of the view that the young person is capable of understanding the nature and probable consequences of the medical treatment or procedure: Age of Legal Capacity (Scotland) Act 1991, s 2(4). This provision is only enabling, ie it gives the child capacity to consent. If the child were to refuse medical treatment that was clearly in the interests of the child, the medical practitioner could, it is submitted, look to the child's guardian for a valid consent. The position in England is similar: *Re W (a minor)* [1992] 4 All ER 627.
6 However, in an emergency, if the patient is, for example, unconscious, a doctor may proceed without the patient's consent if it is *necessary* for the patient's well-being to do so.

delictual liability. It is clear that a patient must be given sufficient information upon which to give consent. All medical and dental procedures involve a risk to the patient even if *properly* carried out. This could be, for example, side effects of a drug or an operation or other medical procedure. In the United States,[1] there has evolved a doctrine known as 'informed consent'. Under this doctrine, if the patient is not informed of all the risks inherent in the proposed medical procedure which a reasonable *patient* should know, then the patient's apparent consent is vitiated and the doctor or dentist can be sued for assault.

An attempt to introduce this doctrine into English law was rejected by a majority of the House of Lords in *Sidaway v Board of Governors of the Bethlem Royal Hospital*.[2] Instead, it was held that a doctor need only disclose to a patient the risks inherent in a medical procedure which were regarded by *a responsible body of medical opinion* as proper to disclose. Two important points follow. First, provided the doctor or dentist has disclosed those risks which a responsible body of medical or dental opinion would disclose, the patient's consent is valid and the patient cannot sue in assault where an injury is sustained, the risk of which it was *not* necessary to disclose. The injury must, of course, be inherent in the medical procedure when properly carried out; if the injury arose as a result of careless treatment, the patient can sue the doctor or dentist for breach of a duty of care since the patient has *not* consented to the risk of injury as a result of professional incompetence.[3] Second, if the doctor or dentist has not disclosed those risks which a responsible body of medical or dental opinion would disclose, then if the patient sustains *any* injury which is inherent in the medical procedure when properly carried out, the patient can sue the doctor or dentist; but it would appear from *Sidaway* that the patient sues for a breach by the doctor or dentist of the duty of care which they owe to their patients to disclose those risks inherent in the medical procedure which a responsible body of medical or dental opinion would disclose, ie for an unintentional wrong and not an assault. In other words, the general principles of liability for *culpa* rather than assault apply to this particular issue. While *Sidaway* is an English case, it has been followed in Scotland.[4]

---

1 *Canterbury v Spence* (1972) 464 F 2d 772.
2 [1985] AC 871, [1985] 1 All ER 643, HL (Lord Scarman dissenting).
3 On professional delictual liability, see Chapter 7 below.
4 *Moyes v Lothian Health Board* 1990 SLT 444. There it was observed by the Lord Ordinary (Caplan) at 447 that provided there was a failure to warn of risks, which amounted to a breach of a duty to care (ie that a responsible body of medical opinion would have disclosed some risks) it did not matter that the injury sustained by the pursuer was one the risk of which it was not necessary to disclose. However, the patient must show that he would not have agreed to the operation if the risks which should have been disclosed, had been disclosed.

In practice, most patients simply sign a general consent form in respect of risks inherent in treatment. Nor is it clear when a reasonably prudent doctor should inform a patient of a particular risk inherent in a medical procedure. In *Sidaway* the risk of injury was slight, less than 1 per cent, but if it materialised the injury could have been severe. Yet the House of Lords took the view that since a majority of responsible medical practitioners would not have informed the patient of such a risk, no delictual liability was incurred.

As we have seen,[1] consent of the victim prevents delictual liability for assault from arising. This explains why there is no liability for assault in sports involving physical contact: boxing, rugby, soccer etc[2]. But the players give consent only to the physical contact inherent in the sport, so that there will be liability if injury is sustained as a result of conduct outwith the rules of the sport, if, for example, a rugby player punches, as opposed to tackles, an opponent. While an assault usually takes the form of physical contact this is not strictly necessary; thus to spit at a person or shake a fist in a threatening manner is an assault.

There is a complete defence to an action of assault if it was the result of an unavoidable accident or carried out in self-defence. If the assault took place as a result of the pursuer's provocation, the damages can be reduced. 'No verbal provocation whatever can justify a blow . . . But . . . verbal provocation is a good ground for mitigating damages . . .'[3] The rationale is that as reparation for intentional wrong is based on *culpa*, the pursuer must come to the court with clean hands; if the pursuer's hands are not clean, the pursuer's damages can be reduced.[4]

One group of persons in Scotland remains without a remedy if assaulted. These are children who have been physically chastised by their parents. The force used by a parent when physically chastising a child must be reasonable but it is irrelevant that a parent loses his or her temper at the time.[5] Parents can delegate the right physically to chastise their children to persons who have *de facto* care of the child.[6] At common law, school teachers had an *independent* right physically to discipline their pupils; however, local authority schools and private schools have now banned the use of corporal punishment.[7] The

1 Page 12 above.
2 Cf non-physical sports, for example, golf: *Lewis v Buckpool Golf Club* 1993 SLT (Sh Ct) 43.
3 *Anderson v Marshall* (1835) 13 S 1130 at 1131 per the Lord President (Hope).
4 *Ross v Bryce* 1972 SLT (Sh Ct) 76.
5 *B v Harris* 1989 SCLR 644, 1990 SLT 208 (mother strapped her 7-year-old child who had called the mother 'a fucking bastard'). Cf *Cowie v Tudhope* 1987 GWD 12-395 (father hit 15-year-old son with the leg of a table).
6 *Stewart v Thain* 1981 JC 13, 1981 SLT (Notes) 2.
7 Education (Scotland) Act 1980, s 48A (local authority schools); Education Act 1993, s 295 (private schools).

Scottish Law Commission has recommended that parents should not have a defence to an action of assault on their children on the grounds that they were disciplining the child, if the child was struck with a stick, belt or other object, or in such a way as to cause or risk causing, pain or discomfort lasting more than a very short time.[1] It is also recommended that a person who has care and control of the child should have no greater right to discipline a child than a parent.[2]

Where an assault constitutes a crime, the victim may receive compensation under the Criminal Injuries Compensation Scheme.

(2) Seduction and entrapment

Closely related to assault is the delict of seduction. In a case of assault the essence of the delict is the invasion of a person's bodily integrity without consent. Thus, for example, rape is actionable as an assault because sexual intercourse was obtained without the woman's consent. Conversely, if a woman consents to sexual intercourse, no assault is committed as she has consented. In the case of seduction, the woman gives consent to sexual intercourse, but her consent is vitiated because it was obtained by the man as a result of deception or abuse of position. In the leading case of *Murray v Fraser*,[3] a young girl who was naive in sexual matters allowed a trusted member of the family to have sexual intercourse with her on his assurance that nothing would happen to her; in fact she became pregnant. The defender was held liable in seduction because he had abused a position of trust and had taken advantage of the girl's innocence. A common example of deception was where a girl allowed a man to have sexual intercourse with her because he promised to marry her but had no intention to do so.[4]

Entrapment arises when a person has been fraudulently induced to enter into a marriage which is void. The most common example is when the defender purports to marry the pursuer, knowing that he is already married to another and has therefore fraudulently misrepresented that he was in a position validly to marry the pursuer.[5]

---

1 Report on Family Law (SLC no 135) rec 11 (a).
2 Ibid rec 11(b).
3 1916 SC 623.
4 It is thought that an action in seduction would continue to arise in these circumstances in spite of s 1(1) of the Law Reform (Husband and Wife) Scotland Act 1984 which declares *inter alia* that a promise to marry does not create any rights or obligations; this is because the delict of seduction does not arise solely from the breach of promise.
5 See, for example, *Burke v Burke* 1983 SLT 331, OH.

(3) Enticement

It is a delict for A to entice B to leave B's family without justification. The most obvious reason why A would wish to entice B away from B's family is for sexual purposes but it could, for example, arise if A wished B to join A's religious sect. The pursuers are B's family.[1] However, there is now no longer delictual liability if A induces B to leave his or her spouse.[2] A *husband* no longer has the right to sue his wife's paramour in damages;[3] these damages were awarded as *solatium* to the husband in respect of the unlawful sexual intercourse, ie his wife's adultery with the defender. It is, however, arguable that a husband can still sue a man for *solatium* if he raped the husband's wife; the wife, of course, would sue the rapist in assault.

(4) Injuries to liberty

'Next to life is liberty; and the delinquence against it are restraint and constraint. And though liberty itself be inestimable, yet the damages sustained through these delinquencies are reparable'.[4] A slight infringement of liberty is *prima facie* actionable: so, for example, where a lady was alleged to have been detained against her will for a quarter of an hour by the manager of a hydropathic establishment, her action in delict was held to be relevant.[5] Thus, as a general principle, no one can be detained against his or her will; if this occurs, there is liability in delict. The loss suffered is both the loss of liberty and the affront caused to the pursuer. However, detention can be justified at common law if, for example, a store detective arrests a person suspected of shoplifting and detains that person for a reasonable time until the police arrive.[6]

---

1 It has, however, been held that parents cannot sue for the loss of society of a child where the child has been removed from the parents as a result of intervention by the police in the interests of the child: *McKeen v Chief Constable, Lothian and Borders Police* 1994 SLT 93. If the removal is not justified, the *child* may have the right to sue for infringement of liberty.
2 Law Reform (Husband and Wife)(Scotland) Act 1984, s 2(2).
3 Divorce (Scotland) Act 1976, s 10.
4 *Stair* I, 9, 4.
5 *MacKenzie v Cluny Hill Hydropathic Co* 1908 SC 200, 15 SLT 518. In the course of his judgment, Lord Low said: 'It is averred that the manager detained this lady for fifteen minutes . . . and refused to let her go until she made an apology. If that be true it was an outrage . . .' (1908 SC 200 at 206).
6 Where, as in the example, the arrest is made without a warrant, the defender must establish that the suspicions were justified: *Pringle v Bremner & Stirling* (1865) 5 M (HL) 55; *Dahl v Chief Constable, Central Scotland Police* 1983 SLT 420. If an arrest is made under authority of a warrant, it is presumed that the detention was lawful and the onus rests on the pursuer to show that the detention was not justified.

In practice, cases of wrongful detention by ordinary members of the public are rare; instead, they arise when the person has been held under what purports to be lawful legal process. Even so, an action in delict may still arise, but there are formidable hurdles to success. This can be illustrated by *Henderson v Chief Constable, Fife Police*.[1] Medical laboratory scientific officers (MLSOs) staged a 'work in' at a hospital laboratory. When they refused to leave, the police were summoned. When they still refused to leave, the police broke down the door and arrested the MLSOs. They were taken to a police station where they were cautioned and charged; they were then placed in cells for one or two hours while the particulars they had given the police were checked. However, one of the men was handcuffed and a woman was required to remove her brassiere while in the cells. In an action for wrongful arrest and detention, it was conceded that the handcuffing was unjustified. The Lord Ordinary (Jauncey) held that the arrests were justified, that the police were entitled to take the MLSOs to the police station and that it was reasonable to detain them in the cells while the particulars were checked, as it was a small police station. However, although it was normal police practice to ask women to remove their brassieres while in custody to prevent them harming themselves, it was unjustified in this case as the woman had been co-operative, had made no attempt to escape and was not mentally unbalanced so as to cause harm to herself or others. The request that she remove the garment was unjustified and therefore constituted an interference with her liberty. It should be noticed, however, that the onus rests on the pursuer to prove that the exercise by the police of their discretion was neither reasonable nor necessary and accordingly unjustified.[2]

Where a person is wrongfully imprisoned by a court, superior court judges are immune from liability. Inferior judges, such as justices of the peace or magistrates can, however, be liable if the sentence is imposed maliciously and without probable cause.[3] If, for example, a magistrate lacks jurisdiction, he will be acting ultra vires, but there is no liability for a bona fide error in relation to statutory interpretation of his jurisdiction. Before he can succeed the pursuer must also prove that the magistrate was acting maliciously.[4] Where there has been a miscarriage of justice by the superior courts, the Secretary of State may make an *ex gratia* award of compensation to the victim.

---

1 1988 SCLR 77, 1988 SLT 361.
2 Ie that the detention was effected maliciously and without probable cause.
3 Criminal Procedure (Scotland) Act 1975, s 456(1).
4 *MacPhee v Macfarlane's Exr* 1933 SC 163, 1933 SLT 148.

In certain circumstances, statute provides for the lawful detention of an individual. The most important, perhaps, are the provisions which allow the compulsory detention of a person in a mental hospital. An application is made to a sheriff by a mental welfare officer or the patient's nearest relative[1] with the recommendation of two doctors, one of whom must be a psychiatrist, that the patient is suffering from a mental illness and is a danger to himself or others.[2] If the sheriff agrees that the statutory criteria are satisfied, an order is made for the compulsory detention of the patient in a mental hospital for a period of up to six months. The patient's nearest relative has the power to object to an application by a mental welfare officer. The detention can be renewed for further periods without recourse to the sheriff, but the patient has the right to appeal to a sheriff. The nearest relative can seek the discharge of the patient, and if it is refused, the nearest relative has the right to appeal to the sheriff for the patient's discharge.

C. INTENTIONAL DELICTS RELATING TO PROPERTY

(1) Heritable property

(a) Trespass

It is often wrongly assumed that Scots law does not recognise the delict of trespass. Indeed, it has been judicially opined that the word 'trespasser' means nothing more in Scots law than 'a person who intrudes on the lands of another without that other's permission'.[3] However, as we shall see, a person who deliberately enters another's land may be interdicted from doing so again and is liable to pay damages if he has caused any damage to the property. Trespass is a *temporary* intrusion into property owned by another, without the permission of the owner; for example, playing football in the owner's field or taking a short cut through his garden. Because heritable property is owned *a coelo usque ad centrum* (from the heavens to the centre of the earth) trespass protects an owner's air space as well as his land and the ground below his property. Thus, for example, the

---

1 For the list of nearest relatives, see the Mental Health (Scotland) Act 1984, ss 53–55; usually the nearest relative is the relative who is the highest on the list.
2 Ibid, s 18.
3 *Dumbreck v Addie* 1928 SC 547 at 554 per the Lord President (Clyde), 1928 SLT 341.

owner of a house successfully obtained an interdict preventing the respondent's crane from sweeping over his property, when the respondent was building on adjacent land.[1] Because of this, statute provides that aircraft may fly over a person's land without liability for trespass.[2]

The primary remedy for trespass is interdict. No damages are available unless there has been actual damage to the property as a result of the intrusion. There is therefore no liability for damages in Scots law merely for entering another's property. But the proprietor is entitled to use self help to remove a trespasser provided it is reasonable in the circumstances; for example, the owner could ask a trespasser playing football in his field to leave but not threaten him with violence if the trespasser refuses to do so. Interdict is an equitable remedy and is not granted automatically merely on proof of an unauthorised entry onto land. Before an interdict will be granted, further intrusions must be likely and the intention of the trespasser is important. Any potential damage to the land as a result of the trespass will also be a relevant consideration. In *Winans v Macrae*[3], for example, a shooting tenant of a lease of 200,000 acres was, perhaps understandably, refused an interdict to prevent a cottar's pet lamb from entering the property.

In summary, apart from specific statutory offences, in Scots law trespass is not per se criminal, does not give rise to an action in damages unless actual damage has been done to the property and will only result in an interdict if likely to recur again and any potential damage is not *de minimis*. However, the landowner is allowed a reasonable degree of self help to remove the trespasser.

In this section, trespass has been defined as a *temporary* intrusion on to land. If a person enters on to another's property with the intention of occupying it for an indefinite period, for example, a squatter, he does commit a criminal offence under the Trespass (Scotland) Act 1865. If the owner is not in possession at the time, the squatter is liable for the delict of intrusion; if the owner is in possession and has been wrongfully removed by the squatter, the squatter is liable for the delict of ejection. The rightful owner can seek summary ejection, violent profits[4] and compensation for actual losses incurred.

---

1 *Brown v Lee Constructions Ltd* 1977 SLT (Notes) 61, OH.
2 Civil Aviation Act 1982, s 76.
3 (1885) 12 R 1051.
4 Violent profits are the greatest profits the owner could have made if he was in actual possession of the land.

(b) Aemulatio vicini

When A owns land (X) which adjoins B's land (Y), A will be liable to B
if he uses his land (X) in such a way that is detrimental to B's
enjoyment of his land (Y). Before A is liable for using his land *in*
aemulationem vicini, A must use his land with the predominant motive
of harming B and not to further A's legitimate interests. If A's
predominant motive is not to harm B, then A cannot be liable for this
delict but A's conduct may amount to nuisance.[1]

An example of use of land *in aemulationem vicini* would be where A
intercepted water flowing below his land, with the predominant purpose of preventing the water percolating on to his neighbour, B's,
land.[2] However, when these facts were litigated in the English case of
Bradford v Pickles,[3] the House of Lords held that *aemulatio vicini* was
not part of English law. The case is important because Lord Watson,
the Scottish Lord of Appeal in Ordinary, stated obiter that *aemulatio*
vicini was also not part of Scots law.[4] This obiter dictum was, of
course, contrary to institutional authority. In *Campbell v Muir*[5] where
the defender spitefully exercised his right to fish from a boat in a river
in such a way that it prevented anglers on the opposite bank from
being able to cast their rods, the Lord President (Dunedin) held that
the pursuer would have been entitled to interdict because 'the defender was on the particular occasion acting *in aemulationem vicini* against
his neighbour's right, and that that was a just ground for complaint'.[6]
In *More v Boyle*[7] it was accepted by the sheriff that the doctrine of
aemulatio vicini is still part of Scots law.

As we have seen, liability arises only if it can be shown that the
defender acted with the predominant motive of harming the pursuer.
It is, of course, difficult to establish malice, so an objective assessment
must be made of the defender's conduct in order to infer malice. But
unlike nuisance, which is concerned with a continuing wrong,[8]
liability for use of land *in aemulationem vicini* can arise from a single act
of the defender, provided the predominant motive of harm to the
pursuer can be established.

---

1 On nuisance, see pp 159 ff below.
2 See Kames *Principles of Equity* (4th edn, 1800) p 42.
3 [1895] AC 587, HL.
4 [1895] AC 587 at 597–598.
5 1908 SC 387, 15 SLT 737.
6 1908 SC 387 at 393.
7 1967 SLT (Sh Ct) 38.
8 See pp 159 ff below.

(2) Moveable property

(a) Trespass

In *Leitch v Leydon*[1] the complainers sold soda water to their customers. Since the bottles were more expensive than the contents, it was a term of their contract with their customers that the complainers retained the ownership of the siphons which should be returned to them when the contents were used. Instead, some customers went to the respondent to have the bottles filled with *his* soda water. The House of Lords held that the complainers were not entitled to an interdict preventing the respondent from filling their bottles with soda water. While the complainers might have an action for breach of contract against their customers, the respondent had not incurred any delictual liability in filling the bottles with soda water at the request of the complainers' customers who had lawful possession of the siphons.[2] In the course of his speech, Viscount Dunedin said that the concept of trespass to moveables 'in a Scottish lawyer's mouth is a perfectly unmeaning phrase'.[3]

Nevertheless, where there have been 'sit-ins' on board a ship[4] or off-shore oil installations,[5] it has been held that the delict of trespass was committed even although neither the ship nor off-shore oil installations constitute heritable property. The Lord Ordinary (Dunpark) maintained that 'Scots law offers remedies for the unlawful *occupation* of property, be it heritable or moveable'.[6] It would appear, therefore, that where the trespass consists of the unlawful occupation of moveable property, for example, a car or caravan, a ship or oil installation, there is delictual liability even although the property concerned is technically moveable rather than heritable. Where the moveable property cannot be occupied, like the soda siphons in *Leitch v Leydon*,[7] merely to handle the property does not per se constitute the delict of trespass.

1 1931 SC (HL) 1.
2 Delictual liability would however arise if the respondent had intended to 'pass off' the soda water as that of the complainer. On passing off, see p 25 below.
3 1931 SC (HL) 1 at 12.
4 *Phestos Shipping Co Ltd v Kurmiawan* 1983 SC 165, 1983 SLT 388.
5 *Shell UK Ltd v McGillivray* 1991 SLT 667.
6 *Phestos Shipping Co Ltd v Kurmiawan* 1983 SLT 388 at 391.
7 1931 SC (HL) 1.

(b) Wrongful interference with moveable property

As we have seen,[1] unless moveable property is actually occupied, the delict of trespass is not available to the owner in Scots law. This does not mean that the owner of a moveable is without legal redress if a person wrongfully interferes with the property. However, the owner's remedy may lie in areas of the law other than the law of delict. Consider the following examples:

(1) A owns a horse. B steals the horse. Under the law of property, A is entitled to sue B for the return of the horse, ie A can vindicate (claim ownership of) the horse. If B had sold the horse to C, a bona fide purchaser for value, A can still vindicate against C because a *vitium reale* attaches to the horse.

(2) A owns a horse. B steals the horse and sells it to C. C slaughters the horse and boils it down to make glue. Under the law of property, the glue belongs to C. A can no longer vindicate as the horse, ie A's property, no longer exists. What remedies are available to A? First, if the delict still exists, A could sue B for spuilzie.[2] Second, he may have a delictual action against C on the general principles of *culpa*. If C knew the horse belonged to A, then A can sue C for intentionally destroying the horse. But even if C did not know that the horse belonged to A, A may be able to sue C if, in the circumstances, C was at fault in going ahead in boiling down the horse without inquiring whether or not B was the animal's true owner. Thus, in *Faulds v Townsend*,[3] a thief stole a horse which he sold in the middle of the night to the defender, who turned the unfortunate animal into glue. Because of the circumstances of the sale and the fact that the horse was in good condition, the court held that the defender was under a duty to inquire as to the ownership of the horse; he had not done so and was therefore at fault, and the owner could sue for damages under the general principles of *culpa*.[4] Finally, even if fault could not be established, A may have an action in restitution against C, in so far as C is *lucratus* as a result of his mistake as to the ownership of the horse.

(3) The modern equivalent of the horse, is, of course, the motor car. As a general rule, the same principles would apply if A's car was

---

1 Page 21 above.
2 See p 5 above. For an attempt to revive the delict see *FC Finance Ltd v Brown & Son* 1969 SLT (Sh Ct) 41.
3 (1861) 23 D 437, 33 SJ 224.
4 Ie because of his careless conduct in not satisfying himself as to the true ownership of the horse.

stolen. However, difficulties can arise where A is technically the owner of a car, for example, a finance company, which is being purchased by B, a hirer, on a contract of hire purchase; what is A's remedy if B sells the car in breach of the hire contract to C, a third party? These difficulties are illustrated by *FC Finance v Langtry Investment Co Ltd*.[1] FC Finance owned a motor car which was hired to Allan under a contract of hire purchase. In breach of the contract, Allan sold the car to McKay who traded as Medwin Motors. McKay sold the car on hire purchase to Kennedy. The hire purchase was financed by Langtry Investment Co and Kennedy paid the instalments. Part III of the Hire Purchase Act 1964 provides an exception to the *nemo dat quod non habet* principle and Kennedy as an innocent private purchaser acquired a good title to the car. Therefore FC Finance could not vindicate against Kennedy. McKay was a man of straw. FC Finance had registered the car with HP Information Ltd; any finance company could telephone HP Information Ltd and discover, before buying the car, whether it was subject to an existing hire purchase agreement. These complex facts are summarised in the diagram on page 24.

FC Finance's primary remedy was to sue Allan for breach of contract. However, Allan had emigrated to Canada. In these circumstances, FC Finance sought redress against Langtry Investment. It was held that there was no duty on Langtry Investment to check with HP Information Ltd before financing Kennedy's hire purchase of the motor car. However, because Medwin Motors had offered them cars subject to subsisting hire purchase agreements on previous occasions, Langtry Investment should have been on their guard and were therefore at fault – like the defender in *Faulds v Townsend*[2] – in not making inquiries. Therefore they were liable on general principles of *culpa*. The parties agreed that if the defenders were liable, the measure of damages would be the balance of the outstanding hire purchase payments owed by Allan to FC Finance.

This decision is controversial. The pursuer's loss was purely economic – there was no physical damage to the car. As we shall see below, in cases of unintentional wrongs, the courts are reluctant to allow recovery for pure economic loss. It is therefore doubtful whether there was sufficient proximity between the parties to impose a duty of care on the defenders to prevent the pursuer suffering pure economic loss as a result of the defender's careless conduct. This might have been a case where spuilzie should have been resurrected,

---

1 1973 SLT (Sh Ct) 11.
2 (1861) 23 D 437, discussed at p 22 above.

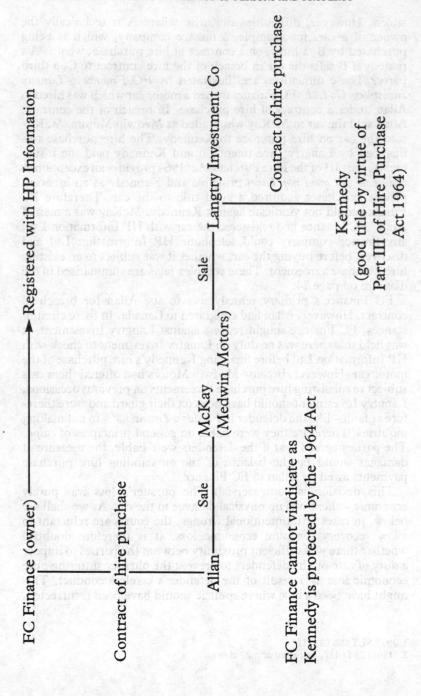

since the defender had wrongfully interfered with the possession of
the pursuer's moveable property. Another solution might have been
for the pursuer to have sued in restitution for the amount that the
defender was *lucratus* as a result of the mistaken dealings with the car.
Whatever the solution, the case is an important example of how the
law of delict cannot be treated in isolation from other areas of law
when considering the difficult issues that can arise in modern
commercial dealings.

(c) Goodwill – passing off

The goodwill and reputation of a business can be a very valuable asset.
Important elements of goodwill are the marketing devices used to
enable customers to recognise the product and distinguish it from the
products of competitors. These devices include trade names, personal
and geographical names associated with a product, for example,
Rennie Mackintosh jewellery[1] or Glenfiddich whisky,[2] and the 'get
up' of the product, for example, a distinctive container.[3] If a competitor markets a product using a similar name or get up, this may cause
confusion among actual or potential customers resulting in damage to
the goodwill of the original trader through loss of custom or loss of
reputation if the rival product is inferior. In order to protect a trader's
goodwill, the delict of passing off has been developed.

Goodwill consists of the features of a business which attract customers to trade with that business. Marketing devices such as a
particular name or get up constitute goodwill. Before there is an action
for passing off it must be established that there is a close association
between the trader and the particular device which identifies the
product or services for existing or potential customers, ie that the
device is part of the goodwill of the trader. It may be very difficult,
particularly in relation to ordinary words, as opposed to invented
words, to show that the word is a marketing device peculiar to the
goodwill of a particular trader. Some words, such as hoover, may
become part of ordinary usage and lose their distinctive quality of
being associated with a particular manufacturer. On the other hand,
other words, such as Scotch, while describing a geographical situation
may, as in relation to whisky, acquire a secondary meaning peculiar to

---

1 *Carrick Jewellery Ltd v Ortak* 1989 GWD 35–162.44.
2 *William Grant & Sons Ltd v William Cadenhead Ltd* 1985 SC 121, 1985 SLT 291.
3 *John Haig & Co Ltd v Forth Blending Co Ltd* 1954 SC 35 (Dimple bottle); *Reckitt and
   Colman Products Ltd v Borden Inc* [1990] 1 All ER 873, (1990) 134 So Jo 784 (Jif
   plastic lemon).

a particular product. Similar difficulties can arise if a trader claims that the shape of a product is sufficiently distinctive to constitute a protectable device; but a lemon-shaped container of lemon juice has been held to have a secondary meaning associated with a particular product.[1] Once it is established that the device is part of his goodwill, the law will protect the goodwill of the trader from being undermined by a competitor 'passing-off' his own product by using a similar name or get up.

The criteria of the delict were articulated by Lord Diplock in the leading case of *Erven Warnink BV v J Townend & Sons (Hull) Ltd*.[2] Passing off consists of

'(1) a misrepresentation (2) made by a trader in the course of trade, (3) to prospective customers of his or ultimate consumers of goods or services supplied by him, (4) which is calculated to injure the business or goodwill of another (in the sense that this is a reasonably foreseeable consequence) and (5) which caused actual damage to a business or goodwill of the trader by whom the action is brought or (in a *quia timet* action) will probably do so.'[3]

The essence of the delict is that by using the same or similar device which forms part of the goodwill of the pursuer, the defender misrepresents his product as that of the pursuer thus causing actual or potential damage to the pursuer's business. There is little difficulty if the exact device is used, but an action of passing off will lie even where there are differences, provided there is likelihood of confusion among the pursuer's customers or potential customers. If there is no likelihood of confusion, then there is no passing off, even if, for example, the same name is used. Thus, in *Dunlop Pneumatic Tyre Co v Dunlop Motor Co*[4] it was held that the pursuers, a large manufacturer of tyres, would not be confused with a small family owned garage of a similar name in Kilmarnock. There is less likelihood of confusion where the products do not belong to a 'common field of activity'. Accordingly, in *Scottish Milk Marketing Board v Dryborough & Co Ltd*,[5] the pursuer who marketed 'Scottish Pride' butter failed to interdict the defender from selling 'Scottish Pride' lager, since it was unlikely that the products – being so different – would be confused. However,

1 *Reckitt and Colman Products Ltd v Borden Inc* above.
2 [1979] AC 731 at 742, [1979] 2 All ER 927, HL. This approach was applied by the Second Division of the Inner House of the Court of Session in *Lang Bros Ltd v Goldwell Ltd* 1980 SC 237, 1982 SLT 309.
3 For a slightly different formulation, see also the speech of Lord Fraser of Tullybelton in *Erven Warnink BV v J Townend & Sons (Hull) Ltd* [1979] AC 731 at 755 and 756, [1979] 2 All ER 927, HL.
4 1907 SC (HL) 15, 15 SLT 362.
5 1985 SLT 253.

although confusion is more likely to be established where there is a common field of activity, a common field of activity is not essential where the device to be protected is, for example, a household name.[1] If there is sufficient likelihood of confusion, it may not be permissible for the defender to use his own name.[2]

In *John Haig & Co Ltd v Forth Blending Co Ltd*[3] the pursuers established that a particular type of bottle (Dimple) was distinctive to their product's 'get up' and successfully interdicted a rival from using a similar shaped bottle, in spite of its having a different label and stopper. The court was satisfied that when in use in a bar, there was a sufficient degree of likelihood of confusion to constitute passing off.

It has been held that manufacturers of Scotch whisky may interdict persons from exporting Scotch whisky, which they know will be mixed with local spirit abroad and passed off in the foreign country as the genuine article.[4] Similarly, passing off actions will lie where a spirit not distilled in Scotland is marketed as Scotch.[5] In *Lang Bros Ltd v Goldwell Ltd*[6] the defender manufactured 'Wee McGlen', a whisky Mac, a blend of Scotch whisky and ginger wine, made in England. This 'get up' consisted of various words and phrases as well as a caricature of a betartaned Scotsman, which were likely to confuse customers that the whole of the product was manufactured in Scotland. The Lord Ordinary (Wheatley), a well-known teetotaller, held that the action was relevant. The get up could mislead the public that the whole product ie the ginger wine as well as the whisky was made in Scotland. This misrepresentation as to the origin of the ginger wine could endanger the reputation and goodwill which attaches to Scotch whisky because of its origins. This decision seems to push the delict to its limits since the defender was not misrepresenting his product as Scotch whisky, nor was the 'get up' proved to be part of the exclusive goodwill of the pursuer.[7]

---

1 In *Lego System A/S v Lego M Lemelstrich Ltd* [1983] FSR 155, a toy manufacturer successfully obtained an injunction preventing the manufacturers of irrigation equipment from using the name 'Lego' on the basis that their goodwill might be affected if they entered the same type of business as the defendant sometime in the future.
2 *Parker Knoll v Knoll International* [1962] RPC 265, HL.
3 1954 SC 35.
4 *John Walker & Sons Ltd v Douglas Laing & Co* 1993 SLT 156.
5 *John Walker & Sons Ltd v Douglas McGibbon & Co Ltd* 1972 SLT 128; *John Walker & Sons Ltd v Henry Ost & Co Ltd* [1970] 2 All ER 106, [1971] 1 WLR 917. Nevertheless, the author has noted that 'House of Lords' whisky, sold in the Crush Bar at Covent Garden, is manufactured in England!
6 1982 SLT 309, [1983] RPC 289.
7 See, further, H L McQueen 'Wee McGlen and the Action of Passing Off' 1982 SLT (News) 225.

At one time it was thought that passing off was simply a particular aspect of the delict of fraud.[1] This is no longer thought to be sound – at least if the only remedy sought is interdict as opposed to damages. However, the misrepresentation which constitutes passing off must be 'calculated to injure' the pursuer's business or goodwill. It is, however, enough if this is a reasonably foreseeable consequence of the misrepresentation.[1] In other words, 'the calculated to injure' element is objectively ascertained. Nevertheless, it is thought that it remains appropriate to discuss passing off in the context of intentional delicts.

The primary remedy is interdict. Damages may be restricted to cases of actual fraud. However, it is extremely difficult to assess and quantify damages in respect of loss of custom, potential custom and goodwill.[2]

(d) Confidential information

Information can be very valuable. However the law has not yet been prepared to regard information per se as a form of property.[3] Nevertheless, it is now clear that Scots law recognises a general obligation arising *ex lege* not to divulge information given in confidence.[4] But what is not clear is whether this obligation is delictual *stricto sensu* or whether, given the influence of equitable principles on the development of the obligation in English law,[5] it is better treated as an obligation *sui generis*. In these circumstances, only a basic outline of the law will be discussed in this section.[6]

The essence of the obligation is the duty not to disclose information given in confidence. There is generally no limit on the type of information which is protected; it is the fact that it is given in confidence which is important.[7] Information which has been protected includes

---

1 *Erven Warnink BV v J Townend & Sons (Hull) Ltd* [1979] AC 731 at 742 per Lord Diplock.
2 On passing off generally, see 18 *Stair Memorial Encyclopaedia* paras 1451–1500.
3 *Grant v Allan* 1988 SLT 11.
4 *Lord Advocate v Scotsman Publications Ltd* 1988 SLT 490 at 502–503 per Lord Justice Clerk (Ross), at 508–509 per Lord Dunpark and at 514 per Lord McDonald; 1989 SLT 705 at 708 per Lord Keith of Kinkel.
5 The view has been taken that the *substance* of the law is the same in both Scotland and England: *Lord Advocate v Scotsman Publications Ltd* 1989 SLT 705 at 708 per Lord Keith.
6 For a full account, see 18 *Stair Memorial Encyclopaedia* paras 1451–1500.
7 However an employee may use information given in confidence by a former employer provided it is not a trade secret and there is no valid restrictive covenant: *Faccenda Chicken Ltd v Fowler* [1987] 1 Ch 117.

sensitive government intelligence, trade secrets and personal information as to a person's sexual activities.

At first, the obligation not to disclose information given in confidence arose from a contractual relationship between the parties. The classic example is, of course, employer and employee. In *Argyll v Argyll*[1] the Duke of Argyll obtained an interdict to prevent the Duchess divulging information as to his private life which he had given to her while they were married. While there is, of course, a contractual nexus between husband and wife, the obligation is also recognised where there is no contract between the parties but the relationship is clearly one of confidence, for example, doctor and patient, priest and parishioner, co-habitees whether heterosexual or homosexual or even friends.[2]

It is therefore clear that if A gives information to B, where there is a confidential relationship between the parties, then even if there is no contract between A and B, B is under an obligation not to divulge the information. If B divulges the information to C, the question then arises whether C owes an obligation to A not to disclose the information. At first, the Scottish courts were reluctant to impose an obligation on C, unless there was an agreement between A and C that the information was given in confidence.[3] However, it is now settled that C does owe an obligation to A if C knows or ought to have known that the information was confidential.[4] The test would appear to be that an obligation arises if a reasonable person would have realised in all the circumstances that he/she was bound to treat the information as confidential.

The reasonable person test explains not only why, in the example above, C owes an obligation to A not to disclose the information, but also why B owes a similar obligation to A. For where there is an agreement between A and B not to disclose the information, or where there is a confidential relationship with or without a contractual nexus, a reasonable person in B's position would realise that the information is given in confidence. It is therefore submitted that there should only be one test for determining whether a person owes an obligation not to disclose information, viz whether in all the circumstances a reasonable person in that position would have realised that the information was confidential. Factors to be considered would include the nature of the information itself, for example, love letters or

---

1 [1967] Ch 302, [1965] 1 All ER 611.
2 *Stephens v Avery* [1988] Ch 449, [1988] 2 All ER 477.
3 *Roxburgh v Seven Seas Engineering Ltd* 1980 SLT (Notes) 49, OH.
4 *Lord Advocate v Scotsman Publications Ltd* 1988 SLT 490, affd 1989 SLT 705, HL.

government information; the relationship between the parties, for example, employer and employee or lovers; whether or not there is an express statement as to confidentiality or an implied term as to confidentiality between the parties; whether or not the information was obtained by illegal or improper means, for example, industrial espionage or computer 'hacking'.[1] If the reasonable person test is satisfied, then the obligation not to divulge the information arises.

The obligation not to disclose information only continues if the information remains confidential. But merely because the information is known to some other people, for example, specialists in a scientific field, does not prevent the information being confidential. In *Exchange Telegraph Co Ltd v Giulianotti*,[2] the pursuer transmitted the results of races to subscribers. It was held that the information was still confidential even though the spectators at the event knew the result. But if the information is clearly in the public domain, it is no longer confidential and the obligation ceases to exist.[3] Thus, if A gives confidential information to B, and A later divulges the information to the world, B's obligation not to disclose the information comes to an end.[4] This principle has also been extended to the following situation: A gives information in confidence to B and B gives the information to C in circumstances where C as a reasonable person would realise it is confidential; if B divulges the information to the world, then C's obligation comes to an end. A will, of course, have a remedy in damages against B for breach of confidence.[5]

While it has been held in England that there can be liability for unintential breach of confidence,[6] it is thought that a pursuer would be unlikely to obtain damages in Scots law unless he intended to breach the confidence.[7]

The obligation not to disclose information given in confidence is not absolute. A defence is available if disclosure was in the public interest. Thus disclosure is justifiable if the information concerned the

---

1 See further 'Breach of Confidence' (SLC no 90; Cmnd 9385 (1984)) p 64.
2 1959 SC 19, 1959 SLT 293, OH.
3 *Attorney-General v Guardian Newspaper Ltd (No 2)* [1990] 1 AC 109, [1988] 3 All ER 545, HL.
4 *O Mustad & Son v S Allcock & Co Ltd and Dosen* [1963] 3 All ER 416, HL.
5 *Attorney-General v Guardian Newspaper Ltd (No 2)* above. A would not obtain an interdict against B to prevent further disclosure as the information is no longer confidential.
6 *Seager v Copydex* [1967] 2 All ER 415, [1967] 1 WLR 923, CA.
7 However, since the test of confidentiality is that of the reasonable person, ie an objective test, it is theoretically possible that a person could breach the obligation when he or she did not subjectively know that the information was confidential, ie because the person had not in fact reached the standard of the reasonable person.

commission of a crime or a civil wrong.[1] Information disclosed to a public official or agency which could take appropriate action, for example, the police, is more likely to provide justification than simple disclosure to the media.[2] The courts must engage in a balancing exercise between the public interest in protecting confidential information and the public interest in access to information which should be known. In $X v Y$[3] a newspaper disclosed the identity of two doctors suffering from AIDS. The newspaper argued that it was in the public interest that patients should know the HIV status of their medical practitioners. In rejecting this defence, the court took the view that the public interest in maintaining confidentiality prevailed because it encouraged persons suffering from AIDS, including doctors, to seek treatment. In the case of government information, the Crown cannot obtain an interdict merely because the information is confidential; the public interest in open government will justify disclosure.[4] However, the public interest in disclosure will be 'trumped' if the disclosure of the information would be damaging to national security.[5]

The primary remedy for breach of confidence is interdict. Damages are possible though difficult to assess. The person divulging the information may be required to account for any profits made from doing so.[5]

1 *Initial Services Ltd v Putterill* [1968] 1 QB 396, [1967] 3 All ER 145, CA.
2 *British Steel Corpn v Granada Television Ltd* [1982] AC 1096, [1981] 1 All ER 417, HL.
3 [1988] 2 All ER 648, [1988] RPC 379.
4 *Lord Advocate v Scotsman Publications* 1988 SLT 490, affd 1989 SLT 705.
5 *Attorney-General v Guardian Newspaper Ltd (No 2)* [1990] 1 AC 109. Although the information in that case was prima facie damaging to national security, by the time the case reached the House of Lords knowledge of the material was so widespread that an injunction on further serialisation of the information was refused; in other words, the information was no longer confidential.

CHAPTER 2

The economic delicts and fraud

A. THE ECONOMIC DELICTS

(1) Introduction – the general principle

In a free market, competition is regarded as essential and in the public interest. This can result in one business being successful while another goes to the wall. The common law therefore took the view that A was entitled to harm B economically, provided A used lawful means, for example, undercutting the price of his product, in order to do so. However, towards the end of the nineteenth century and during the twentieth century, the courts developed a range of delicts which set parameters beyond which parties could not wield their economic and social power. These are known as the economic delicts. Since then, important statutory provisions and principles of EC law have been introduced directly to regulate competition, for example, the Office of Fair Trading. Competition law is outwith the scope of this book. However, the economic delicts remain important and will be treated in this chapter.

The basic principle was laid down by the House of Lords in *Allen v Flood*.[1] In this case boilermakers objected to the practice of employing shipwrights to repair ironwork on board ships. The plaintiffs were shipwrights who were employed to repair woodwork on certain ships. Members of the boilermakers' union discovered that they had previously been employed by another employer to repair ironwork on ships. Incensed, a trade union representative approached the current employer of the shipwrights and informed him that unless he dismissed the plaintiffs, his other employees would strike. This was done maliciously to punish the plaintiffs. The employer dismissed the plaintiffs who brought the action against the trade union representative.

Three points should be noticed. First, the case proceeded on the

1 [1898] AC 1, HL.

basis that there was no conspiracy, ie no agreement among the boiler-makers that they would strike; it was simply the individual trade unionist who said that there would be a strike. Second, if there had been a strike, the employees would have terminated their contracts of employment lawfully. Third, when the employer dismissed the plaintiffs he did so by lawfully terminating their contracts. In other words, the individual trade unionist used lawful means (the threat of a lawful strike) to compel the employer to use lawful means (the lawful dismissal) to harm the plaintiffs economically (the loss of their employment). In these circumstances, the House of Lords held that no delict was committed even although the defendant had acted maliciously.

Accordingly, *Allen v Flood* is authority that an individual, A, can wield economic pressure to force B to act to his own or another's economic harm provided the means used by A are lawful; if, as in this case, the means used are lawful, no delict is committed even if A acts maliciously to harm B or another person, rather than to further A's economic interests. This result, while harsh, is, however, an inevitable consequence of a free market economy. But if the means used are *not* lawful, as a result of later developments, delictual liability may arise. It is to these that we shall now turn.

(2) Inducing breach of contract – procuring breach of contract

If A induces B to break his contract with C, C can sue B for breach of contract. In addition, or as an alternative, C can sue A *in delict* for inducing B to break his contract with C. This delict was recognised as part of Scots law in *British Motor Trade Association v Gray*.[1] There Lord Russell approved counsel's concession that

'by the law of Scotland an actionable wrong is committed by one who intentionally and without lawful justification induces or procures someone to break a contract made by him with another, if damage has resulted to that other, provided the contract creates contractual relations recognised by law.'[2]

The delict can be represented by the diagram on page 34.

Thus if A, with the intention of harming C, induces B to break his contract with C, C can sue A *in delict* for inducing the breach, as well as suing B for breach of contract.

Before A is liable, A must know of the existence of the contract between B and C. It is not enough in Scots law that A was reckless or turned a blind eye to whether or not a contract existed between B and

1 1951 SC 586, 1951 SLT 247.
2 1951 SC 586 at 603.

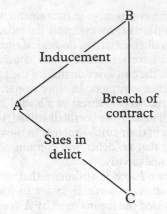

C.[1] However, A does not need to know the specific terms of the contract between B and C. The court will readily infer that A knew of the existence of the contract if a reasonable person in A's position would know that a contract existed between B and C. A must intend that B should break his contract with C in order to harm C. A must in fact induce B to break the contract. It is not necessary that A's inducement takes the form of unlawful means, for example, threatening to assault B; A will still be liable to C if the means used are lawful and, indeed, beneficial to B, for example, giving B a gift to break his contract with C. C must suffer loss as a result of the inducement, but proof of specific damage is not required and once inducement of the breach is established, some damage will be readily inferred by the court.[2] Finally, A will have a defence if the inducement of the breach is justified, for example, inducing female artistes to break their contracts of employment to obtain better wages so that they do not have to resort to prostitution.[3]

We have been considering the situation where A induces or persuades B to break his contract with C. However, if B is unwilling to break his contract with C, A may nevertheless be able to procure the breach of contract by B. Before there is liability in this situation, A must use *unlawful* means to procure the breach. Procurement can arise directly if, for example, A steals B's tools with the result that B cannot fulfil his contract and breaks his contract with C: the theft constitutes the unlawful means. However, it is much more likely that

1 *Rossleigh v Leader Cars Ltd* 1987 SLT 355, OH. Cf the position in England: *Emerald Construction Co Ltd v Lowthian* [1966] 1 All ER 1013, [1966] 1 WLR 691, CA.
2 *British Motor Trade Association v Gray* 1951 SC 586, 1951 SLT 247.
3 *Brimelow v Casson* [1924] 1 Ch 302.

procurement will be done indirectly, ie if A with the intention of harming C induces D to break his contract with B so that B cannot perform his contract with C. The delict can be represented as follows:

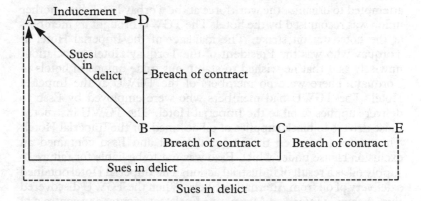

Here B could sue A in delict for inducing a breach of his contract with D. But C can also sue A for procuring a breach of C's contract with B: A's inducement of a breach of B's contract with D (ie a delict) and the breach of contract between D and B itself, constitute the unlawful means which are essential for A's liability for procuring the breach of contract between B and C.[1]

Before there is liability, A must know of the existence of B's contract with C. If, as a result, C is unable to fulfil his contract with E, E will also be able to sue A in delict provided A knows of C's contract with E and intended to harm E.[2] As we have emphasised, A must use unlawful means before there is liability for procurement. Justification can be a defence to procuring a breach of contract in the same way as in a case of inducement.

(3) Wrongful interference with performance of contract

Arising from the delict of inducement of breach of contract, the English courts have developed the delict of wrongful interference with performance of a contract, where there has technically been no breach. Like the delict discussed above this can take two forms –

---

1 *Stratford (JT) & Son Ltd v Lindley* [1965] AC 269, [1964] 3 All ER 102, HL.
2 *Merkur Island Shipping Co v Laughton* [1983] 2 AC 570, [1983] ICR 490. A's liability could continue indefinitely; for example, if E cannot fulfil his contract with F, F can sue A provided A has knowledge of the contract between E and F.

direct interference where unlawful means are not required and indirect interference where unlawful means are essential.

The origin of the delict is the case of *Torquay Hotel Co Ltd v Cousins*.[1] The Transport and General Workers Union (TGWU) attempted to organise the workforce at the Torbay hotel, but another union was recognised by the hotel. The TGWU brought its members at the hotel out on strike. The manager of the Imperial Hotel at Torquay who was the President of the Torquay Hotel Association, unwisely said that he wished to stamp out trade unions in hotels in Torquay. There were no members of the TGWU at the Imperial Hotel. The TGWU had members who were employed by Esso to deliver supplies of oil to the Imperial Hotel. The TGWU instructed those drivers to black supplies of oil destined for the Imperial Hotel. The contract between the Imperial Hotel and Esso contained an exclusion clause under which Esso was not to be liable for failure to supply oil as a result of industrial action. The Imperial Hotel obtained a delivery of oil from Alternative Fuels. When the TGWU discovered this, the union informed Alternative Fuels not to enter any contract to supply the hotel with oil or else their drivers who were members of TGWU would black the hotel. In refusing to deliver oil to the hotel, the drivers were in breach of their contracts of employment with Esso and would have been in breach of their contracts of employment with Alternative Fuels. This complex factual situation can be shown by the diagram on page 37.

Although the TGWU had directly persuaded Esso not to perform the contract with the Imperial Hotel and had indirectly procured the non performance of the contract by using unlawful means (the breach of the drivers' contracts of employment in refusing to deliver the oil to the hotel), the delicts of inducement or procurement of *breach* of contract were not applicable as there was no breach of contract by Esso in failing to perform, because of the exclusion clause in the contract. The Court of Appeal nevertheless held that it was not necessary to have a technical breach of contract before the TGWU was liable to Imperial Hotels.[2] It was enough that the TGWU had wrongfully interfered with Esso's performance of the contract with Imperial Hotel. Thus, a new delict, wrongful interference with performance of a contract, was born. As in the case of inducement/ procurement of a breach of contract, the defender must know of the existence of the contract and intend to interfere with its performance. If there is direct interference, unlawful means are not required; if

---

1 [1969] 2 Ch 106, [1969] 1 All ER 522, CA.
2 Esso could, of course, sue the TGWU for inducing its employees to breach their contracts of employment.

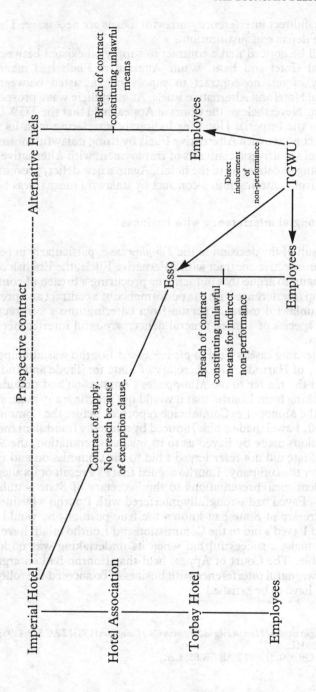

there is indirect interference, unlawful means are necessary. There is also the defence of justification.

It will be noticed that a contract to supply oil existed between the Imperial Hotel and Esso. While Alternative Fuels had made one delivery of oil, no contract to supply oil subsisted between the Imperial Hotel and Alternative Fuels. At most there was a prospective contract. Nevertheless, the Court of Appeal held that the TGWU was liable to the Imperial Hotel for indirectly interfering with its prospective contract with Alternative Fuels by using unlawful means (the breach of the drivers' contracts of employment with Alternative Fuel in refusing to deliver oil to the hotel). Again a new delict, preventing a person from entering into a contract by unlawful means, was born.

(4) Wrongful interference with business

As a result of the decision in the *Torquay* case, particularly in respect of the prospective contract with Alternative Fuels, the English courts have begun to argue that inducing or procuring a breach of contract, wrongful interference with the performance of a contract and preventing by unlawful means a person from entering into a contract, are merely species of a more general delict, wrongful interference with business.[1]

The leading case is *Lonrho plc v Fayed*.[2] Lonrho was attempting a takeover of Harrods. The Secretary of State for Trade and Industry referred the matter to the Monopolies Commission and obtained an undertaking from Lonrho that it would not purchase any more shares before the Monopolies Commission reported. Before the Commission reported, Fayed made a bid. Induced by allegedly fraudulent misrepresentations made by Fayed as to its business reputation, the Secretary of State did not refer Fayed's bid to the Commission and Fayed took over the company. Lonrho argued that as a result of its allegedly fraudulent misrepresentations to the Secretary of State – unlawful means – Fayed had wrongfully interfered with Lonrho's business. If the Secretary of State had known the true position, he would have referred Fayed's bid to the Commission and Lonrho might have been able to make a successful bid when its undertaking was no longer applicable. The Court of Appeal held that Lonrho had an arguable case of wrongful interference with business. To succeed the following criteria have to be satisfied:

---

1 See, in particular, *Merkur Island Shipping Co v Laughton* [1983] 2 AC 570, [1983] 2 All ER 189, HL.
2 [1990] QB 490, [1989] 2 All ER 65, CA.

(1) the plaintiff has to establish that the defendant intended to harm the plaintiff's business; this intention does not, however, have to be the defendant's predominant intention or motive;
(2) the plaintiff has to establish that a business interest has been damaged by the defendant's conduct;
(3) the defendant's actions have to constitute unlawful means and there has to be a causal nexus between the unlawful act and the alleged loss;
(4) the loss sustained by the plaintiff has to be sufficient to sustain an action in damages.

Because of the need for *unlawful* means, the new delict can be distinguished from the general principle of non-liability for causing economic harm laid down in *Allen v Flood*.[1]

(5) Intimidation

Intimidation arises when A threatens B with an unlawful act unless B harms C economically. If B yields to the threat and harms C, C can sue A. The delict can be represented as follows:

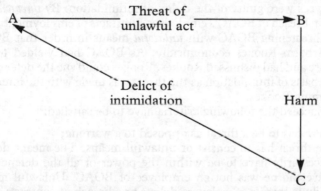

The existence of this delict was 'discovered' by the House of Lords in *Rookes v Barnard*[2]. BOAC and the draughtsmen's union, AESD, had an informal 100 per cent union membership agreement (closed shop). Rookes was an employee of BOAC who had left the union. Two trade union officials who were employees of BOAC, and Silverthorne who was not an employee, told BOAC that unless Rookes was dismissed within three days, the AESD employees would withdraw their labour. As a result of a 'no strike' clause which had been incorporated

1 [1898] AC 1 discussed at p 32 above.
2 [1964] AC 1129, [1964] 1 All ER 367, HL.

from a collective agreement into the employees' contracts of employment, the threatened strike would have been a breach of the employees' contracts of employment. Under this pressure, BOAC lawfully dismissed Rookes. Rookes sued the three officials. This complex factual situation can be shown thus:

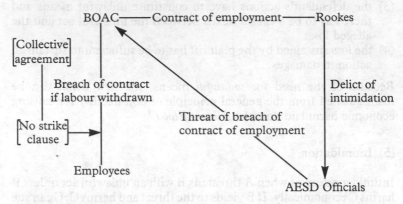

The House of Lords held that Silverthorne and the other two employees were guilty of the delict of intimidation. By *threatening* a strike in breach of BOAC's employees' contracts of employment, they were threatening BOAC with *unlawful* means in order that BOAC should harm Rookes economically. As BOAC had yielded to the pressure and had dismissed Rookes, Rookes could sue the defendants on the basis of intimidation as the threat was made with the intention of harming Rookes.

To succeed the following criteria have to be satisfied:

(1) there has to be a threat as opposed to a warning;
(2) the threat has to consist of unlawful means. The means do not necessarily have to be within the power of all the defendants: Silverthorne was not an employee of BOAC. Unlawful means include threats of violence, delicts or a breach of contract;
(3) the threat must be made with the intention that the person threatened will harm the pursuer;
(4) the person threatened must yield to the threat and harm the pursuer; if he does not comply with the threat, it is not intimidation. If the person threatened resists and the threat is carried out, depending on the nature of the unlawful act, he may have a remedy in delict or for breach of contract.

There is always the possibility of the defence of justification, if, for example, Rookes had been a dealer in drugs who upset the rest of the workforce.

Rookes was concerned with three-party intimidation, ie A threatens B with unlawful means in order that B should harm C; if B yields, C can sue A for intimidation. The question arises whether there can be two-party intimidation, ie if A threatens B with unlawful means, can B sue A for intimidation? In the present writer's view, there is no delict of two-party intimidation because it is unnecessary. If A threatens B with violence, that is itself an assault and B can sue in delict. If A threatens B with breach of contract by A, that is an anticipatory breach of contract and B can sue A in contract. If A threatens B with other delictual conduct, then B must be robust and wait until the threat is carried out and then sue in delict; B cannot sue on an 'anticipatory' delict as he has not yet suffered any loss. If, however, the threat of unlawful means interferes with B's business, A could be liable for the delict of wrongful interference with B's business.[1]

(5) Conspiracy

Allen v Flood[2] was concerned with the situation where A uses lawful means to harm B economically. There it was held that A was not liable in delict to B, even if his predominant motive or intention was to harm B rather than further A's legitimate business interests. Only three years later, in *Quinn v Leathem*,[3] the House of Lords held that if A and B combine together with the intention to harm C, then A and B are liable in delict for harm caused to C as a result of their combination or conspiracy against him. The rationale of the delict of conspiracy is that while a person can be expected to withstand the harmful but lawful acts of another, he cannot be expected to withstand the harm caused by a combination or conspiracy of persons to harm him.[4] This rationalisation has been doubted, for a multi-national conglomerate or oil company may exercise far greater economic power than a combination of small businesses.[5]

The essence of conspiracy is therefore a combination of persons, who combine together with the intention of harming the pursuer economically. There are two types of conspiracy: (a) where the means used by the conspirators are lawful in the sense that they would not be

---

1 Discussed at p 38 above.
2 [1898] AC 1. Discussed at p 32 above.
3 [1901] AC 495, HL.
4 *Mogul SS Co v McGregor* (1889) 23 QBD 598 at 616 per Bowen LJ.
5 *Lonrho v Shell Petroleum Co Ltd (No 2)* [1982] AC 173, [1981] 2 All ER 456 at 464 per Lord Diplock; see also *Crofter Handwoven Harris Tweed Co Ltd v Veitch* 1942 SC (HL) 1 at 8 per Viscount Simon LC, 1943 SLT 2, HL.

actionable if carried out by one person alone (lawful means conspiracy); (b) where the means used by the conspirators are unlawful in the sense that *either* they would be actionable if carried out by one person alone, for example, if the means constitute a delict or breach of contract, *or* they involve a crime or a breach of statute which does not provide a civil remedy for breach (unlawful means conspiracy).

(a) Lawful means conspiracy

A combination of persons will be liable in conspiracy if they combine together with the predominant motive or intention of harming the pursuer rather than furthering their own legitimate interests. Thus, if A and B combine together with the predominant motive or intention to harm C, A and B are liable in conspiracy even if their actions, for example undercutting C's prices, would not be actionable in delict if carried out by A or B alone. It is the *combination* of A and B together *and* their predominant motive or intention of harming C which renders their conspiracy delictual. If the predominant motive or intention of A and B is not to harm C but to further their own legitimate interests, the conspiracy is not delictual even though C suffers economic loss as a result of the actions of A and B, provided these actions are lawful. Where lawful means are used, a conspiracy is delictual only if the predominant motive or intention of the conspirators was to harm the pursuer.

These principles were laid down in the leading case of *Crofter Handwoven Harris Tweed Co Ltd v Veitch*.[1] Millowners on the Island of Lewis who made and sold tweed cloth from yarn spun on the island were unable to agree a 100 per cent union membership agreement (closed shop) with the TGWU because of competition from rival producers on the island (the pursuers) who obtained cheaper yarn from the mainland, wove it into cloth and sold it at a lower price than the millowners. The TGWU and the millowners combined together. They instructed the members of the TGWU who were employed at the port to refuse to handle the yarn being imported by the pursuers to the island from the mainland. The case proceeded on the basis that the dockers were not in breach of their contracts of employment with the port authority in refusing to handle the imported yarn because they were never asked by their employer to do so. The question was whether the combination amounted to an actionable conspiracy. This complex factual situation can be shown thus:

1 1942 SC (HL) 1, 1943 SLT 2.

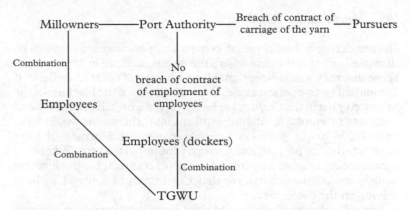

Millowners———Port Authority———Breach of contract of carriage of the yarn———Pursuers

Combination

Employees

No breach of contract of employment of employees

Employees (dockers)

Combination

Combination

TGWU

The House of Lords held that since no unlawful means were used as the dockers were not in breach of their contracts of employment, ie there was no conduct which would be actionable if done by one person alone, the conspiracy would be delictual only if the pursuers could establish that the predominant motive or intention of the conspirators was to harm the pursuers. In this case, the predominant motive or intention was to further the union's legitimate interests, ie 100 per cent union membership. Harm to the pursuers was not their primary intention, it was only incidental to achieving their goal. Accordingly, the defenders were not liable.

It can, of course, be a very difficult issue of fact to establish whether the predominant purpose of the conspiracy is to harm the pursuer or whether the damage done to the pursuer is simply incidental to the furtherance of the conspirators' legitimate interests, be they commercial[1] or trade union interests, as in the *Crofter* case. In *Scala Ballroom (Wolverhampton) Ltd v Radcliffe*[2] it was held to be legitimate for trade union officials to organise a boycott among their members from playing at a dance hall which operated a colour bar; although this objective did not bring any financial benefits to the members of the union, it was genuinely thought by them to be in the interests of the union.

To summarise: when the combination uses lawful means, ie means which would not be actionable if done by one person alone, then the conspiracy is not delictual unless the predominant motive or intention of the conspirators was to injure the pursuer. The onus rests on the pursuer to prove that the predominant purpose of the conspiracy was to harm the pursuer economically.

1 As in *Mogul SS Co v McGregor* (1889) 23 QBD 598.
2 [1958] 3 All ER 220, [1958] 1 WLR 1057.

(b) Unlawful means conspiracy

In considering unlawful means conspiracy, two situations have to be discussed. First is the case where the means used are unlawful in the sense that they would be actionable as a breach of contract or delict if committed by one person alone. So, for example, if the blacking of the imported yarn in the Crofter case had involved a breach of the dockers' contracts of employment (unlawful means), the union would have been liable to the pursuers for procurement of a breach of their contract with the port authority to carry the imported yarn. Where the means are delictual or amount to a breach of contract, the pursuer will usually sue on the substantive delict or breach of contract without relying on the conspiracy.[1]

Second, the means may be unlawful but not actionable as a breach of contract or a delict if committed by one person alone. This will usually arise where the means used involve a breach of a statutory provision. While breach of some statutes gives rise to an action in delict,[2] not all breaches of statute give a person who suffers harm as a result the right to sue in delict. In particular, the pursuer will not generally have title to sue in delict unless the statute was specifically designed to protect the interests of a class of persons to which the pursuer belongs.[3] In this situation, as the means used do not constitute a substantive delict, conspiracy may be the only form of redress.

The criteria for an actionable unlawful means conspiracy have been the subject of two decisions of the House of Lords concerned with Lonrho. The first is Lonrho v Shell Petroleum Co Ltd (No 2).[4] Lonrho owned a pipeline running from Beira in Mozambique to a refinery in Southern Rhodesia. The pipeline was operated under an agreement between Lonrho and oil companies, including Shell. When Southern Rhodesia declared unilateral independence, the British government made a sanctions order under the Southern Rhodesia Act 1965. As a result of the sanctions order, oil was no longer shipped to Beira, the pipeline ceased to be used and Lonrho lost profits. Before unilateral independence was declared, the oil companies gave assurances to the Rhodesian government that they would supply petroleum products to Rhodesia through South Africa. After independence had been declared, the defendants supplied the oil to Rhodesia in breach of the

---

1 Similarly, in Rookes v Barnard [1964] AC 1129, Silverthorne was sued for the substantive delict of intimidation rather than conspiracy to break the employees' contracts. See p 39 above.
2 See Chapter 11 below.
3 RCA Corpn v Pollard [1983] Ch 135, [1982] 3 All ER 771.
4 [1982] AC 173, [1981] 2 All ER 456, HL.

sanctions order. In an action of conspiracy against the defendants, Lonrho argued that the breach of the sanctions order enabled unilateral independence to last longer and thereby led to a loss of its revenue as a result of the prolonged non-use of its pipeline.

While the supply of the oil was a breach of the sanctions order, this was simply a criminal offence. In other words, the sanction order was not imposed for the benefit of persons, like Lonrho, who had traded with Rhodesia before independence. There was therefore no substantive delict arising from the defendants' breach of the order. The only delictual claim had to be based on conspiracy. Both the Court of Appeal and the House of Lords held that the conspiracy was not actionable because Lonrho had failed to establish that the defendants had *intended* to harm Lonrho when they breached the sanctions order. In the course of his speech in the House of Lords, Lord Diplock expressed the view that he did not wish to extend the delict of conspiracy beyond its existing limits.[1] As the previous cases were concerned with lawful means conspiracy, where there is no liability unless the predominant motive or intention of the conspirators was to harm the pursuer, Lord Diplock's dicta were subsequently taken as authority that there was also no liability for an unlawful means conspiracy unless the primary aim of the combination was to harm the pursuer.[2]

The issue was finally clarified by the House of Lords in the second Lonrho case, *Lonrho plc v Fayed*.[3] In addition to the claim based on wrongful interference with business,[4] Lonrho also argued that the defendants had committed an unlawful means conspiracy against them, the alleged fraudulent misrepresentation to the Secretary of State constituting unlawful means. The House of Lords held that Lord Diplock's analysis in *Lonrho v Shell Petroleum Co Ltd (No 2)*[5] was not intended as a definitive account of the law relating to unlawful means conspiracy.[6] While accepting that a lawful means conspiracy was delictual only if the predominant motive or intention of the conspirators was to harm the pursuer, an unlawful means conspiracy was actionable if the pursuer could establish that the conspirators had *an* intention to harm the pursuer, even though that was not their

---

1 [1981] 2 All ER 456 at 464.
2 *Allied Arab Bank Ltd v Hajjar (No 2)* [1988] QB 944, [1988] 3 All ER 103; *Metall und Rohstoff v Donaldson Lufkin and Jenrette Inc* [1990] QB 391, [1989] 3 All ER 14, CA.
3 [1991] 3 All ER 303. For the facts, see p 38 above.
4 Discussed at p 38 above.
5 [1981] 2 All ER 456.
6 *Lonrho v Fayed* [1991] 3 All ER 303 at 312 per Lord Bridge; Lord Bridge had been a member of the House of Lords in *Lonrho v Shell Petroleum*.

predominant motive or intention. This intention could not be proved merely by showing that the defenders had used unlawful means: otherwise, Lonrho should have succeeded in the *Shell Petroleum* case. However, if the conspirators have an intention to harm the pursuer, an unlawful means conspiracy is delictual even if the unlawful means used would not be actionable if done by one person alone.

To summarise: if the means used are lawful, a conspiracy is delictual only if the *predominant* motive or intention of the conspirators is to harm the pursuer; if the means used are unlawful, a conspiracy is actionable if *an* intention of the conspirators was to harm the pursuer, even although that was not their primary purpose. Unlawful means include means which are delictual if done by one person alone or constitute a breach of contract or amount to a breach of criminal law, even although this would not give rise to a delictual action if done by one person alone.

(7) Postscript

As we have seen, many of these economic delicts were developed in the context of industrial conflict between employers and trade unions. Most forms of effective industrial action will involve the commission of one or more of the economic delicts. In order to obtain a balance between the power of capital and labour for the purpose of collective bargaining, legislation has been passed to give immunity to trade unions and trade unionists from civil liability in respect of some, at least, of these delicts. Immunity arises only if the acts which prima facie constitute an economic delict are carried out in contemplation or furtherance of a trade dispute. There are now stringent balloting requirements of the members of a trade union which must be satisfied before the statutory defences are applicable; and the defences do not apply to some forms of secondary industrial action. The law has now been consolidated in the Trade Union and Labour Relations (Consolidation) Act 1992 and the reader seeking an account of the law relating to industrial action is referred to the textbooks on labour law.

B. FRAUD

Fraud is the paradigm example of an intentional delict in Scots law. It has been defined as 'a machination or contrivance to deceive'.[1] Fraud

---

1 Erskine *Institute* III, 1, 16.

will usually cause pure economic loss to the pursuer. As we shall see, this provides a stark contrast to the situation where unintentional conduct results in pure economic loss; there the courts have been unwilling to allow recovery in delict. However, fraud is not restricted to economic loss. If A lies to B when A tells B that B's wife and children have been seriously injured with the result that B suffers nervous shock, B can recover damages from A for fraud.[1]

Much confusion has arisen in this area because the fraudulent conduct will often take the form of a misrepresentation which induces the misrepresentee to enter into a contract with the misrepresentor. In these circumstances, the misrepresentee may have two sets of remedies, viz contractual and delictual. If the fraudulent misrepresentation prevented the formation of the contract, the contract is null;[2] if, however, a contract is concluded but the misrepresentee was induced by the fraudulent misrepresentation to contract under essential error, the contract may be reduced or rescinded provided *restitutio in integrum* is possible.[3] But, in addition, the misrepresentee can sue in *delict* for damages. Thus, if A lies to B to induce B to enter a contract with A, A will have contractual remedies against B, for example, rescission and the right to sue B for damages in delict. However, if A lies to B who as a result enters into a contract with C, B may have no contractual remedies against C (unless A was acting as C's agent) but B will be able to sue A in delict.

While the institutional writers had a flexible view of the concept of fraud, as a result of developments in the nineteenth century, fraud as a delict was confined to a relatively narrow range of situations where the defender intended to harm the pursuer. In effect, the Scots delict of fraud was equated with the English tort of deceit.[4]

Before delictual liability arises for fraud, there must be a positive act by the defender which causes loss to the pursuer. This will often take the form of a misrepresentation by words. However, positive conduct can amount to a fraudulent misrepresentation, for example, supplying reconditioned as opposed to new cash registers[5] or selling reproduction furniture 'got up' to look like antiques.[6] As a general rule, non-disclosure does not amount to a misrepresentation

---

1 *Wilkinson v Downtown* [1897] 2 QB 57. Similarly if A obtained sexual intercourse with B as a result of fraudulent misrepresentation.
2 *Morrisson v Robertson* 1908 SC 332.
3 *MacLeod v Kerr* 1965 SC 253, 1965 SLT 358.
4 On these developments see, generally, 11 *Stair Memorial Encyclopaedia* paras 701–789.
5 *Gibson v National Cash Register Co Ltd* 1925 SC 500.
6 *Patterson v H Landsberg & Son* (1905) 7 F 675, 13 SLT 62.

unless there is a fiduciary relationship between the parties or the contract is a contract *uberrimae fidei*.[1]

Before there is liability for fraud, the pursuer must establish that the defender had the requisite mental element, *mens rea*. In other words, the pursuer has to show that at the time of the misrepresentation the defender's state of mind was such that he did not, or could not, believe his statement was true. It is, of course, extremely difficult to prove this mental element; as a result, the law has developed liability for negligent – as opposed to fraudulent – misrepresentation where the defender's conduct can be tested objectively.[2]

What, then, will constitute the *mens rea* of fraud? The first situation is where the defender makes a statement which he knows is false. For example, A tells B there is a gold seam in A's garden when A knows that no seam is there. In these circumstances, A is lying. The second situation is where the defender makes a statement which he does not positively *know* is false but which he positively *believes* to be false. For example, A tells B there is a gold seam in A's garden; A has not dug up his garden and therefore does not know that there is no gold seam, but A believes no gold seam is there. If in fact there is no gold seam, then A can be sued by B for fraud. B will have great difficulty in proving that A believed his statement was false if A maintains he believed it was true. However, the court will infer fraud if the statement was destitute of all reasonable grounds for believing it was true or the least inquiry would immediately correct.[3]

The final situation is where the defender makes a statement which he does not positively know is false and does not positively believe is false but is recklessly indifferent to whether it is true or false. If the matter is of no importance to speaker and listener, this is not dishonesty. But if it is a matter of importance between them, it is fraud, since the speaker has attempted to induce a belief in the listener, ie that the statement is true, which the speaker does not actually entertain.[4] For example, A tells B there is a gold seam in A's garden. A has done tests which establish that the strata is not inconsistent with a gold seam but A, nevertheless, has serious doubts whether a gold seam is actually there. Assuming B has an interest in the statement, although A does not positively know that the statement is false and does not positively believe that it is false, if he does not care whether it is true or false, he is liable in fraud to B if in fact there is no gold seam in the

---

1 For example, a contract of insurance.
2 On these developments, see pp 68 ff below.
3 *Western Bank of Scotland v Addie* (1867) 5 M (HL) 80.
4 *Lees v Tod* (1882) 9 R 807.

garden.[1] Proof of the requisite *mens rea* in this situation will be difficult, but again will be inferred if the statement was destitute of all reasonable grounds for believing it was true or the least inquiry would immediately correct.

To summarise,[2] *mens rea* for the purposes of fraud arises if the misrepresentor:

(1) positively knows the statement is false; or
(2) positively believes the statement is false even though he does not positively know it is false: liability if in fact untrue;
(3) does not positively believe the statement is true, even though he does not positively know or believe it is false: liability if in fact untrue provided both parties have an interest in what has been said.

There can, therefore, be no liability in fraud if the defender positively believes that the statement is true. However, in these circumstances, if he did not take reasonable care in making the statement, there may be liability for negligent misrepresentation.[3] Theoretically, even if he did take reasonable care, there could nevertheless be liability in fraud if he did not positively believe the statement was true;[4] but, in practice, this would be almost impossible to establish since the *mens rea* of fraud is usually inferred from the fact that the grounds upon which the statement was based were so unreasonable that the defender could have no bona fide belief that the statement was true.

Because fraud is an intentional delict, the pursuer is entitled to recover damages for all the losses directly arising from the fraud – even if the losses are not reasonably foreseeable by the defender. It is not possible to exclude liability for fraud by an exemption clause.[5]

1 *H & JM Bennet (Potatoes) Ltd v Secretary of State for Scotland* 1986 SLT 665, OH (revsd on another point 1988 SLT 390).
2 The *locus classicus* is to be found in *Derry v Peek* (1889) 14 App Cas 337 at 374 per Lord Herschell.
3 See pp 68 ff below.
4 The third situation of fraud.
5 Thus the necessity to plead fraud in *H & JM Bennet (Potatoes) Ltd v Secretary of State for Scotland* above.

Part II
UNINTENTIONAL DELICT – GENERAL PRINCIPLES OF LIABILITY

CHAPTER 3

The duty of care

A. INTRODUCTION

In the first part of this book we examined the intentional delicts. *Culpa* or fault is the basis of delictual liability and is present in those delicts because the defender intended to harm the pursuer. Moreover, and this is important, the range of potential pursuers in those delicts is automatically restricted to those persons whom the defender intended to harm. However, in Scots law the concept of *culpa* also covers conduct which is merely careless, ie where the defender causes harm to the pursuer *unintentionally*. Immediately a difficulty arises. If A acts in a careless manner, ie his conduct fails to meet the standard of care demanded by society of a person in his position, then prima facie A is liable to anyone who suffers harm as a result of A's careless conduct.[1] In order to *limit* A's potential liability in delict to an indeterminate class of persons, the law has had to develop devices which restrict the number of persons who can claim damages for harm incurred by A's unintentional, but careless, conduct.

While there are many ways to restrict A's potential liability,[2] modern Scots law has accepted as a general principle that A will be liable for careless conduct only if he owed a duty of care to the person harmed by his actions. This duty of care must pre-exist the careless conduct. Whether a duty of care is owed by A to a particular person or class of persons, is ultimately a question of law to be determined by the courts. In deciding whether or not to recognise the existence of a duty of care in particular circumstances, the courts are influenced by issues of policy as well as legal principle. By recognising – or refusing to recognise – the existence of a duty of care, the courts in effect set the parameters of delictual liability for unintentional, but careless, conduct.

1 Cardozo J's phrase 'liability in an indeterminate amount for an indeterminate time, to an indeterminate class' elegantly summarises the point: *Ultramares Corporation v Touche* (1931) 255 NY 170 at 179.
2 For example, by developing a doctrine of proximate causation before A will be liable.

53

B. *DONOGHUE v STEVENSON*: THE NEIGHBOURHOOD PRINCIPLE

The starting point of any discussion of the duty of care is the famous case of *Donoghue v Stevenson*.[1] One Sunday evening, Mrs Donoghue went to visit a friend in Paisley.[2] They went to Wellmeadow Cafe at Wellmeadow Place, Paisley. The cafe was owned by Mr Minchella. They decided to have 'iced drinks' ie ice cream over which was poured lemonade. Mrs Donoghue's friend bought the ice cream and a bottle of 'ginger'.[3] The case proceeded on the assumption that Mrs Donoghue's friend had in fact bought a bottle of ginger beer, which would be contained in an opaque bottle. The friend poured some of the ginger beer over Mrs Donoghue's ice cream; but when, later in the evening, the friend poured the remainder of the contents of the bottle over Mrs Donoghue's melting ice, out floated the decomposing remains of a snail. The sight of the snail and her consumption of the snail-tainted iced drink resulted in Mrs Donoghue becoming ill. Mrs Donoghue sued Stevenson, the manufacturers of the ginger beer, in delict. The question before the courts was whether the manufacturer was liable to Mrs Donoghue in delict, even if she could prove the facts alleged and Stevenson had, in fact, been careless.

A most important point to notice is that there was no contractual nexus between Mrs Donoghue and Stevenson. The facts of the case can be shown thus:

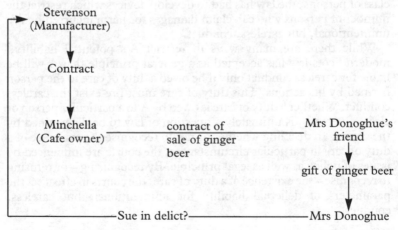

1 1932 SC (HL) 31, 1932 SLT 317. The literature on this case is voluminous. But see in particular A F Rodger 'Mrs Donoghue and Alfenus Varus' 1988 CLP 1.
2 The sex of the friend is not disclosed in the law reports!
3 In the parlance of the West Coast of Scotland at the time, 'ginger' was a generic term covering all kinds of aereated drinks.

Mrs Donoghue's friend could sue Minchella for breach of the contract of sale on the grounds that the ginger beer was not of merchantable quality; however, the friend's damages would be minimal as the friend did not suffer any ill-effects.[1] Mrs Donoghue could not sue Minchella, as she was not a party to the contract. Minchella could also have sued Stevenson in contract if he had suffered any loss. However, Mrs Donoghue had no contractual remedy. Therefore the issue before the House of Lords was whether *in the absence* of any contractual nexus between them, Mrs Donoghue, the ultimate consumer of the product, could sue the manufacturer in delict.

It was held by a majority of the House of Lords[2] that Mrs Donoghue was entitled to sue Stevenson in delict, because he owed her a duty of care; if he had in fact broken his duty towards her by his careless conduct and she had suffered loss, then she would succeed.[3] In other words, the relationship between the pursuer and defender was sufficiently proximate that the majority was prepared to hold that Stevenson owed Mrs Donoghue a duty of care for the purpose of liability in delict. Lord Atkin concluded:[4]

'. . . a manufacturer of products, which he sells in such a form as to show that he intends them to reach the ultimate consumer in the form in which they left him, with no reasonable possibility of intermediate examination, and with the knowledge that the absence of reasonable care in the preparation or putting up of the product will result in an injury to the consumer's life or property, owes a duty to the consumer to take that reasonable care'.

Lord Macmillan had

'no hesitation in affirming that a person, who for gain engages in the business of manufacturing articles of food and drink intended for consumption by members of the public in the form which he issues them, is under a duty to take care in the manufacture of these articles. That duty, in my opinion, he owes to those whom he intends to consume his produce . . .'[5]

At its most specific level *Donoghue v Stevenson* is authority that a manufacturer of food and drink, which he intends to be used by the ultimate consumer without the opportunity of inspection or interference before use, owes a duty of care to the ultimate consumer to

---

1 For that reason it would have been pointless for the friend to have assigned his or her rights under the contract to Mrs Donoghue.
2 Lord Atkin, Lord Thankerton, Lord Macmillan; Lord Buckmaster, Lord Tomlin (diss).
3 After the decision of the House of Lords on the relevancy point, the case was settled and did not go to proof.
4 1932 SC (HL) 31 at 57.
5 1932 SC (HL) 31 at 71. On the genesis of Lord Macmillan's speech, see A F Rodger (1992) 168 LQR 236.

prevent him suffering injury to his person or property as a result of the manufacturer's carelessness when manufacturing the product. In other words, the relationship between manufacturer and ultimate consumer was sufficiently proximate in these circumstances that the court was prepared to impose a duty of care on the manufacturer towards the ultimate consumer. However, four years later, the Privy Council refused to interpret *Donoghue v Stevenson* in such a narrow way and held that the manufacturer of underpants owed a duty of care to the ultimate consumer even although the product was not for internal consumption, the underpants had been removed by the retailer from packets in which they had been delivered and they could have been – but had not been – washed by the ultimate consumer before use.[1] *Donoghue v Stevenson* thus becomes authority for the more general principle that a manufacturer of *any* product owes a duty of care to the ultimate consumer not to cause injury to his person or property as a result of a latent defect in a product which could not be discovered by inspection before use and was intended by the manufacturer to be used by the ultimate consumer in the same condition as it left the manufacturer. If, by his careless conduct, the manufacturer breaches this duty causing injury to the ultimate consumer's person or property, then he is liable in delict to make reparation for the damage suffered by the consumer.

Even at this more general level, there are two important limitations on the extent of the duty of care laid down in *Donoghue*:

(1) The duty only extends to *latent* defects; the bottle of ginger beer was opaque and the snail could not be seen before the contents were used.[2] If the defect is patent, ie obvious and the consumer chooses to use it, the manufacturer may escape liability because the chain of causation is broken[3] or, at least, the damages will be reduced by the ultimate consumer's contributory negligence.[4]

(2) The duty is to prevent injury to the ultimate consumer's person or property. If A is injured by a defective product, carelessly manufactured by B, A can sue B for damages for pain and suffering (*solatium*). A can also sue B for economic loss which derives from

---

1 *Grant v Australian Knitting Mills* [1936] AC 85. The plaintiff suffered dermatitis because free sulphites used in the manufacturing process had not been washed out of the garments before they were marketed. The fact that the plaintiff could have sued the retailer for breach of contract did not prevent recovery against the manufacturer in delict.
2 Similarly the defect in the underpants in *Grant* was latent.
3 On causation see Chapter 6 below.
4 On contributory negligence, see pp 125 ff below.

his injuries (derivative economic loss), for example, loss of wages when in hospital, loss of wages in the future if A is permanently incapacitated and so forth.[1] If A's property is damaged by a defective product, carelessly manufactured by B, then A can recover damages from B in respect of the damage to his property, for example, if A's dog dies as a result of contaminated dog food or a defective vacuum cleaner damages A's carpet. But A is not able to sue B in delict if the only property damaged is the defective product itself. A cannot sue B in delict for the cost of repairing a defective car or for replacing a defective vacuum cleaner which blew up without injuring A's person or damaging any property, other than the vacuum cleaner itself. In these situations, A has suffered *pure*, as opposed to derivative, economic loss viz the cost of repair or replacement or the difference in value between the property with and without the defect. As we shall see, the courts are reluctant to allow a person to recover damages for pure economic loss in *delict*; A's remedy lies in *contract* against the person who sold him the goods, not the manufacturer.[2] Similarly, if the defect is discovered before there has been any damage done to A's person or property, the cost of repairing the defect is pure economic loss and cannot be recovered in delict.[3]

Donoghue is therefore an important decision in relation to product liability. But what makes the case remarkable is that two of the judges attempted to lay down criteria to determine the existence of a duty of care which would be applicable whenever an action for reparation as a result of unintentional, but careless, conduct arose. Lord Macmillan sets the scene:[4]

'The law takes no cognisance of carelessness in the abstract. It concerns itself with carelessness only where there is a duty to take care and where failure in that duty has caused damage. In such circumstances carelessness assumes the legal quality of negligence and entails the consequences in law of negligence. What then are the circumstances which give rise to this duty to take care? In the daily contacts of social and business life, human beings are thrown into, or place themselves in, an infinite variety of relations with their fellows; and *the law can refer only to the standards of the reasonable man in order to determine whether any particular relationship gives rise to a duty to take care as between those who stand in relation to each other.* The grounds of action may be as various and

1 On damages generally see Chapter 16 below.
2 Of course A may not have a contract; for example, if the goods were a gift. But the purchaser could assign his contractual rights against the seller to A.
3 On economic loss, see further pp 67 ff below. There is no such restriction in the case of the intentional delicts: see, for example, pp 46–47 above.
4 1932 SC (HL) 31 at 70 (italics added).

manifold as human errancy; and the conception of legal responsibility may develop in adaption to altering social conditions and the changing circumstances of life. *The categories of negligence are never closed.* The cardinal principle of liability is that the party complained of should owe to the party complaining a duty to take care, and that the party complaining should be able to prove that he has suffered damage in consequence of a breach of that duty.'

Lord Macmillan is arguing that given changes in society, the courts, using as a yardstick the values of the reasonable man, may consider that new relationships are sufficiently proximate to impose a duty of care, breach of which gives rise to delictual liability for unintentional, but careless, conduct. *Donoghue v Stevenson* thus introduces a dynamic into the law which can extend the parameters within which there is delictual liability for careless conduct; this is done by the court deciding that a duty of care exists between parties in new social or economic relationships. Conversely, the court can refuse to extend the boundaries of delictual liability for careless conduct by deciding that a duty of care does not exist between parties in the circumstances of the case. As we shall see, during the period 1960–1980 the courts were prepared to expand the scope of delictual liability by recognising the existence of a duty of care in many new areas of social and economic life; but since the 1980s, the House of Lords has entered into a period of retrenchment and has refused to recognise the existence of a duty of care unless there is a direct precedent for doing so. Indeed, the House of Lords has overruled or distinguished earlier precedents where a duty of care had been recognised on the basis that they extended liability too far.[1] It will be clear that in determining whether or not to impose a duty of care, the courts will be influenced by policy considerations as well as legal principle.

However, in *Donoghue v Stevenson* Lord Atkin attempted to provide a criterion for the existence of a duty of care which, at first sight, appears to be more objective. In a famous passage, he said:[2]

'The liability for negligence, whether you style it such or treat it as in other systems as a species of *"culpa"*, is no doubt based upon a general public sentiment of moral wrongdoing for which the offender must pay. But acts or omissions which any moral code would censure cannot, in a practical world, be treated so as to give a right to every person injured by them to demand relief. *In this way rules of law arise which limit the range of complaints, and the extent of their remedy.* The rule that you are to love your neighbour becomes in law, you must not injure your neighbour; and the lawyer's question, Who is my neighbour? receives a *restricted* reply. You must take reasonable care to

1 See p 84 below.
2 1932 SC (HL) 31 at 44 (italics added).

avoid acts or omissions which you can *reasonably foresee* would be likely to injure your neighbour. Who, then, in law, is my neighbour? The answer seems to be – persons who are so *closely and directly* affected by my act that I ought reasonably to have them in contemplation when I am directing my mind to the acts or omissions which are called in question.'

Thus, for Lord Atkin, a duty of care arises when it is reasonably foreseeable by the defender that a person in the position of the pursuer would be affected by the defender's acts or omissions. The neighbourhood principle therefore explains why a duty of care arises in many situations. A driver owes a duty of care to other road users because it is reasonably foreseeable that if he drives carelessly he may harm other road users. The occupier of property owes a duty of care to those who enter the property because it is reasonably foreseeable that they may be injured if the occupier is careless in the way he maintains the property. An employer owes a duty of care to his employee because it is reasonably foreseeable that if he is careless in the way he runs his system of working the employee may be injured. A manufacturer of a product owes a duty of care to the ultimate consumer because it is reasonably foreseeable that the ultimate consumer may be injured or suffer harm to his property if the product is defective.

It will be noticed, however, that in these examples the duty of care is to prevent *physical* harm to the pursuer or physical damage to his property, and will enable the pursuer only to recover economic loss which is *derivative* from the injuries or damage sustained. But in situations where the pursuer does not suffer physical injury or damage to property, for example, pure economic loss, the courts have been reluctant to impose a duty of care even though the loss to the pursuer would have been reasonably foreseeable by a person in the position of the defender. In other words, the reasonable foreseeability criterion, while a necessary condition for the existence of a duty of care, may not be sufficient to persuade the court to impose a duty of care in areas where no precedent for such a duty exists. Particularly in relation to recovery in delict for pure economic loss[1] the courts have refused to impose a duty of care merely because the loss was reasonably foreseeable; there has to be additional factors present which demonstrate a closer degree of proximity between the parties than mere reasonable foreseeability of economic harm. In these areas, where the courts are being asked to extend delictual liability into hitherto uncharted waters, the courts, under the guise of determining whether or not there is a sufficient degree of proximity for the imposition of a duty of care, are undoubtedly influenced by policy considerations. In doing

1 For full discussion, see pp 67 ff below.

so the courts are governed by their concept of a fair distribution of risk in contemporary society – allowing the loss to be compensated in some areas, letting the risk lie where it has fallen in others.[1]

To summarise: Lord Atkin's neighbourhood principle, based on reasonable foreseeability of harm, undoubtedly explains why a duty of care arises in many situations where there is the risk of physical harm to the pursuer or physical damage to the pursuer's property. But at the parameters of the field of existing delictual liability, the courts, for policy reasons, may refuse to extend the frontiers even though loss to the pursuer is reasonably foreseeable. On the other hand, there may be other factors present – as well as reasonable foreseeability of harm – which will persuade the courts that a duty of care should be imposed in the particular circumstances. The duty of care is here being used as a *threshold* device, enabling the courts to extend the scope of delictual liability or to refuse to do so depending on policy considerations. The duty of care allows the courts, if they so wish, to give an inch without fear that pursuers will take the proverbial mile. In the next chapter, we shall consider some important examples of this process.

1 In *Marc Rich & Co AG v Bishop Rock Marine Co Ltd* The Times, 23 Feb 1994, a surveyor (the defendant) advised the owner of a damaged vessel to continue on her voyage. The vessel sank and the cargo was lost. The Court of Appeal held that the surveyor did not owe a duty of care to the owner of the *cargo* (the plaintiff) to avoid damage to his property. Although it was reasonably foreseeable that the surveyor's careless advice could result in *physical* harm to the plaintiff's property, nevertheless no duty of care arose as the relationship between the parties was not sufficiently proximate and it would have been unfair, unjust and unreasonable to do so. In other words, the duty of care can still be used as a threshold device even in cases where physical harm to the victim's property is reasonably foreseeable, if there is no direct precedent for a duty of care arising in such circumstances. To have imposed a duty of care in this case would have disturbed 'the intricate blend' of internationally accepted rules of shipping law, under which the owner of the cargo has a remedy against the owner of the ship in *contract*. As Balcombe LJ bluntly recognised, the imposition of a duty of care 'is essentially a question of policy'; and policy considerations demanded that a duty of care towards the cargo owner should *not* be imposed upon the surveyor in this case.

CHAPTER 4

Duty of care as a threshold device

We shall now consider four examples of how the existence or non-existence of a duty of care has been used to extend or limit liability in delict for careless acts or omissions.

A. PURE OMISSIONS

A, a professor of law, is standing in the quadrangle of the university. He sees B, another professor, who is very shortsighted, walking with a white stick across the quadrangle. There is a banana skin lying in B's path. Instead of warning B, A merely stands and watches. B slips on the banana skin. A walks away giggling. Is A liable to B in delict for A's failure to warn B about the banana skin? The answer is no. Why? In spite of the fact that it is reasonably foreseeable by A that B may slip on the banana skin if A does not warn him, A does not owe B a duty of care. As a matter of policy, the law does not compel us to be good Samaritans. There must be additional factors creating a closer degree of proximity between the parties before the defender is liable in delict for an omission to act. Thus, for example, a parent is under a duty to rescue his child provided it is reasonable to do so; similarly, a nurse or a doctor owes a duty of care to tend their patients. But unless , as in these examples,[1] there is some pre-existing relationship between the parties, the law does not impose a duty of care on the defender to rescue the pursuer or to act in such a way that the pursuer will avoid an accident.

Returning to the example, it does not follow that B is without remedy. The university, as his employer, owes B a duty to take reasonable care for his safety at work;[2] moreover, as the occupier of the premises,[3] the university owes B a duty to take reasonable care that

---

1 Another example would be a policeman or fireman.
2 On employer's liability, see Chapter 12 below.
3 On occupier's liability, see Chapter 10 below.

he is not harmed as a result of the state of the premises. If, of course, A deliberately dropped the banana skin in B's path, A would be liable for assault if A intended that B should slip. If A had carelessly dropped the banana skin, he could be liable since it is reasonably foreseeable that another person in the quadrangle could slip on the skin. But that duty of care is triggered by A's positive act in dropping the banana skin; it is no longer a case of a 'pure' omission.[1]

We must be careful to distinguish the cases of 'pure' omission where there is no liability, from the situation where there is a duty of care to prevent harm to the pursuer caused by the defender's careless conduct. In the latter situation, for example, in the case of the driver of a vehicle and other road users or the manufacturer of a product and the ultimate consumer, it is irrelevant for the purpose of the law of delict that the carelessness involves an omission to act, as opposed to a positive action. Overtaking without first checking in the mirror is just as careless as driving too fast: failing to check whether a product is infested by a snail is just as careless as giving the wrong instructions on how a product is to be used.

B. NERVOUS SHOCK

The law has long recognised that A can owe a duty of care to B to prevent B suffering nervous shock as a result of A's unintentional, but careless, conduct.[2] In order to succeed, the nervous shock must amount to a nervous illness, not simply a fright. However, initially at least, the duty of care arose only when the pursuer was in danger of suffering potential physical harm as a result of the defender's conduct. Put another way, where it was reasonably foreseeable by the defender that the pursuer could be physically injured as a result of the defender's conduct, it was also reasonably foreseeable that the pursuer might suffer a nervous shock if the defender's conduct did not actually cause physical injury to the pursuer but the pursuer had been terrified that it might do so. There was therefore a duty of care not to cause a nervous shock to a person who was within the area of risk of physical harm as a result of the defender's careless conduct. It followed as a corollary that there was no duty of care to prevent the pursuer suffering a nervous shock if the pursuer was not within the

---

1 For an interesting discussion of pure omissions, see T B Smith *A Short Commentary on the Law of Scotland* (Greens, 1962) p 672.
2 See, for example, *Dulieu v White & Sons* [1901] 2 KB 669.

area of risk of physical harm. Here, the absence of a duty of care was being used by the courts as a threshold device to *limit* the defender's potential liability.

The leading case in Scots law is *Bourhill v Young*.[1] Young was a motorcyclist. Driving too fast, he overtook a stationary tramcar on its near side. He then crashed into a car which was turning right into a side street, some 50 feet from the tramcar. Young was killed. It was accepted that the accident was caused by Young's careless driving. At the time of the accident the pursuer, Mrs Bourhill, a fishwife, was on the far side of the tramcar putting her creel on her back. She therefore did not see the collision but she heard the crash and, after Young's body was removed, saw the blood on the road. She maintained that as a result of the accident she suffered a nervous shock which had caused her to miscarry. She sued Young's executor in delict. The complex factual situation can be shown as follows:

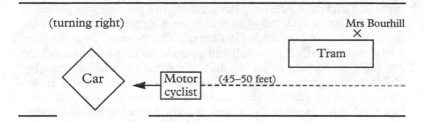

At the time of the accident Mrs Bourhill was 45–50 feet from the collision and on the far side of the tramcar ie she was not within the area of risk of potential physical harm. In those circumstances, the House of Lords held that Young did not owe the pursuer a duty of care to prevent her suffering nervous shock as a result of his careless driving. It was accepted that a driver owes a duty of care to other road users or persons in premises adjoining the highway, but only when they were 'so placed' that they could reasonably be expected to be injured by the defender's failure to take care.[2] Lord Macmillan stated[3] that:

'The duty to take care is the duty to avoid doing or omitting to do anything the doing or omitting to do which may have as its reasonable and probable consequence injury to others, and the duty is owed to those to whom injury may reasonably and probably be anticipated if the duty is not observed.'

1 1942 SC (HL) 78, 1943 SLT 105. For a discussion of this case, see W W McBryde 'Bourhill v Young: the Case of the Pregnant Fishwife' in *Comparative and Historical Essays in Scots Law* (Butterworths, 1992) pp 66ff.
2 1942 SC (HL) 78 at 86 per Lord Russell of Killowen.
3 1942 SC (HL) 78 at 88.

But while Young owed such a duty to the occupants of the motor car, he did not owe it to Mrs Bourhill because she was outwith the area of risk of potential physical harm. As Lord Wright observed[1] she 'was completely outside the range of the collision. She merely heard a noise which upset her . . . She saw nothing of the actual accident, or indeed any marks of blood until later'. Lord Porter expressly articulated the policy considerations involved:[2]

'In the case of a civil action there is no such thing as negligence in the abstract. There must be neglect of the use of care towards a person towards whom the defendant owes the duty of observing care . . . The driver of a car or vehicle, even though careless, is entitled to assume that the ordinary frequenter of the streets has sufficient fortitude to endure such incidents as may from time to time be expected to occur in them, including the noise of a collision and the sight of injury to others, and is not to be considered negligent towards one who does not possess the customary phlegm.'

Thus, as a general rule, there is no duty of care to prevent the pursuer suffering a nervous shock unless the pursuer was placed in bodily danger or reasonably in fear of such danger as a result of the defender's careless conduct. However, in *Hanbrook v Stokes Brothers*[3] a lorry ran violently down a hill and passed a mother who had just left her children further down the hill. Terrified for the safety of her children, the woman suffered a serious nervous illness and subsequently died. It was held that the owners of the lorry who had left it unattended and improperly braked, owed a duty of care to the mother of children who were within the area of risk of injury. In that case, of course, the mother was present at the incident.

However, in *McLoughlin v O'Brian*[4] the House of Lords was persuaded to widen the scope of potential delictual liability for nervous shock. In this case, the plaintiff's husband and three children were involved in a road accident at 4 pm. They were taken to hospital where it was discovered that one child was dead. The plaintiff was told of the accident at 6 pm and went to the hospital where she saw the victims. She later suffered a psychiatric illness. The Court of Appeal took the view that while it was reasonably foreseeable that a wife and mother might suffer nervous shock in these circumstances, the defendant did not owe the plaintiff a duty of care as she was not present at the accident. The House of Lords rejected this argument and held that a duty of care existed in spite of the fact that the plaintiff had not

---

1 1942 SC (HL) 78 at 93.
2 1942 SC (HL) 78 at 98.
3 [1925] KB 141.
4 [1983] AC 410, [1982] 2 All ER 298.

witnessed the accident directly. While it was reasonably foreseeable that the spouse and mother of persons injured in an accident might suffer nervous shock, this in itself was not sufficient to create a duty of care. However, there were additional factors present in the case which provided the necessary degree of proximity between the parties from which a duty of care could be inferred. First, the plaintiff was with the victims shortly after the accident; accordingly, she had witnessed the aftermath of the accident. Second, she had personally *seen* the effects of the accident on her family and had not simply learned of the accident by letter or on television or from a third party.[1] It follows from *McLoughlin* that not only must the risk of nervous shock to the pursuer be reasonably foreseeable but other factors must be present which show a sufficient degree of proximity between the parties. If these additional factors are *not* present, the court will not impose a duty of care.

These issues were further explored by the House of Lords in *Alcock v Chief Constable of South Yorkshire*.[2] Friends and relations of persons crushed to death at Hillsborough football ground brought claims for nervous shock. The House of Lords held that before a duty of care arose, it had to be reasonably foreseeable that the plaintiffs would suffer a nervous shock. The criterion was whether there was a close tie of love and affection between the plaintiff and the victim. This would be presumed if they were spouses or parent and child, but merely because they were related in some way would not per se be sufficient. Conversely, if they were not related, a plaintiff might still succeed if it could be shown that the requisite degree of love and affection *in fact* existed between the plaintiff and the victim. However, reasonable foreseeability was not sufficient and the two *extra* factors for proximity had also to exist. Thus, the plaintiff had to witness the calamity or its aftermath (for example, if the plaintiff had been at the stadium): identifying a dead relative or friend eight hours after the event was not enough. Secondly, the plaintiff must have seen or heard the accident: watching the event on television did not suffice as the defender knew that it was the policy of the television company in such circumstances to ensure that no specific person who was injured could be identified.

The court indicated that in terrible circumstances a duty might arise even where the plaintiff was not a friend of the victim. However, to qualify the plaintiff would have to have been a bystander at the event in which case, as the accident has *ex hypothesi* to be horrific, the plaintiff will usually be in fear of his own life and a duty of care

1 [1983] AC 410 at 421–423 per Lord Wilberforce.
2 [1992] 1 AC 310, [1991] 4 All ER 907.

would arise in the usual way. Secondly, there could be circumstances where seeing the event on television would be sufficient; for example, if parents watching television see their children flying in a hot air balloon which blows up in the air, there could be liability as they know their children have died. At Hillsborough, because of the way in which the television company filmed the disaster, the plaintiffs could not have known for sure that their loved ones had been killed. Finally, neither *McLoughlin* nor *Alcock* undermine the *ratio* of *Bourhill v Young*, as Mrs Bourhill was not a close friend of the passengers in the motor car; therefore it was not reasonably foreseeable that she would suffer a nervous shock if they were injured by Young's careless conduct.[1]

C. WRONGFUL LIFE ACTIONS

It is generally accepted that a person owes a duty of care not to harm a foetus, ie a child *in utero*.[2] If a foetus is injured in its mother's womb, if the child is subsequently born alive, the *child* can sue the defender in delict in respect of its injuries even although they were sustained when the child was a foetus. However, in *McKay v Essex Area Health Authority*[3] a mother contracted rubella (German measles) during her pregnancy. When her child was born, the baby was badly deformed as a result of the mother's illness. The mother alleged that owing to the hospital's carelessness, she had not been informed that her baby might be born with deformities. Since no tests had been carried out, the mother had been denied the opportunity of a lawful termination of her pregnancy. The Court of Appeal held that the hospital may have been in breach of a duty of care towards the *mother* which might entitle her to damages for having to bring up a deformed child. However, the hospital did not owe a duty of care towards the *child*, to allow the child's mother the opportunity to terminate the pregnancy. A child has no right to be born whole or not at all. This denial of the existence of a duty of care towards a foetus to terminate the pregnancy, if the foetus is deformed, is clearly based on principles of public policy.[4] Thus the law

---

1 It is submitted that the accident was not so horrific as to qualify Mrs Bourhill merely as a bystander.
2 For full discussion, see pp 190 ff below.
3 [1982] QB 1166, [1982] 2 WLR 890.
4 Moreover, even if such a duty existed, the child's deformities were not caused by the careless conduct of the hospital, but by the rubella; on the necessity for causation, see Chapter 6 below. Of course, if the hospital had caused the injuries, it *would* have been liable to the child, if born alive.

has refused to recognise wrongful life actions by denying the existence of a duty of care: again, we see the duty of care being used as a threshold device.

While there was no duty of care towards the foetus to terminate the pregnancy because it was born deformed, the Court of Appeal emphasised that the defendant could have been in breach of its duty towards the *mother*, in not allowing her the opportunity of termination. It has been held that a doctor owes a duty towards a man or a woman who undergoes sterilisation; if owing to the doctor's careless conduct, a child is conceived, the patient may sue in delict for the birth of an unplanned child. In other words, the law recognises wrongful *birth*, as opposed to wrongful life, actions.[1] As well as compensation for pain and suffering arising from the pregnancy and birth, damages include the cost of alimenting the unplanned child. These damages constitute pure economic loss and do not technically derive from any physical injury to the pursuer – particularly if the failed sterilisation was concerned with the father! This is an example of the law being prepared to allow recovery for pure economic loss in delict. Damages are not reduced if the mother is given the opportunity to have a lawful termination of the pregnancy but chooses not to do so.[2]

D. ECONOMIC LOSS[3]

It is in the area of liability in delict for economic loss that the concept of a duty of care has been extensively used by the courts as a threshold device. *Donoghue v Stevenson*[4] is authority for the principle that a duty of care arises when it is reasonably foreseeable by the defender that his careless acts or omissions would cause physical injury to the pursuer or physical damage to the pursuer's property. However, the pursuer can recover damages for economic loss which derives from the pursuer's injuries or the physical damage to his property, for example, loss of earnings while in hospital, loss of earnings in the future when

---

1 See generally, K Norrie 'Actionability of Birth' 1983 SLT (News) 121; 'Damages for Birth of a Child' 1985 SLT (News) 121; 'Liability for Failed Sterilisation' 1986 SLT (News) 145.
2 See, for examples, *Thake v Maurice* [1986] QB 644, [1984] 2 All ER 513; *Gold v Haringey Health Authority* [1987] QB 481, [1987] 2 All ER 888, CA.
3 In this section I have largely relied upon the terminology used by Wilkinson and Forte in their important article, 'Pure Economic Loss – a Scottish Perspective' 1985 JR 1.
4 1932 SC (HL) 31, discussed at pp 54 ff above.

the pursuer is unable to work.[1] This is known as *derivative* economic loss, economic loss which derives from the pursuer's physical injuries or the physical damage to the pursuer's property. However, the law does not, as a general rule, allow recovery in *delict* where the pursuer only suffers economic loss as a result of the defender's careless conduct. In the case of a defective product, for example, which has not physically injured the pursuer or damaged other property belonging to the pursuer, the cost of repair or the difference in value between a defective and non-defective product, is not recoverable in *delict*.[2] The pursuer has suffered pure economic loss and the courts have refused to impose a duty of care on the manufacturer in respect of such losses, even although such a loss is reasonably foreseeable. This is because the courts seek to protect the defender from potentially indeterminate liability. Although it is reasonably foreseeable that the defender's careless conduct would cause a power cut and loss of production at many factories, the defender does not owe a duty of care to the owners of the factories for loss of production. This is pure economic loss and is not generally recoverable in delict. Of course, if the power cut caused physical injury to a worker in the factory or damage to a machine, liability would arise if the injury or physical damage was reasonably foreseeable; the pursuer could sue in delict for damages, including any derivative economic loss.

While reasonable foreseeability of pure economic loss is not sufficient for the imposition of a duty of care, the courts have, in certain situations, been prepared to hold that a duty of care does exist. However, there must be factors *in addition* to reasonable foreseeability of pure economic loss, which demonstrate that there is a sufficient degree of proximity between the parties for a duty of care to be inferred. This requirement of proximity is, as we have seen,[3] simply a rationalisation by the courts of why they are, or are not, prepared to extend the parameters of liability in delict. It is the paradigm of the duty of care being used as a threshold device.

We shall now examine these developments in detail.

(1) Careless misrepresentation

A may make a statement to B which causes B physical injury or damage to B's property: for example, A tells B that it is safe to drink

---

1 On damages, generally, see Chapter 16 below. Derivative economic losses may not be recoverable if they are too remote: see pp 225 ff below.
2 See the discussion at p 57 above.
3 See pp 59 ff above.

contaminated water. A will owe B a duty of care if it is reasonably foreseeable that B will suffer physical injury or damage to his property if A's statement is made carelessly. This is a simple application of the *Donoghue* neighbourhood principle.[1] However, A may make a statement to B which causes B pure economic loss. For example, A tells B that B should enter into a contract with C. Relying on A's advice, B enters into the contract with C. As a result, B loses money. Can B sue A in delict for the pure economic loss B has suffered, if A's statement was made carelessly?[2] The answer depends on whether A owes a duty of care to B not to make careless statements which cause B pure economic loss.

The criteria for the existence of such a duty were laid down by the House of Lords in *Hedley Byrne v Heller*.[3] The plaintiffs through their bankers asked E's bankers, the defendants, whether E was a respectably constituted company. E's bankers replied that E was. On reliance of this statement, the plaintiffs became E's advertising agents. E later went into liquidation. As a result, the plaintiffs suffered economic loss. The facts of the case can be shown as follows:

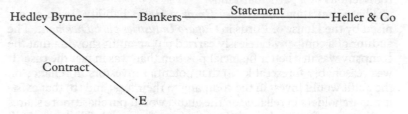

It will be clear that there was no contract between Hedley Byrne and Heller & Co. The question was whether the plaintiffs could sue the defendants in delict. The House of Lords held that the defendants owed a duty of care to the plaintiffs, if the defendants had undertaken responsibility for the accuracy of the statement and knew or ought to have known that the plaintiffs would rely on that statement. If the duty was broken as a result of the statement being made carelessly, the defendants could be liable for the plaintiffs' pure economic loss. In the course of his speech, Lord Devlin[4] stated that before there was liability, the plaintiffs had to show that the defendants owed the plaintiffs 'a special duty' to take care. The categories of relationships where this duty arose were not limited to contractual relationships (ie

1 For full discussion, see pp 58 ff above.
2 Cf if A made the statement fraudulently, when, of course, A is liable for fraud. On fraud, see pp 46 ff above.
3 [1964] AC 465, [1963] 2 All ER 575, HL.
4 [1963] 2 All ER 575 at 610.

where there was a contract between the parties) or fiduciary relationships (for example, parent and child, trustee and beneficiary) but also to relationships which were the 'equivalent to contract'. This would arise where the defender had voluntarily assumed responsibility for the accuracy of the statement and knew or ought to have known that the pursuer would rely on the information. The paradigm situation is where the defender is a professional business man, for example a banker, solicitor or accountant, who in the absence of a contract between them, gives advice to the pursuer in the course of the defender's business, knowing that it would be relied on by the pursuer.

It is important to notice that reasonable foreseeability of loss to the pursuer is not per se sufficient to establish a duty of care. There must be additional factors present from which the courts will infer the necessary proximity of relationship between the parties. These factors include the defender's knowledge of the identity of the pursuer, either as an individual or a member of an identifiable class; and the defender's knowledge that the information will be communicated to and used by the pursuer in connection with a particular transaction or transactions of a particular kind.

These limitations on *Hedley Byrne v Heller* liability, were recognised by the House of Lords in *Caparo Industries plc v Dickman*.[1] The auditor of a company carelessly carried out an audit showing that the company was in a better financial position than was in fact the case. It was reasonably foreseeable (a) that potential investors in reliance on the audit would invest in the company to their loss; and (b) that existing shareholders in reliance on the audit, would purchase more shares in the company to their loss. This, in fact, happened. While the auditor had a contract with the company, he did not have a contract with existing and potential shareholders. While the losses which had been incurred were reasonably foreseeable, the House of Lords held that the auditor did not owe a duty of care to the shareholders or potential shareholders to prevent them suffering economic loss as a result of the careless audit. The reason was that their relationships were not sufficiently proximate, ie the factors additional to reasonable foreseeability did not exist in this case. Lord Bridge explains:[2]

'The salient feature of all these cases [ie where a *Hedley Byrne v Heller* duty of care was recognised] is that the defendant giving advice or information was fully aware of the nature of the transaction which the plaintiff had in contemplation, knew that the advice or information would be communicated to him directly or indirectly and knew that it was very likely that the plaintiff would rely on that advice or information in deciding whether or not to engage in the

1 [1990] AC 605, [1990] 1 All ER 568, HL.
2 [1990] 1 All ER 568 at 576.

transaction in contemplation. In these circumstances the defendant could clearly be expected . . . specifically to anticipate that the plaintiff would rely on the advice or information given by the defendant for the very purpose for which he did in the event rely on it. So also the plaintiff . . . would in that situation reasonably suppose that he was entitled to rely on the advice or information communicated to him for the very purpose for which he required it. The situation is entirely different where a statement is put into more or less general circulation and may foreseeably be relied on by strangers to the maker of the statement for any one of a variety of different purposes which the speaker has no specific reason to anticipate. To hold the maker of the statement to be under a duty of care in respect of the accuracy of the statement to all and sundry for any purpose for which they may choose to rely on it is not only to subject him, in the classic words of Cardozo CJ to "liability in an indeterminate amount for an indeterminate time to an indeterminate class",[1] it is also to confer on the world at large a quite unwarranted entitlement to appropriate for their own purposes the benefit of the expert knowledge or professional expertise attributed to the maker of the statement.'

Accordingly, the House of Lords held that an auditor did not owe a duty of care to a member of the public at large who relied on the audit to purchase shares or increase an existing shareholding in the company: such a duty would arise only if the auditor knew that his statement would be communicated to the plaintiff and relied upon by the plaintiff in a particular transaction of a particular kind.[2]

Hedley Byrne v Heller was an English case. The principle has been accepted as part of Scots law.[3] One area where it has been applied is in relation to the liability of surveyors. Consider the following example. A wishes to purchase a house from B. He approaches a building society for a loan. Before it can give the loan the building society must obtain a report on the value of the property from a surveyor. It is a term of A's contract with the building society that A will pay the surveyor's fee. Instead of obtaining an independent survey, A relies on the valuation report commissioned for the building society and goes ahead with the purchase. The house turns out to have faulty foundations which will cost £20,000 to repair. The facts of the case can be represented in the following diagram.

Since A has not been physically injured and the faulty foundations have not caused physical damage to any other property owned by A, A has

1 *Ultramares Corp v Touche* (1931) 255 NY 170 at 179.
2 In *Nordic Oil Services Ltd v Berman* 1993 SLT 1164, the Lord Ordinary (Osborne) held that directors of a company did not owe a duty of care to creditors of the company to prevent them suffering economic loss as a result of the acts or omissions of the company.
3 *John Kenway v Orcantic Ltd* 1979 SC 422, 1980 SLT 46, OH; *Eastern Marine Services (and Supplies) Ltd v Dickson Motors Ltd* 1981 SC 355, OH; *Twomax Ltd v Dickson, McFarlane and Robinson* 1982 SC 113, 1983 SLT 98, OH. The last decision must now be read in the light of the limitations laid down in *Caparo*.

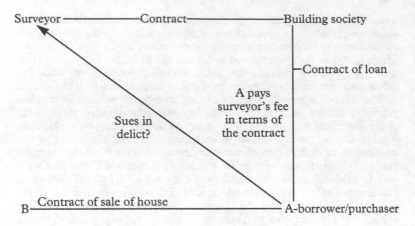

only suffered pure economic loss. This is either the cost of repairs or the difference in value between the house with faulty foundations and the house if the foundations were sound. While A has a contract of sale with B, the seller of heritage does not usually warrant that a house built on the land conveyed is sound. Therefore A has no *contractual* remedy against B. Moreover, although A paid for the survey, he has no contract with the surveyor: the surveyor's contract is with the building society. However, it has been held that the surveyor owes a duty of care to A, if the surveyor knows that the report will be used by A and will be relied upon by A to purchase the house.[1] As well as reasonable foreseeability of loss to A, the surveyor's knowledge of A and the particular transaction, A's reliance on the report and the fact that A paid for the report, provide the additional factors which create a sufficient degree of proximity between A and the surveyor for a *Hedley Byrne v Heller* duty of care to arise. Accordingly, if the report was made carelessly, A can recover damages for pure economic loss from the surveyor. If, however, A later sold the house to C and C relied on the valuation report rather than commission a new survey, the surveyor would not owe a duty of care to C. For although it is reasonably foreseeable that the report would be relied on by a singular successor of A (ie a subsequent purchaser of the house), as the surveyor did not know the identity of C at the time of the survey and the fact that C did not pay the fee, the additional factors are not present and the duty of care does not arise.[2]

1 *Martin v Bell-Ingram* 1986 SLT 575; *Smith v Eric S Bush and Harris v Wyre Forest District Council* [1990] 1 AC 831, [1989] 2 WLR 790.
2 This would follow from the *ratio* of *Caparo Industries plc v Dickman* [1990] 1 All ER 568. Similarly, the absence of such additional factors prevented the surveyor owing a duty of care to the owner of the lost cargo in *Marc Rich & Co v Bishop Rock Marine Co Ltd*, discussed at p 60, n 1.

While the existence of a duty of care to prevent economic loss to the plaintiff was recognised in *Hedley Byrne v Heller*,[1] in fact the plaintiff did not obtain damages in that case. When they provided the information, the defendants expressly stated that it was given 'without responsibility on the part of the bank'. The House of Lords held that this disclaimer was effective to protect the defendants from liability. After their potential delictual liability towards purchasers of property was established, surveyors inserted a similar disclaimer in their valuation reports or in the building society's contract with the borrower/purchaser. Provided the disclaimer came to the notice of the purchaser before the purchaser entered into the contract of sale,[2] for a time these disclaimers were effective to protect the surveyor from liability in delict.[3] However, where the disclaimer is a term of the purchaser's contract with the building society,[4] it cannot be relied on unless it satisfies the requirement of reasonableness under the Unfair Contract Terms Act 1977.[5] Moreover, the controls in the 1977 Act now extend to disclaimers which are not contractual terms.[6] This would include a disclaimer in the surveyor's valuation report. Accordingly, a surveyor cannot escape delictual liability by relying on a disclaimer, unless it satisfies the requirement of reasonableness. In *Smith v Eric S Bush and Harris v Wyre Forest District Council*,[7] the House of Lords, applying the parallel English provisions of the Unfair Contract Terms Act 1977, held that a disclaimer was not reasonable when the purchaser was of limited means and buying domestic property. If the purchaser was wealthy or the property bought was commercial, then a surveyor might be able to establish that the disclaimer was reasonable. It is thought that a similar view would be taken by the courts in Scotland.[8]

The classic example of *Hedley Byrne v Heller* liability is where A makes a misrepresentation to B which B relies on to enter a contract with C: A owes B a duty of care which enables B to sue A in *delict* for pure economic loss. However, does A owe B a *Hedley Byrne v Heller*

---

1 [1964] AC 465, [1963] 2 All ER 575.
2 If it did not come to the purchaser's notice before the contract of sale was agreed, the disclaimer was not effective: *Martin v Bell-Ingram* 1986 SLT 575.
3 *Robbie v Graham and Sibbald* 1989 SCLR 578, 1989 SLT 870.
4 *Melrose v Davidson* 1993 SLT 611.
5 Section 16; *Melrose v Davidson* above.
6 Law Reform (Miscellaneous Provisions) (Scotland) Act 1990, s 68.
7 [1990] 1 AC 831, [1989] 2 WLR 790.
8 The House of Lords in this case also rejected the argument that the disclaimer prevented a duty of care arising in the first place; instead, it held that the duty of care existed in spite of the disclaimer and that the disclaimer was therefore an exemption clause purporting to exclude liability. *Sed quaere*.

duty of care when A makes a misrepresentation to B which induces B to enter a contract with A? For many years, as a result of the decision in *Manners v Whitehead*,[1] B was denied a remedy in delict against A unless A's misrepresentation was fraudulent.[2] The rule in *Manners v Whitehead* has been abolished.[3] Accordingly, provided the *Hedley Byrne v Heller* criteria are established,[4] A will owe B a duty of care so that B can sue A in *delict* if the misrepresentation was made carelessly and caused B pure economic loss. In addition or as an alternative, B will have contractual remedies, for example, reduction or rescission, arising from the misrepresentation.[5] There has, as yet, been no reported decision in Scotland where an action for negligent misrepresentation in delict has been successfully brought against the other party to the contract.[6]

This discussion has illustrated the way in which the concept of a duty of care has been used as a threshold device to extend – and at the same time keep in check – liability in delict for pure economic loss caused by a careless misrepresentation.

To summarise, a duty of care to prevent pure economic loss arising from a negligent misrepresentation will arise if:

(1) advice is given for a purpose, particularly specified or generally described, which is made known, either actually or inferentially, to the defender at the time when the advice is given;
(2) the defender knows, actually or inferentially, that his advice will be communicated to the pursuer, either specifically or as a member of an ascertainable class, in order that it should be used by the pursuer for that purpose;
(3) the defender, actually or inferentially, knows that the advice so communicated is likely to be acted on by the pursuer for that purpose without independent inquiry; and
(4) is acted upon by the pursuer to the pursuer's detriment.

In practice, liability will arise only when the advice is given by the defender in the course of the defender's profession or business. Any disclaimer of liability will have to satisfy the requirement of

---

1 (1898) 1 F 171.
2 On fraud, see pp 46 ff above.
3 Law Reform (Miscellaneous Provisions) (Scotland) Act 1985, s 10.
4 And it is submitted that in this situation they usually are.
5 These are the same as the contractual remedies available after a fraudulent misrepresentation, discussed at p 47 above.
6 An attempt failed in *Palmer v Beck* 1993 SLT 485 on the ground that s 10 of the 1985 Act was not retrospective.

reasonableness under the Unfair Contract Terms Act 1977 if it is to be effective.

(2) Liability arising from defective performance of a contract

A enters a contract with B. In order to fulfil his contract with A, B enters into a contract with C. C's performance of his contract with B is carried out carelessly. As a result, A suffers pure economic loss. The facts can be represented as follows:

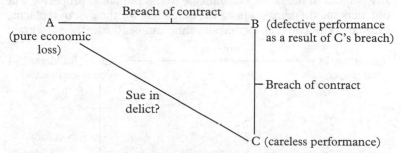

A's obvious remedy is to sue B for breach of contract. But if this is not possible (for example, if there is an exemption clause in A's contract with B) or not desirable (for example, if B is bankrupt) can A sue C in delict?

If C's careless performance of his contract with B had caused physical injury to A or physical damage to A's property, C would owe A a duty of care provided A's injury or damage to A's property was reasonably foreseeable: ie the *Donoghue v Stevenson* neighbourhood principle would apply.[1] As A only suffers pure economic loss, reasonable foreseeability of such loss is not sufficient to give rise to a duty of care. But A, B and C are connected by a series of contracts. If C had broken his contract with B, with the intention of harming A, A can sue C in *delict* for wrongful interference with B's performance of his contract with A and can recover for pure economic loss.[2] In this case, however, C has not broken his contract with B in order to harm A. Instead, C has by his *careless* conduct broken his contract with B with the result that B's performance of his contract with A is defective causing A economic loss. In these circumstances, does C owe a duty of care to A not to perform his contract with B in a careless manner, when it will cause A economic loss to do so?

1 For discussion, see pp 58 ff above.
2 On the relevant delicts see pp 33 ff above.

In *Junior Books v Veitchi*,[1] the House of Lords held that such a duty of care could exist. The pursuers entered into a contract with Ogilvie (Builders) Ltd (the main contractor) for the construction of a factory. The pursuers' architects nominated Veitchi, a floor specialist, to lay a floor in the factory, ie Veitchi was a nominated sub-contractor. However, Veitchi's contract to lay the floor was with the main contractor, not Junior Books. The floor laid was seriously defective and would have to be replaced by the pursuers. There was no averment that the floor laid was dangerous so as to be likely to cause physical injuries to any persons in the factory or damage to the pursuers' property. The pursuers sought damages from the defenders for the cost of replacing the floor. This complex factual situation can be illustrated as follows:

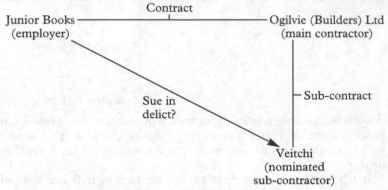

Although nominated by Junior Books' architect, Veitchi has no contractual relationship with Junior Books. While Junior Books could have sued the main contractor for breach of contract, they chose not to do so. Their only remedy against Veitchi, therefore, lay in delict. As there was no danger of any physical injury to persons in the factory or damage to the pursuer's property, the case fell outside the neighbourhood principle of reasonable foreseeability of harm laid down in *Donoghue v Stevenson*.[2] In other words, the case was concerned with the recovery of pure economic loss ie the cost of replacing the defective floor. Nevertheless, the House of Lords held[3] that, in the

---

1 1982 SC (HL) 244, 1982 SLT 492.
2 However, Lord Keith of Kinkel took the view (1982 SC (HL) 244 at 267) that if such a danger was present, the neighbourhood principle in *Donoghue* was wide enough to cover the cost of averting such a danger. This is doubtful after the decision of the House of Lords in *Murphy v Brentwood District Council* [1991] 1 AC 398, [1990] 2 All ER 908 discussed at pp 84 ff below.
3 Lords Fraser of Tullybelton, Russell of Killowen, Keith of Kinkel, Roskill; Lord Brandon dissenting.

circumstances, there was sufficient proximity between the parties for a duty of care to arise, ie the defenders were under a duty to prevent loss to the pursuers as a result of the defenders' careless performance of their contract with Ogilvie (Builders) Ltd.

Lord Roskill identified[1] eight factors from which the requisite proximity for a duty of care could be inferred viz:

'(1) The appellants [Veitchi] were nominated sub-contractors. (2) The appellants were specialists in flooring. (3) The appellants knew what products were required by the respondents [Junior Books] and their main contractors and specialised in the production of those products. (4) The appellants alone were responsible for the composition and construction of the flooring. (5) The respondents relied upon the appellants' skill and experience. (6) The appellants as nominated subcontractors must have known that the respondents relied upon their skill and experience. (7) The relationship between the parties was as close as it could be, short of actual privity of contract. (8) The appellants must be taken to have known that if they did the work negligently (as it must be assumed that they did) the resulting defects would at some time require remedying by the respondents expending money upon the remedial measures as a consequence of which the respondents would suffer financial or economic loss.'

Several points should be noted. First, the defender and the pursuer are connected by a series of contracts which are subsisting at the time of the defenders' careless acts (ie the installation of the defective floor). Second, Veitchi had been nominated by the pursuers' architect. This is important because as a nominated sub-contractor, Veitchi must have known the identity of the employer, Junior Books, who was contracting with the main contractor, Ogilvie (Builders) Ltd. Third, because Veitchi knew that Junior Books required their services, knew that Junior Books relied upon their expertise, knew that careless performance of their contract would require the floor to be repaired by Junior Books, Veitchi must have *known* that careless performance by them of their contract with Ogilvie (Builders) Ltd would cause *economic* loss to the pursuer.

Thus, for a *Junior Books* duty of care to arise, the pursuer A and defender C must be connected by a series of contracts viz A–B–C.[2] In

---

1 1982 SC (HL) 244 at 277.
2 *Comex Houlder Diving Ltd v Colne Fishing Co Ltd (No 2)* 1992 SLT 89; *Scott Lithgow v GEC Electrical Products Ltd* 1992 SLT 244. The pursuer and defender must not be parties to the same contract, for example, A–D; if so, A's remedy for D's careless defective performance is restricted to an action for breach of contract; there is no liability in delict if A only suffers economic loss (cf physical injury or harm to A's property) as a result of D's breach: see *Middleton v Douglass* 1991 SLT 726; *Parkhead Housing Association v Phoenix Preservation* 1990 SLT 812.

addition to reasonable foreseeability of loss as a result of his careless acts, C must know the identity of the pursuer A, know that A has a contract with B and know that A will suffer economic loss as a result of C's careless performance of his contract with B, since this will, in turn, render defective B's performance of his contract with A. In establishing this degree of knowledge, the fact that C is a nominated sub-contractor is important but not necessary.[1] Similarly, A's reliance on C's expertise etc is merely, albeit important, *evidence* that C knows that his careless performance will cause A economic loss; but reliance per se is neither necessary nor sufficient. The crucial point is that C must know that the careless performance of his contract with B will cause A economic loss as a result of B's consequent defective performance of his contract with A.

Thus, it is the present writer's submission that *Junior Books* liability should be seen as an extension of the economic delict of wrongful interference with performance of a contract. If, in the above example, C broke his contract with B with the result that B renders defective performance of his contract with A, it is long settled that A can sue C in delict for pure economic loss if C broke his contract with B *with the intention* of harming A.[2] *Junior Books* goes a step further by providing that A can sue C in delict where C carelessly performs his contract with B with the result that B renders defective performance of his contract with A, provided C *knew* that his careless performance of his contract with B would cause economic loss to A; ie C owes a duty of care to A not to perform his contract with B in a careless manner.

Read this way, the duty of care held to exist in *Junior Books* is kept within the narrowest of limits. First, it only applies where the parties are connected by contracts which are *existing* at the time of the defender's careless acts. In *D and F Estates v Church Commissioners for England*,[3] the Church Commissioners owned a block of flats built by the main contractors. The main contractors sub-contracted the plaster work to sub-contractors. The plaster was defective but was not a source of danger. *After* the flats were built, a flat was leased to the plaintiffs. The plaintiffs sued *inter alia* the main contractors in delict for the cost of repairing the plaster work. The House of Lords held that the main contractors and the sub-contractors were not under a duty of care to prevent economic loss to the plaintiffs as a result of the

---

1 In *Scott Lithgow v GEC Electrical Products Ltd* 1992 SLT 244, the Lord Ordinary (Clyde) thought at 250 ff that it would be enough if the defender had been approved by the pursuer.
2 For discussion of the relevant delicts, see pp 33 ff above.
3 [1989] AC 177, [1988] 2 All ER 992, HL.

defective plaster.[1] In the present writer's view, there was also no possibility of a *Junior Books* duty of care in this case as there was no contractual nexus between the plaintiffs and the main contractor or sub-contractor at the time of the careless act viz:

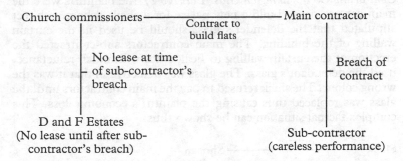

Second, even if there is an existing contractual nexus, no *Junior Books* duty of care will arise unless the defender knows the identity of the pursuer; this will therefore prevent such a duty of care arising in most cases involving mass production. For example, if A manufactures components for B who uses them to produce products which he sells to C, a distributor, which C sells to X, Y and Z etc, A does not owe a *Junior Books* duty of care to X, Y or Z to prevent *economic loss*[2] due to A's careless performance of his contract with B in supplying B with defective components: this is because A will generally not know of the contracts between C and X, Y, and Z:

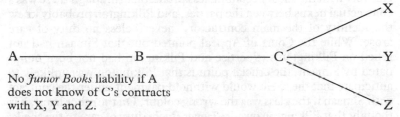

Third, even if there is an existing contractual nexus and the defender knows the identity of the pursuer, the terms of the contracts between the parties, for example exemption or indemnity clauses, may indicate that the parties intended to exclude potential liability in delict. In

1 For discussion of the absence of a duty of care to prevent economic loss arising from a defective product, see pp 81 ff below.
2 Of course, A may owe a *Donoghue v Stevenson* duty of care to X, Y and Z to prevent them suffering physical injury or damage to their property as a result of A's careless manufacture of the components.

those circumstances, the court is unlikely to find the existence of a *Junior Books* duty of care.

Finally, the defender must anticipate loss to the particular pursuer as a result of the defender's defective performance. In *Simaan General Contracting Co v Pilkington Glass Ltd (No 2)*[1] the plaintiffs were the main contractors to build a new palace for a sheik, whose architect stipulated that the defender's glass should be used in the curtain walling of the building. The main contractors sub-contracted the erection of the curtain walling to Feal, who, with much reluctance, used the defendant's glass. The glass was defective in that it was the wrong colour. The sheik refused to pay the main contractors until the glass was replaced thus causing the plaintiff's economic loss. This complex factual situation can be shown thus:

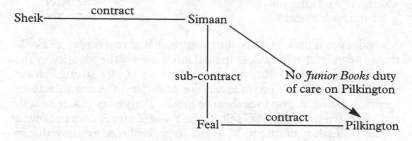

The Court of Appeal held that Pilkington did not owe Simaan a duty of care to prevent Simaan suffering loss as a result of Simaan's contract with the sheik becoming less profitable. Although there was a contractual nexus between the parties, and Pilkington probably knew the identity of the main contractor,[2] nevertheless no duty of care arose. While the Court of Appeal pointed out that Simaan had not relied on Pilkington's expertise and Pilkington had not been nominated by Simaan, the crucial point is that Pilkington was unlikely to anticipate that the sheik would withhold payment under the contract with Simaan if the glass was the wrong colour. On the other hand, it is thought that Pilkington owed a *Junior Books* duty of care to the sheik, and would have been liable in delict if the sheik had suffered economic loss as a result of Pilkington's defective performance of its contract with Feal.[3]

1 [1988] QB 758, [1988] 1 All ER 791, CA.
2 There was no technical discussions between Simaan and Pilkington about the glass; the only reason Pilkington was used was because the sheik's architect insisted on Pilkington's glass.
3 *Simaan General Contracting Co v Pilkington Glass Ltd (No 2)* [1988] 1 All ER 791 at 803 per Bingham LJ.

The limitations which are inherent in the *Junior Books* duty of care are therefore sufficient to keep potential liability for economic loss within relatively narrow parameters. Once again we see the duty of care operating as a threshold device.

If it is accepted that the *Junior Books* duty of care is simply an extension of the delict of wrongful interference with the performance of a contract, so as to trigger liability as a result of the defender's careless conduct as well as conduct intended to harm the pursuer, then it is thought that there is a future for *Junior Books* liability. As we have seen, because of the criteria for the duty viz an existing contractual chain or nexus between the parties, the defender's knowledge of the identity of the pursuer, the defender's knowledge that his conduct will cause the pursuer economic loss etc, potential liability under *Junior Books* is kept within relatively narrow parameters.

While followed in Scotland, *Junior Books* has been consistently distinguished in cases south of the border. In *D and F Estates Ltd v Church Commissioners*[1] Lord Bridge opined[2] of *Junior Books*:

'The consensus of judicial opinion, with which I concur, seems to be that the decision of the majority is so far dependent on the unique, albeit non-contractual, relationship between the pursuer and the defender in that case and the unique scope of the duty of care owed by the defender to the pursuer arising from that relationship that the decision cannot be regarded as laying down any principle of general application in the law of tort or delict.'

The reason for this scepticism is that *Junior Books* has *not* been regarded as a case which is only concerned with wrongful interference with the pursuer's existing contracts. Instead, it has been read as laying down potential liability for economic loss arising from the careless manufacture of a defective product, which is not dangerous, in the sense of causing injury to the pursuer or damage to property. If this were the case, then there would, indeed, be cause for concern. But if analysed as above, *Junior Books* liability does not have this potential. Within its relatively narrow sphere, *Junior Books* is both an important and principled decision.

(3) Liability arising from defective products and buildings

As we have seen[3] A owes a duty of care to B when it is reasonably foreseeable that B will suffer physical injury or physical harm to his

---

1 [1988] 2 All ER 992.
2 [1988] 2 All ER 992 at 1003.
3 Page 59 above.

property as a result of A's careless acts or omissions. In *Donoghue v Stevenson*[1] it was held that the manufacturer of a product owed a duty of care to the ultimate consumer to prevent the consumer suffering personal injury or physical damage to his property as a result of a defect in the product caused by the manufacturer's carelessness. The consumer is not only entitled to damages for pain and suffering but also for economic loss which derives from the injury or damage to his property ie derivative economic loss.

There is an important limitation on the scope of *Donoghue v Stevenson* liability. The duty of care only extends to physical injuries to the pursuer or damage to the pursuer's property caused by the defective product. The damage must be done to property other than the defective product itself. For example, if a defective vacuum cleaner explodes and burns the pursuer or burns the pursuer's carpet, there is *Donoghue v Stevenson* liability. But if the defective vacuum simply does not work or it explodes and does not injure the pursuer or does not damage any other property of the pursuer there is no *Donoghue v Stevenson* liability. Why? In these circumstances, the pursuer has suffered only *pure* economic loss, ie the cost of repairing the vacuum cleaner or the difference in value between a defective or non-defective cleaner. The courts have consistently refused to allow the pursuer to recover compensation *in delict* for such losses; instead, the pursuer must resort to the law of contract to obtain compensation viz:

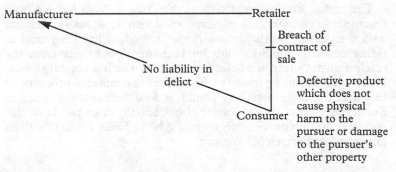

The consumer cannot sue the manufacturer in delict as the consumer has suffered only pure economic loss. The consumer must sue the retailer for *breach of contract* to recover any loss suffered as a result of the product being defective. If the ultimate consumer does not have a contract with the retailer, if, for example, the defective product was a gift from a third party, the consumer has prima facie no remedy;

---

1   1932 SC (HL) 31, discussed at pp 54 ff above.

however, the third party could assign his rights under *his* contract with the retailer to the consumer, thus enabling the consumer to recover damages for breach of contract.

It should also be noticed that there will generally be no possibility of *Junior Books* liability in this situation. This is for two reasons viz: (i) no contractual chain or nexus exists between the manufacturer and the consumer at the time of the careless act as the consumer will only enter into a contract with the retailer *after* the product has been manufactured; and (ii) the manufacturer will not know the identity of the consumer.[1]

This principle of non-liability for economic loss also applies to the provision of services as well as the manufacture of goods. In *D and F Ltd v Church Commissioners for England*[2] the plaintiffs incurred expense in repairing defective plasterwork. The defective plasterwork was not a danger to the plaintiffs' person or property. The House of Lords held that the plaintiffs could not sue the defendants, who were responsible for the defective plasterwork, in *delict* because they had only suffered pure economic loss ie the cost of repair. The plaintiffs' only remedy could be in contract.

However, at one time, there appeared to be an exception in respect of defective buildings. Local authorities are under a duty to ensure that buildings conform to building regulations and bye-laws: this is done by a local authority engineer approving the plans and the design of the proposed building. In *Anns v Merton London Borough Council*[3] the defendants approved the design of the foundations of a building. After it was built, the foundations were discovered to be defective. The House of Lords held that the local authority owed the owner[4] of the house a duty of care in this situation and that damages could include the cost of repair. It was also decided that the builder owed a similar duty of care to the owner of the property. The fact that the plaintiff had only suffered pure economic loss appeared to be irrelevant. The concept of the duty of care was clearly being used as a threshold device significantly to extend the parameters of delictual liability for pure economic loss. In a famous passage, Lord Wilberforce explained:[5]

'The position has now been reached that in order to establish that a duty of care arises in a particular situation, it is not necessary to bring the facts of that situation within those of previous situations in which a duty of care has been held to exist. Rather the question has to be approached in two stages. First one

1 It might, of course, be different in both respects if the manufacturer was supplying a product specifically designed for the consumer: see discussion at p 80 above.
2 [1988] 2 All ER 992. There was no *Junior Books* liability in this case. See p 79 above.
3 [1978] AC 728, [1977] 2 All ER 492, HL.
4 Technically the plaintiff in this case was a lessee of the property.
5 [1978] AC 728 at 751–752.

has to ask whether, as between the alleged wrongdoer and the person who has suffered damage there is a sufficient relationship of proximity or neighbourhood such that, in the reasonable contemplation of the former, carelessness on his part may be likely to cause damage to the latter, in which case a prima facie duty of care arises. Secondly, if the first question is answered affirmatively, it is necessary to consider whether there are any considerations which ought to negative, or to reduce or limit the scope of the duty or the class of person to whom it is owed or the damages to which a breach of it may give rise.'

Applying these principles, Lord Wilberforce held that the local authority owed a duty of care to the owner of a building which was subject to latent defects in construction when the plans had been inspected and approved by the local authority; the fact that the owner may only suffer pure economic loss was not sufficient to deny the existence of the duty on policy grounds as the class of potential plaintiffs was restricted to the owners or lessees of the property.

This was to prove to be the high-water mark of the extension of the parameters of delictual liability for defective buildings. The courts thereafter refused to use Lord Wilberforce's two-stage test further to extend the scope of liability. At length, *Anns* itself came to be doubted and was ultimately overruled in *Murphy v Brentwood District Council*.[1] In this case, a builder laid foundations of a house in accordance with designs approved by the local authority. The foundations proved to be defective. The owner could not afford the £45,000 required for repairs; instead he sold the house for £35,000 less than its market value if the foundations had been sound. The owner sued the local authority for the loss of the value of the house. The House of Lords held that *Anns* was wrongly decided. Neither a local authority nor a builder owed the owner of a house a duty of care in respect of pure economic loss arising from the defective construction of the property; pure economic loss included the cost of repairs or the loss of the property's value.

The House of Lords was also sceptical of what is known as the 'complex structure' doctrine. It can be argued that the foundations should be regarded as separate from the rest of the house; if they were defective and caused physical damage to another part of the house, for example, cracks in the walls, this would be damage to 'other' property

---

1 [1990] 2 All ER 908. The House of Lords doubted the value of Lord Wilberforce's two-stage test for the existence of a duty of care. Instead, it should only be imposed by analogy with earlier precedents ie it is an incremental process. In this respect, *Murphy* has been followed in Scotland: *Nordic Oil Services Ltd v Berman*. '[I]n determining the existence and scope of a duty of care in a context in which a claim is made for economic loss, the court must have particular regard to the traditional categorisation of situations in which duties may or may not have been recognised in particular circumstances': 1993 SLT 1164 at 1171 per the Lord Ordinary (Osborne).

and fall within the *Donoghue v Stevenson* duty of care. However, the view was taken that this is unrealistic:[1]

'The reality is that the structural elements in any building form a single indivisible unit of which the different parts are essentially interdependent. To the extent that there is any defect in one part of the structure it must to a greater or lesser degree necessarily affect all other parts of the structure. Therefore any defect in the structure is a defect in the quality of the whole and it is quite artificial, in order to impose a legal liability which the law would not otherwise impose, to treat a defect in an integral structure, so far as it weakens the structure, as a dangerous defect liable to cause damage to "other property".'

But where a distinct item is incorporated into the structure, for example, a central heating boiler, then there can be *Donoghue v Stevenson* liability if, as a result of a defect, it causes damage to the house. The owner in these circumstances could sue the manufacturer of the boiler for physical damage to his 'other' property ie the house.

It is important to examine the implications of *Murphy* for purchasers of heritable property. Consider the following example. A, a company, enters into a contract with B to build a block of flats. After the flats are completed, A feus the flats to various purchasers (vassals) including C. After a few years, cracks appear in C's flat. It is discovered that the foundations are unsound and that it will cost approximately £10,000 to have them repaired viz:

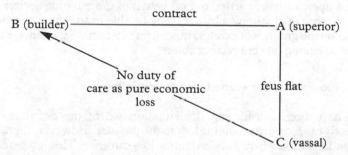

As a result of *Murphy*, C has no delictual remedy against B as C has only suffered pure economic loss, ie B does not owe C a duty of care in respect of the cost of repairs.[2] While there is a contractual relationship between A and B, this will not help B as a superior does not warrant the quality of the buildings on the land feued. Similarly, if B enters

---

1 [1990] 2 All ER 908 at 928 per Lord Bridge.
2 If C was injured or any property of C's other than the house was damaged, C can sue B in delict as B owes C a duty of care under the *Donoghue v Stevenson* neighbourhood principle.

into a contract to build a house for A who later sells the house to C (a singular successor), B does not owe C a duty of care to prevent C suffering pure economic loss as a result of defects in the building viz:

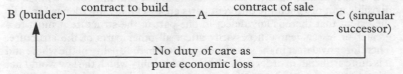

Again, although there is a contract between A and C, C will have no contractual remedy against A as A does not usually warrant the quality of the buildings on the land disponed.

Moreover, B does not owe a *Junior Books* duty of care to C in either of these examples. This is because there is no contractual nexus between B and C at the time of the careless act as C only purchases the property *after* it is built; even if C had an option from A to purchase a flat while it was being built, a *Junior Books* duty of care will not arise unless B knows the identity of the purchaser, C.

Because of the absence of a delictual claim against B or a contractual claim against A, in order to protect his interests C should obtain an independent survey *before* purchasing the property. If as a result of the surveyor's carelessness the defects are not discovered, C can sue the surveyor for breach of contract. And, as we have seen,[1] even if C relied upon a survey carried out on behalf of C's building society for the purpose of obtaining a loan, C may be able to sue the surveyor in delict on the grounds of careless misrepresentation where damages for pure economic loss are recoverable.

(4) Non-liability for secondary economic loss

We have been considering the situation where the defender has directly caused pure economic loss to the pursuer. However, there is a second situation where pure economic loss can arise. This is where the defender has caused physical harm to A or A's property, but as a result B suffers economic loss. This will most often arise where, as a consequence of A's injury or damage to A's property, B suffers economic loss because a contract which B had with A cannot be fulfilled or is no longer profitable. This is known as secondary economic loss.

In *Reavis v Clan Line Steamers*[2] Mrs Reavis and her orchestra were involved in a collision at sea which was caused *inter alia* by the fault of

---

1 Pages 77 ff above.
2 1925 SC 725.

the defender, the owner of the ship in which they were sailing. Some members of the orchestra were drowned and the orchestra had to be disbanded. Mrs Reavis claimed that the services of the players had been secured by contracts of employment and she sought damages from the defender for the loss of profits she had sustained as a result of the deaths and injuries of her employees. The court held that she was not entitled to recover. An employer is not entitled to sue in delict in respect of secondary economic loss sustained as a result of the death or injury of an employee caused by the negligence of a third party. In other words, the defender did not owe Mrs Reavis a duty of care to prevent her suffering economic loss as a result of her employees being no longer able to perform their contracts of employment with her. If Mrs Reavis had been injured, she could, of course, recover for derivative economic loss arising from her *own* injuries – but she could not sue in respect of the death or injury of her employees. The injured employees and the families of the deceased employees, would, of course, have separate claims in delict against the defender.

Thus, where a person is injured or property is damaged, prima facie, it is only the injured person or the owner of the property who has title to sue. Third parties who suffer economic loss as a result of the injuries or damage to the property are not entitled to sue for secondary economic loss as the defender does not owe them a duty of care. Thus, for example, in *Dynamco v Holland*[1] the defender's excavator damaged an underground electric supply cable owned by the South of Scotland Electricity Board. As a result, there was a power cut at the pursuer's factory which lasted for 15½ hours. The pursuer sued for the loss of profits while the factory was closed. The court held that while the defender owed a duty of care to the electricity board not to damage its property, ie the cable, the defender did not owe a duty to the pursuer in respect of secondary economic loss, even although such loss was reasonably foreseeable. If, of course, the power cut had damaged the pursuer's machinery, an action would lie and the pursuer could recover any derivative economic loss.

In the important case of *Nacap v Moffat Plant Ltd*,[2] the pursuers entered into a contract with British Gas to lay a pipeline owned by British Gas in the North Sea. During the work, the defenders damaged the pipeline. As a result, Nacap was unable to complete the work in the time agreed in their contract with British Gas and consequently suffered economic loss. The Inner House held that the pursuers had no title to sue as they were not the owners of the pipeline; in

1 1971 SC 257, 1972 SLT 38.
2 1987 SLT 221, reversing 1986 SLT 326.

other words, they could not sue in delict for the secondary economic loss they had suffered as a result of the damage to property owned by a third party, viz British Gas.

This approach has been followed in England. In *Candlewood Navigation Corpn v Mitsui OSK Lines Ltd, the Mineral Transporter*[1] the plaintiffs time-chartered a vessel from the owners of a ship. The vessel was damaged by the defendants. The Privy Council held that the plaintiffs could not recover damages for the hire charges they had to continue to pay and the loss of profits they had incurred while the ship underwent repairs. The defendants did not owe a duty of care to the plaintiffs in respect of the secondary economic loss they had suffered as a result of their contract with the owners becoming less profitable viz:

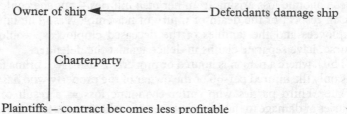

Owner of ship ◄─────────── Defendants damage ship

Charterparty

Plaintiffs – contract becomes less profitable

In this and the previous two cases, a *Junior Books* duty of care does not arise because there is no contractual nexus between the parties. Even if, in *Dynamco*, the defender had been engaged on a contract with the electricity board, who had, of course, a contract with its customer, Dynamco, *Junior Books* liability would still not have arisen because the defender would not have known the identity of the pursuer.

Nevertheless, in other circumstances, it is thought that there could be sufficient proximity between the parties for a *Junior Books* duty to arise. In *Leigh and Sillivan v Aliakmon Shipping*[2] the plaintiff (the buyers) entered into a c & f contract for the purchase of steel coils. Under a c & f contract the seller arranges for the shipping of the goods and obtains a bill of lading from the shipper. The bill of lading is the contract of carriage of the goods. The buyer becomes the owner of the goods when the bill of lading is indorsed by the seller and delivered to the buyer against payment by the buyer of the price. On indorsement, the buyer 'steps into the shoes' of the seller in relation to the bill of lading issued by the shipper. Accordingly, if the goods are damaged in transit, the buyer can sue the shipper for breach of contract. This did

1 [1986] AC 1, [1985] 2 All ER 935.
2 [1986] AC 785, [1986] 2 All ER 145, affirming [1985] 2 All ER 44.

not happen in this case as the c & f contract was varied by the parties with the effect that the seller remained owner even although the risk of damage to the goods passed to the buyers. The bill of lading was not indorsed, so that the buyers did not have title to sue the shippers for breach of contract. When they eventually became the owners of the goods, the plaintiff attempted to sue the shippers in delict. The complex facts can be shown thus:

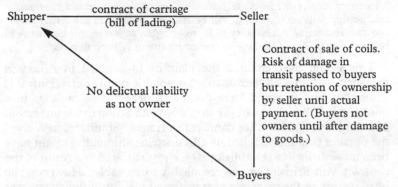

Because the buyers assumed the risk under the contract of sale, they had no right to sue the seller for breach of contract when the goods were damaged. As a result of the variation, the buyers could not use the usual remedy in a c & f situation of suing the shipper for breach of contract. The House of Lords held that the buyers could not sue the shipper in delict, because they were not the owners of the goods at the time the goods were damaged. *Junior Books* was distinguished on the grounds that unlike the buyers the pursuer in that case was the owner of the floor when it was carelessly laid.[1] However, if *Junior Books* had been argued as a wrongful interference with contracts case, there could have been liability if the shipper had known the identity of the buyers and the existence of the c & f contract when they carelessly performed their contract with the sellers. However, such an argument would probably have failed as the shipper had no knowledge of the variation of the contract between the sellers and the buyers and that the buyers had consequently not become the owners of the goods in the usual way.[2]

---

1 [1986] 2 All ER 145 at 155 per Lord Brandon.
2 If, in *Reavis v Clan Line Steamers* 1925 SC 725, Mrs Reavis had been killed or injured with the result that her employees suffered economic loss, it is submitted that there would now be a possibility of their recovering damages for economic loss under *Junior Books* if the defender, who had a contract of carriage with Mrs Reavis, had known the identity of her employees and the existence of the contracts of employment.

In the *Aliakmon* case, an attempt was made to circumvent the principle of non-recovery in delict for secondary economic loss by invoking the doctrine of 'transferred loss'. In the Court of Appeal,[1] Goff LJ formulated the doctrine thus:

'Where A owes a duty of care in tort [delict] not to cause physical damage to B's property, and commits a breach of that duty in circumstances in which the loss of or physical damage to property will ordinarily fall on B but (as is reasonably foreseeable by A) such loss or damage, by reason of a contractual relationship falls on C, then C will be entitled, subject to the terms of any contract restricting A's liability to B, to bring an action in tort against A in respect of such loss or damage to the extent that it falls on him, C.'

This would have enabled the plaintiff to succeed in *Aliakmon* provided such loss was reasonably foreseeable by the defendant; it is submitted that it would have been reasonably foreseeable as in a normal c & f contract the buyer would have an action to sue on the bill of lading if the goods were damaged in transit. Similarly, in *Nacap*[2] the pursuer could have relied on this doctrine although it might have been more difficult to establish that the loss suffered as a result of the contract with British Gas was reasonably foreseeable.[3] However, the introduction of the principle of transferred loss into English law was vigorously rejected by the House of Lords.[4] It is thought, after *Nacap*, that the principle would not fare any better north of the border.

Thus, it appears that the courts have set their face against recovery in delict for secondary economic loss by restricting title to sue to the person injured or the owner of the damaged property. However, where a person has a possessory title to the property, he may be able to sue. For example, if A pledges his watch worth £500 to B in return for a loan of £300, B, the pledgee, has a possessory title to the watch. If the watch is damaged by C, B can sue C in delict to the extent of his interest in the watch ie up to £300.

Cases of possessory title apart, it is clear from *Nacap* that merely to have lawful possession of the property is not sufficient, as the pursuers in that case had lawful possession of the pipeline which they were laying. In *North of Scotland Helicopters Ltd v United Technologies*

---

1 [1985] 2 All ER 44 at 77.
2 1987 SLT 221, discussed at pp 87 ff above.
3 Goff LJ expressly stated ([1985] 2 All ER 44 at 77) that the doctrine would not have helped the plaintiff in the *Mineral Transporter* case [1985] 2 All ER 935; the present writer would have thought that loss to a time-charterer from a collision would be reasonably foreseeable by a shipowner: see p 88 above.
4 [1986] 2 All ER 145 at 157 per Lord Brandon. Since then, however, Lord Brandon has retired and Lord Goff has been appointed to the House of Lords.

Corpn (No 2),[1] however, the pursuers were allowed to sue in respect of economic loss sustained as a result of damage to a helicopter which they leased but did not own. Under the lease agreement with the owner, a finance company, the second pursuer had to maintain the helicopter, indemnify the finance company if the helicopter was damaged or destroyed and replace or repair the helicopter at the pursuer's expense. It was agreed with the finance company that the helicopter could be flown by the first pursuer, a subsidiary company of the second pursuer. The finance company had no obligation to provide a replacement if the helicopter was not operational. Owing to a fault in the manufacturing process, the helicopter went on fire and was destroyed. The pursuers sought damages for the economic loss sustained in indemnifying the finance company in terms of the lease, and loss of profits sustained due to the absence of a helicopter. The complex facts can be shown thus:

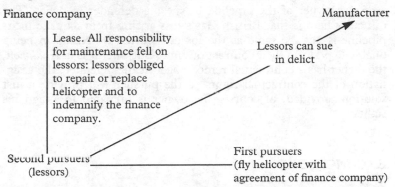

Finance company

Lease. All responsibility for maintenance fell on lessors: lessors obliged to repair or replace helicopter and to indemnify the finance company.

Second pursuers (lessors)

Manufacturer

Lessors can sue in delict

First pursuers (fly helicopter with agreement of finance company)

The Lord Ordinary (Davidson) held that because of the onerous terms of the lease and the fact that the finance company had agreed that the helicopter could be flown by the first pursuers, the second pursuers were 'owners' of the helicopter as a matter of substance even if, technically, the finance company was the owner as a matter of law. In other words, the pursuers had far more than lawful possession of the helicopter and this gave them title to sue, in spite of not being the legal owner of the property. Thus it appears that there can be exceptional circumstances when a non-owner has title to sue.

It was assumed in this case that the manufacturer owed a duty of care to the pursuer. However, it should be noticed that the destruction of the helicopter was pure economic loss, ie the defective product did not cause physical injury to the pursuers or any other property

1 1988 SLT 778n, OH.

owned by the pursuers – it only destroyed itself. The manufacturer's duty of care could therefore not have arisen by virtue of the *Donoghue v Stevenson* neighbourhood principle. Nor could there be a *Junior Books* duty of care owing to the absence of a contractual nexus between the pursuer and defender at the time of the fault in the manufacturing process. The action could therefore have been defended on the ground that the defender did not owe a duty of care to prevent pure economic loss arising to the pursuers and, indeed, the finance company, rather than the absence of the pursuers' title to sue for secondary economic loss.

In the cases we have been discussing, the only remedy available to a person who has suffered secondary economic loss is to obtain an assignation of the owner's rights against the defender. In Scots law, delictual rights as well as contractual rights can be assigned. For example in *Nacap*, British Gas could have assigned to the pursuer its rights as owner of the pipeline to sue the defender in delict. The difficulty here is that British Gas's loss arising from damage to its pipeline is not the same as the losses incurred by Nacap in being unable to perform their contract on time. But where, as in *Aliakmon*, the owner has a contractual remedy against the defender, the assignation of the contractual rights to the pursuer will provide a just solution provided, of course, the owner is prepared to assign his rights.

E. CONCLUSION

In this chapter, we have been considering how the concept of a duty of care has been used as a threshold device to set the parameters of liability in delict. Four important areas have been examined viz pure omissions, nervous shock, wrongful life actions and economic loss. The last has been treated in depth because it has been an area of extensive judicial activity and controversy and, in addition, is conceptually difficult. There are, of course, other areas where the duty of care is used as a threshold device and some of these, at least, will be treated later in this book.[1]

At the end of the day, the imposition of a duty of care is a matter of policy for the courts. As a final example, this is graphically illustrated by the decision of the House of Lords in *Hill v Chief Constable of West*

---

1 For example, delictual liability of public authorities: see pp 171 ff below.

Yorkshire.[1] There, the mother of the last victim of the Yorkshire Ripper brought an action against the Chief Constable of West Yorkshire on the grounds that the police had been careless in their investigation of the earlier murders and should have apprehended the killer before her daughter was murdered. The House of Lords held that the police did not owe a duty of care to individual members of the public to identify and apprehend an unknown criminal, even though it was reasonably foreseeable that a member of the public would be harmed if the criminal was not detected and apprehended. Lord Keith of Kinkel held[2] that on the facts the victim had been at no special distinctive risk as compared with other potential victims and therefore the police did not owe her a duty of care.[3] But he expressly stated that the imposition of such a duty of care was contrary to public policy as it would involve the courts in an elaborate examination of the conduct of a police investigation and would waste valuable police time in defending such actions.[4] As Lord Templeman observed:[5]

'. . . if this action lies, every citizen will be able to require the court to investigate the performance of every policeman. If the policeman concentrates on one crime, he may be accused of neglecting others. If the policeman does not arrest on suspicion a suspect with previous convictions, the police force may be held liable for subsequent crimes. The threat of litigation against the police force would not make a policeman more efficient. The necessity for defending proceedings, successfully or unsuccessfully, would distract the policeman from his duties. This action is, in my opinion misconceived and will do more harm than good.'

A duty of care will therefore be imposed only when in the view of the courts it would achieve more good than harm to do so.

1 [1988] 2 All ER 238, [1988] 2 WLR 1049.
2 [1988] 2 All ER 238 at 243.
3 Of course, an action in delict is available against the criminal.
4 [1988] 2 All ER 238 at 239.
5 [1988] 2 All ER 238 at 245.

CHAPTER 5

Breach of a duty of care

A. INTRODUCTION

We have been considering situations where an action in delict fails at the outset because there is no duty of care owed by the defender to prevent harm to the pursuer as a result of the defender's unintentional, but careless, conduct. This is done by the courts utilising the concept of a duty of care as a threshold device, and the decision whether or not to recognise the existence of a duty of care in particular circumstances ultimately involves issues of policy. The duty of care enables the courts to determine the parameters of liability in delict for unintentional, but careless, conduct.

However, even where it is recognised that the defender owes the pursuer a duty of care, a pursuer is not entitled to succeed unless it can be shown that the harm sustained by the pursuer arose as a result of a *breach* by the defender of the duty of care which he owed to the pursuer. In this chapter we shall examine the criteria which must be satisfied before the defender's act or omission will constitute a *breach* of the duty of care which, *ex hypothesi*, the defender owes to the pursuer. Only when these criteria are satisfied, ie when there is a breach by the defender of the duty of care he owes to the pursuer, will the defender be liable to make reparation to the pursuer for harm sustained as a result of the defender's breach of duty.[1]

B. THE CRITERIA USED TO ESTABLISH A BREACH OF A DUTY OF CARE

(1) Voluntary act or omission of the defender

Before there is a breach by the defender of a duty of care owed to the pursuer, the relevant act or omission must be voluntary on the part of

1 In this chapter, I owe an immense debt to W A Wilson, 'The Analysis of Negligence' in *Introductory Essays on Scots Law* (2nd edn, 1984) pp 126–148.

the defender. In *Waugh v James K Allan Ltd*[1] a lorry driver, Gemmell, suffered symptoms consistent with a gastric attack; after he felt recovered, he drove the lorry. In fact, the symptoms were the onset of thrombosis and he shortly thereafter died at the wheel. The lorry swerved and seriously injured a pedestrian. While the lorry driver clearly owed the pursuer a duty of care, it was held that there was no breach of duty in this case. On the medical evidence, the driver had no reason to anticipate the onset of the thrombosis and had therefore acted reasonably in driving the lorry after he felt better. Accordingly, the driver's act which injured the pursuer was involuntary, ie his death, and there was therefore no breach of the duty of care. If, however, the driver should have realised that he was seriously ill, then the act of driving while unfit to do so would have been a voluntary act which could have amounted to a breach of duty. But, in the circumstances, Lord Reid observed:[2]

'I am therefore of opinion that the appellant [the pursuer] has failed to prove that Gemmell acted rashly or negligently in driving off so soon after his illness, and no other fault can be imputed to him. One must have great sympathy with the appellant who has suffered so severely through no fault of his own, but I find it impossible to blame Gemmell. Accordingly, I would dismiss this appeal.'

(2) The defender's act or omission must have as its reasonable and probable consequence harm to the pursuer

Before there is a breach of a duty of care, harm to the pursuer must be a reasonable and probable consequence of the acts or omissions of the defender. The leading case is *Muir v Glasgow Corporation*.[3] Members of the Milton Free Church were having a Sunday school picnic in King's Park, Glasgow. Although it was a June afternoon, it began to rain. Mrs Alexander, the manageress of a tea room/sweet shop in the park, gave permission to the party to have their tea in the tea room. Access to the tea room was through a narrow passage where the sweet shop was situated. Some of the children were queuing in the passage to purchase sweets from the shop. When two members of the party carried a tea urn full of boiling water through the passage in order to gain entry to the tea room, the tea urn dropped, scalding several children. It was never established how the urn was upset. We can illustrate the case as follows:

1 1964 SC (HL) 102, 1964 SLT 269. The pursuer was suing the driver's employer as vicariously liable for the employee's delict: on vicarious liability, see pp 178 ff below.
2 1964 SC (HL) 102 at 106.
3 1943 SC (HL) 3, 1944 SLT 60.

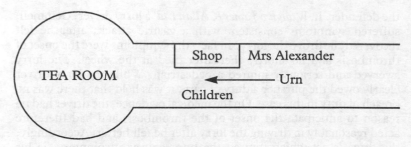

Clearly the persons carrying the urn owed a duty of care to the injured children but no action in delict was brought against them, either because of difficulty in establishing the cause of the accident or, more likely, because they had no assets. Instead, an action was brought against the Glasgow Corporation on the basis that, as Mrs Alexander's employer, the corporation was vicariously liable for any delicts she committed in the course of her employment.[1] It was accepted that as manageress of the tea room Mrs Alexander owed a duty of care to any persons she allowed to enter the premises. But, in order to succeed, the pursuer had to show that by allowing the urn to be carried through the passage crowded with children, Mrs Alexander was in breach of the duty of care she undoubtedly owed to them. The House of Lords took the view that Mrs Alexander could only be liable for those consequences of her actions which a reasonable person in her position would have had in contemplation in the circumstances of the case. Lord Thankerton said:[2] '. . . it has long been held in Scotland that all that a person can be held bound to foresee are the reasonable and probable consequences of the failure to take care, judged by the standard of the ordinary reasonable man [sic]'. Lord Wright considered[3] that:

'It is not, of course, a question of what she [Mrs Alexander] actually thought at the moment, but what the hypothetical reasonable person could have foreseen. That is the standard to determine the scope of her duty. This involves the question: Was the operation of carrying the tea-urn something which a reasonable person in Mrs Alexander's position should have realised would render the place in which it was performed dangerous to the children in the circumstances? This is the crucial issue of fact and the acid test of liability.'

The House of Lords held that the answer to this question was no. Mrs Alexander was entitled to assume that the tea-urn would be carried by responsible persons and that if carried with reasonable care would

1 On vicarious liability, see pp 178 ff below.
2 1943 SC (HL) 3 at 8.
3 1943 SC (HL) 3 at 15.

cause no harm to the children. A reasonable person in her position would not therefore have foreseen as a possibility, let alone a probability, that the urn would slip and the children would be scalded. Thus, because injury to the children could not have been foreseen as a *reasonable* and *probable* consequence of allowing the urn to be carried through the passage, Mrs Alexander had not broken the duty of care she owed the children.[1]

Muir v Glasgow Corporation is therefore authority that before a breach of a duty of care can arise, the defender's acts or omissions must have as their *reasonable* and *probable* consequence injury to the pursuer or damage to the pursuer's property. The test is the reasonable foresight of the hypothetical reasonable person in the position of the defender, as opposed to what the particular defender actually foresaw. But since the hypothetical reasonable person is in effect the court, it will be obvious that the scope of the duty of care in a particular case is, to some extent at least, determined by the judges.

Thus, for example, in *Malcolm v Dickson*[2] a painter who was working on a house, set the house on fire. A guest who was staying there attempted to save some of the property. As a result of his exertions, the guest collapsed and died. The court held that the painter had not broken the duty of care he owed to the deceased because it could not have been anticipated by a reasonable person in the defender's position that an occupant of the house would die as a result of trying to salvage furniture. As Lord Patrick said:[3]

'It would not occur to the ordinary reasonable man that a reasonable and prob able consequence of his being careless in burning paint from a window frame would be that some intervener would suffer a substantial injury through over-exertion, strain and excitement in carrying furniture from the house.'

It is important to note in this case that the deceased died from a heart attack. If he had died as a result of the fire, for example, suffocated by smoke, it is submitted that there would have been a breach of the duty of care as it is foreseeable as a reasonable and probable consequence of carelessly setting a house on fire that an occupant might die from the smoke.

Since policy considerations are inevitably involved in determining what the hypothetical reasonable person can be deemed to foresee, it should occasion little surprise that, as a general rule, the courts take the view that when a person causes an accident, it is a reasonable and

---

1 Lord Wright thought it would have been different if, for example, Mrs Alexander had allowed lions or tigers to be taken through the passage: 1943 SC (HL) 3 at 16.
2 1951 SC 542, 1951 SLT 357.
3 1951 SC 542 at 556.

probable consequence of his carelessness that a rescuer may appear on the scene and be injured. The extent to which the courts are prepared to compensate injured rescuers is illustrated by *Videan v British Transport Commission*.[1] In this case, a child was trespassing on a railway line. A driver of a trolley, who was driving carelessly, did not see the child on the line. The child's father, who was the station master, threw himself from the platform on to the track in order to save his child. As a result, the father was killed by the trolley. The Court of Appeal held that while the driver had not broken his duty of care to the child as the child's presence on the line was not reasonably foreseeable, he had nevertheless broken the duty of care that he owed to the child's father. A reasonable man in the position of the driver would have foreseen as a reasonable and probable consequence of his careless driving that he might endanger someone, in which case it was also a reasonable and probable consequence of his carelessness that another might come to his rescue and be injured attempting to save him.[2]

In determining whether or not the injury was a reasonable and probable consequence of a careless act or omission, the scientific knowledge available to the hypothetical reasonable person at that time can be crucial. In *Roe v Minister of Health*[3] a patient was given a spinal anaesthetic. As was ordinary practice at the time, the phials containing the anaesthetic were kept in a solution of phenol. Unknown to the hospital, the phials developed invisible cracks and the anaesthetic became impregnated with phenol. As a result of the phenol in the anaesthetic, the patient was paralysed. The court held that the defendant had not broken the duty of care owed to the plaintiff: given the state of scientific knowledge at the time, a reasonable medical practitioner could not have foreseen that paralysis of a patient was a reasonable and probable consequence of storing the phials in phenol.

Before there is a breach of the duty of care, the act or omission must have as its reasonable and probable consequence injury to the *pursuer*. In *Bourhill v Young*,[4] for example, even although Young owed pedestrians a duty of care, he did not breach that duty in respect of Mrs Bourhill because a reasonable motor cyclist could not have foreseen as a reasonable and probable consequence of his careless driving that a pedestrian who was 50 feet or so away from the collision, ie outwith the area of potential physical danger, would be injured.

---

1 [1963] 2 QB 650, [1963] 3 WLR 374.
2 See also on rescuers, *Steel v Glasgow Iron and Steel Co Ltd* 1944 SC 237, 1945 SLT 70.
3 [1954] 2 QB 66, [1954] 2 All ER 131, CA.
4 1942 SC (HL) 78: for full discussion see pp 63 ff above.

Nevertheless, in some cases the courts have taken a very liberal view of what the hypothetical reasonable person could foresee as a reasonable and probable consequence of a careless act or omission. In *Carmarthenshire County Council v Lewis*[1] the council ran a nursery school. In the absence of a teacher, a young child left an unlocked room, crossed the playground, went through the gate on to a busy street where a motorist swerved to avoid the child. As a result, the *driver* was killed. The House of Lords held that the motorist's death was foreseeable as a reasonable and probable consequence of leaving a child unattended in an unlocked schoolroom. This surely is taking the concept of reasonable foreseeability to its limits.

It is not, however, necessary reasonably to foresee the *extent* of the pursuer's injuries; it is enough that the injuries actually sustained by the pursuer are of a *kind* which would be foreseeable as a reasonable and probable consequence of the defender's careless conduct. Nor does every aspect of the accident have to be reasonably foreseeable. These points were settled by the House of Lords in the important decision, *Hughes v Lord Advocate*.[2] In order to work on underground cables, Post Office workers uncovered a manhole. They erected a canvas shelter over the manhole. At 5 pm when it was dusk, they left the manhole unattended; they also left outside the shelter a ladder, a rope, and paraffin warning lamps. Two boys[3] saw the shelter and decided to explore. They carried the ladder, the rope and a paraffin lamp inside the tarpaulin. One boy tripped over the lamp which fell into the manhole. The paraffin spilled from the lamp, was vaporised by the heat and there was an explosion. There was a rush of flame and one of the lads fell into the manhole and suffered severe burns. It was agreed by expert witnesses that in the circumstances[4] an explosion was not reasonably foreseeable. But it was accepted that the workmen were careless in leaving the manhole unattended. The House of Lords held that it was foreseeable as a reasonable and probable consequence of leaving the manhole unattended that a child might enter the tent with a lamp, that the paraffin might spill and the child suffer a burn, ie that a boy might be burned by the lamp. This was sufficient to establish a breach of the duty of care which the workmen undoubtedly owed to prevent physical harm to pedestrians by leaving the manhole unattended. The fact that there had been an unforeseeable explosion and that the child's burns were therefore much worse than could have

---

1 [1955] AC 549, [1955] 1 All ER 565, HL.
2 1963 SC (HL) 31, 1963 SLT 150.
3 The pursuer, aged 8, and his 10-year-old *uncle!*
4 Cf if they had been working on a gas main.

been reasonably anticipated, was irrelevant. As Lord Morris of Bor-th-y-Gest explained:[1]

'The circumstances that an explosion as such could not have been contemplated does not alter the fact that it could reasonably have been foreseen that a boy who played in and about the canvas shelter and played with the things that were thereabouts might get hurt and might in some way burn himself. That is just what happened. The pursuer did burn himself, though his burns were more grave than would have been expected. The fact that the features and developments of an accident may not reasonably have been foreseen does not mean that the accident itself was not foreseeable. The pursuer was, in my view, injured as a result of the type or kind of accident or occurrence that could reasonably have been foreseen.'

Hughes v Lord Advocate is therefore authority that a breach of a duty of care will occur when the pursuer suffers the kind or type of injury which is a reasonable and probable consequence of the defender's careless act or omission; the fact that the injuries sustained are greater than could have been reasonably foreseen and/or that some of the causes of the accident were unforeseeable is irrelevant, as long as the type of injury suffered by the pursuer and the fact that an accident could occur as a result of the defender's carelessness are reasonably foreseeable.

It is interesting to contrast this decision with the later case of *Doughty v Turner*.[2] Here it was an employer's practice to cover cauldrons of molten metal with asbestos covers. Owing to the employer's carelessness, a cover was not placed securely over a cauldron. As a result, it slipped into the molten metal. The asbestos reacted with the liquid, caused the cauldron to explode and an employee was blinded by the molten metal. The employer undoubtedly owed a duty of care to his employee. The question was whether the employer was in breach of his duty. The expert evidence established that given the nature of scientific knowledge at the time, it was not reasonably foreseeable that asbestos would react with the molten metal to cause an explosion. However, the Court of Appeal accepted that it was reasonably foreseeable that if the lid was not securely fastened it might slip into the cauldron causing a splash which might burn an employee within the vicinity of the cauldron. It might be thought that following *Hughes v Lord Advocate*, since it was reasonably foreseeable that an employee could be burned as a result of a splash, it was irrelevant that the employee had suffered more severe burns as a result of an unforeseeable explosion. However, the court

1 1963 SC (HL) 31 at 43–44.
2 [1964] 1 QB 518, [1964] 2 WLR 240.

rejected that argument on the basis that a splash is caused by a body displacing a liquid while an explosion is an eruption of the liquid from within.

It might appear difficult to reconcile the two decisions, until it is appreciated that the plaintiff in *Doughty* was not within the area where there was a risk of danger of being burned by a *splash*. In other words, given that an explosion was not reasonably foreseeable, it was not reasonably foreseeable that a person in the physical position of the plaintiff would be burned at all. The boys in *Hughes* were under the tarpaulin and it was reasonably foreseeable that persons in that position could be burned by the lamp. The plaintiff failed in *Doughty* for the same reason that the pursuer failed in *Bourhill v Young*.[1] If, for example, in *Hughes* a pedestrian who was 50 feet from the manhole had been injured by the unforeseeable explosion, it is submitted that he would not have been successful as it was not foreseeable as a reasonable and probable consequence of leaving the manhole unattended that a person so far away from the manhole would have been burnt by a paraffin warning lamp.

Finally, there can be difficulties if a defender has been careless but the damage to the pursuer has been caused as a result of the intervention of a third party. As a general rule, there will be no breach by the defender of his duty of care in these circumstances unless it is foreseeable as a reasonable and probable consequence of the defender's carelessness that a third party would intervene and harm the pursuer. In *Smith v Littlewoods Organisation Ltd; Maloco v Littlewoods Organisation Ltd*[2] the defender owned an empty cinema. Vandals broke in and started a fire which damaged neighbouring property. While the defenders owed the pursuers, as neighbouring proprietors, a duty of care not to damage their property, the House of Lords held that there had been no breach of the duty in the circumstances. The defenders did not know that vandals were trespassing on their property and kindling fires there. Accordingly, it was not foreseeable that the defenders' failure to mount a 24-hour guard on the property would have as a reasonable and probable consequence the destruction by fire of neighbouring properties. As Lord Mackay of Clashfern explained:[3]

'While no doubt in this case . . . it was probable that children and young persons might attempt to break into the vacated cinema, this by no means establishes that it was a probable consequence of its being vacated with no

---

1 1942 SC (HL) 78: see pp 63 ff above.
2 1987 SCLR 489, 1987 SLT 425, HL: discussed in the context of delictual liability of owners of heritage at pp 155 ff below.
3 1987 SLT 425 at pp 155 ff below.

steps being taken to maintain it lockfast that it would be set on fire with consequent risk of damage to neighbouring properties.'

On the other hand, in *Dorset Yacht Co Ltd v Home Office*[1] borstal boys were working on the Isle of Wight under the custody and control of three borstal officers. The officers went to bed leaving the boys to their own devices. Seven boys decided to escape. They went on board a yacht moored off the island, which collided and damaged the plaintiff's yacht. The House of Lords held that the borstal officers owed a duty of care to the plaintiff, which they had broken in the circumstances. The officers were responsible for the boys. It was foreseeable as a reasonable and probable consequence of leaving the boys alone that they would try to abscond: as the only means of escape was by sea, it was also reasonably foreseeable as a probable consequence that they would steal a yacht and, being inexperienced mariners, collide with another vessel.[2] It should be noted, however, that there was a special relationship between the officers and the third party who caused the damage, ie the boys; for the officers were under a duty to guard the lads. It therefore remains a general principle that a person is not liable in delict for damage caused as a result of the deliberate acts of third parties.

(3) The standard of care – negligence

Before a defender is in breach of a duty of care, it must be established that the careless act or omission which caused harm to the pursuer constituted *culpa*. In modern terminology, the careless act or omission must amount to *negligence*. What the law requires is that the defender's conduct should not fall below the standard of the reasonable person in the position of the defender. If the defender's act or omission does not fall below the standard of the reasonable person, ie he is not negligent, there is no breach of duty even though damage to the pursuer was reasonably foreseeable as a reasonable and probable

---

1 [1970] AC 1004, [1970] 2 All ER 294, HL: discussed in the context of delictual liability of public authorities at p 173 below.
2 It is important to note that the duty was only owed to the plaintiff because it was reasonably foreseeable that damage might be caused to his yacht as the only method of effecting escape was by sea. If the boys had broken into a shop to steal food and drink, it is unlikely the court would have imposed a duty of care on the officers towards a member of the general public who suffered damage as a result of the acts of an absconding criminal ie the duty of care would be used as a threshold device to prevent delictual liability as in the case of *Hill v Chief Constable of West Yorkshire* [1988] 2 All ER 238 discussed at pp 92–93 above.

consequence of the defender's conduct. The law demands reparation only when the defender has been negligent, ie when his conduct has not met the standards of the reasonable person in the position of the defender. The law does not expect the defender to go beyond the standards of the reasonable person. The defender is only obliged not to be negligent, he is not expected to ensure that his acts or omissions never harm the pursuer. This point was forcibly made in *Muir v Glasgow Corporation*,[1] where the House of Lords held that the duty of the manageress was only to take reasonable care and not to prevent any accident occurring on the premises.

How then do we determine the standard of care of a reasonable person in any particular circumstance? Once again, as the standard of care is that of the hypothetical reasonable person in the position of the defender, the issue is ultimately a question for the court. What the judges do is to consider a number of relevant factors and then determine what steps a reasonable person would have taken to prevent a foreseeable risk of harm to the pursuer. If the defender did not take these steps – or their equivalent – then he has been negligent and has broken the duty of care which he owed to the pursuer, always pro-vided that harm to the pursuer is a reasonable and probable conse-quence of his failure to do so.

This involves a balancing process. The relevant factors to be con-sidered include the probability of injury, the seriousness of the injury, the practicability of precautions, the cost of the precautions and the utility of the defender's activities. The practice of other persons in the same type of business or profession as the defender can also be important. The court then balances the costs of preventing harm to the pursuer against the risk of injury to the pursuer. By such a calculus of risk, there emerges the standard of the reasonable person in the position of the defender. If the defender's conduct has *in fact* not reached that standard, he has been negligent and therefore in breach of the duty of care owed to the pursuer.

Considering the factors in more detail:

(a) Probability of injury to the pursuer

Even if injury to the pursuer is foreseeable, a defender who causes such an injury is not negligent in failing to take precautions to avoid such injury, if the risk of such an injury is so improbable that a reasonable person in the position of the defender would not have

---

1 1943 SC (HL) 3, discussed at pp 95 ff above.

taken any precautions. Thus, for example, in *Bolton v Stone*[1] the plaintiff was injured by a cricket ball which had been hit out of a cricket ground; this had happened on six occasions in the previous thirty years and no one had been injured. The House of Lords held that the defendants had not been negligent in failing to take precautions since the risk of injury was so slight in the circumstances that a reasonable person in the position of the defendants would not have taken any precautions. Lord Reid explained:

'In my judgment, the test to be applied here is whether the risk of damage to a person on the road was so small that a reasonable man in the position of the appellants [the defendants], considering the matter from the point of view of safety, would have thought it right to refrain from taking steps to prevent the damage. In considering the matter I think that it would be right to take into account, not only how remote is the chance that a person might be struck, but also how serious the consequences are likely to be if a person is struck, but I do not think that it would be right to take into account the difficulty of remedial measures. If cricket cannot be played on a ground without creating a substantial risk, then it should not be played there at all.'[2]

(b) Seriousness of injury to potential pursuer

As Lord Reid indicated in the passage cited immediately above, the seriousness of the consequences for a person if he is injured is a relevant factor. In *Paris v Stepney Borough Council*,[3] a mechanic who had only the use of one eye was not supplied with goggles. When he was removing a rusty bolt from a car with a hammer, a chip of metal flew into his good eye and as a result he became totally blind. The employer had known that the plaintiff had only one eye. It was accepted that it was not the practice in the industry to supply goggles to workers engaged on the plaintiff's tasks. The question, however, was whether the employer had been negligent in failing to provide goggles for an employee whom they knew was already partially sighted. In the Court of Appeal,[4] the plaintiff's claim failed. Asquith LJ took the view that while the greater risk of injury was a relevant factor, the risk of greater injury was not. The House of Lords[5] held, however, that the seriousness of the consequences of an injury for a particular plaintiff was a relevant consideration. Since the

---

1 [1951] AC 850, [1951] 1 All ER 1078, HL.
2 [1951] 1 All ER 1078 at 1086. See in relation to golf balls 'driven' off course where the pursuer succeeded *Whitefield v Bolton* 1987 SCLR 259.
3 [1951] AC 367, [1951] 1 All ER 42, HL.
4 [1949] 2 All ER 843, CA.
5 [1951] AC 367, [1951] 1 All ER 42, HL.

consequences of an eye injury for an already partially sighted person could be total blindness, the court held that the employer had been negligent in failing to provide him with goggles. It was irrelevant that the defendants might not have been negligent in failing to provide goggles to two-eyed workers. Lord Normand observed:[1]

'The court's task of deciding what precautions a reasonable and prudent man would take in the circumstances of a particular case may not be easy. Nevertheless, the judgment of the reasonable and prudent man should be allowed its common every day scope, and it should not be restrained from considering the foreseeable consequences of an accident and their seriousness for the person to whom the duty of care is owed . . . the seriousness of the injury or damage risked and the likelihood of its being in fact caused may not be the only relevant factors. For example Asquith LJ in *Daborn v Bath Tramways Motor Co Ltd* pointed out that it is sometimes necessary to take account of the consequences of not assuming a risk.'

(c) Utility of the activity

In *Daborn v Bath Tramways Motor Co Ltd*[2] during the Second World War an ambulance was used with a left hand drive. The plaintiff had put a sign at the back of the vehicle which said, 'Caution – Left hand drive – No signals'. When she was turning to the right, after having given a hand signal, she collided with a bus which she could not see was trying to overtake her. The plaintiff was injured. The defendant argued that the plaintiff had been negligent as well as the bus driver and that her damages should be reduced on the grounds of her contributory negligence.[3] The Court of Appeal held that the plaintiff had not been negligent. In the course of his judgment Asquith LJ said:[3]

'I think that the plaintiff did all that in the circumstances she could reasonably be required to do if you include in those circumstances, as I think you should: (i) the necessity in time of national emergency of employing all transport resources which were available and (ii) the inherent limitations and incapacities of this particular form of transport. In considering whether reasonable care has been observed, one must balance the risk against the consequences of not assuming that risk, and in the present instance that calculation seems to me to work out in favour of the plaintiff.'

1 [1951] 1 All ER 42 at 49.
2 [1946] 2 All ER 333.
3 On contributory negligence, see pp 125 ff below.
4 [1946] 2 All ER 333 at 336.

Thus, the social utility of the activities which it is foreseeable may cause injury must be taken into account. In *Watt v Hertfordshire County Council*[1] a woman was trapped under a vehicle. The fire service sent a lorry with a jack; when attempting to rescue the woman, the jack slipped and a fireman was injured. He claimed that the defendants, his employers, were negligent in not using a specially adapted lorry. The court held that given the emergency the employers were justified in using the vehicle which was available, ie a reasonable employer would have used the vehicle. They had not therefore fallen below the standard of the reasonable person in their position and therefore had not broken the duty of care which they owed to their employee.

(d) Practicality of precautions

The hypothetical reasonable person in the position of the defender will – indeed, can – only take such precautions as are practicable to avoid the risk of harm. In *Quinn v Cameron and Robertson*,[2] for example, the pursuer developed pneumoconiosis as a result of prolonged exposure to silica dust where he was working. His case against his employers failed on the basis that since the danger to employees from silica dust in iron foundries was not appreciated during the period when the pursuer was working for the employer (nine years prior to 1951) the defenders were not in breach of their duty of care by not providing precautions. However, another reason why they had not been negligent was that effective dust-extraction appliances were not available to the employers until 1950. The Lord President (Clyde) explains:[3]

'The Lord Ordinary has held it proved that the provision of dust-extraction appliances at plough buffs was not general practice between 1946 and 1951, and the expert evidence is really unanimously in favour of this conclusion. Indeed any apparatus to cope with the dangerous dust only seems to have come into the market in 1950, and went into general practice thereafter.'

(e) Cost of precautions

The hypothetical reasonable person in the position of the defender will take into account the cost of precautions and balance this against the probability of risk of harm and the seriousness of any injuries likely to be sustained. The defender's duty is not to be negligent; it is not to act to

---

1 [1954] 2 All ER 368, [1954] 1 WLR 208, CA.
2 1956 SC 224, 1957 SLT 2.
3 1956 SC 224 at 233.

eliminate all risks of injury to the pursuer. Thus, for example, in *Latimer v AEC Ltd*[1] a factory floor became slippery as a result of a phenomenal rainstorm. In an attempt to avoid accidents, the employer spread three tons of sawdust on the floor. Nevertheless, an employee slipped and was injured on a part of the floor *not* covered by sawdust.[2] The plaintiff argued that the employer should have closed down the factory while the floor was properly cleaned, thus eliminating the risk of employees slipping. This would, of course, have involved loss of production. The House of Lords held that the employer did all that a reasonable person would have done and was therefore not negligent. For Lord Tucker[3] the only question was:

'Has it been proved that the floor was so slippery that, remedial steps not being possible, a reasonably prudent employer would have closed down the factory rather than allow his employees to run the risks involved in continuing work? . . . The absence of any evidence that anyone in the factory during the afternoon or night shift, other than the appellant, slipped, or experienced any difficulty, or that any complaint was made by or on behalf of the workers, all points to the conclusion that the danger was, in fact, not such as to impose on a reasonable employer the obligation [to close down the factory].'

In *Charlton v Forrest Printing Ink Co*[4] it was one of the tasks of a group of employees to collect the wages for the workforce from a bank and take them to the factory. The employer had warned them of the possibility of being robbed and advised them to vary the times – and the transport used – when they went to collect the wages. Nevertheless, there was a robbery and the plaintiff was blinded by acid which had been thrown in his face. The Court of Appeal held that the employer had taken reasonable precautions and had not been negligent in failing to use the services of Securicor to uplift the wages, which could have been done at a very modest cost. This case illustrates graphically the importance of the cost of precautions in determining the standard of care of the hypothetical reasonable person in the position of the defender.

---

1 [1953] AC 643, [1953] 2 All ER 449.
2 In spite of using three tons, some areas were left uncovered!
3 [1953] 2 All ER 449 at 455.
4 [1980] IRLR 331, CA. The case was concerned with an employer's *contractual* duty to take reasonable care for the safety of employees; however, the point is also applicable in respect of the employer's *delictual* duty of care towards his employees.

(f) Practice of other persons in the same business, trade or profession as the defender

The standard to be reached is that of the hypothetical reasonable person in the position of the defender. Accordingly, the practice of other persons in the same business, trade or profession as the defender will be at least an indication of the standard expected by a reasonable person in that situation. This was recognised by the Lord President (Dunedin) in *Morton v Wm Dixon Ltd.*[1] There a miner sued his employer on the basis that the employer had been negligent in failing to provide a 'shielding contrivance' to prevent coal falling between a cage and the side of the mine shaft. In determining whether the employer was negligent and in breach of his duty of care, Lord Dunedin said:[2]

'I look upon this matter as one of great importance not merely for this particular case, but for cases of this sort generally. Where the negligence of an employer consists of what I may call a fault of omission, I think that it is absolutely necessary that the proof of fault of omission should be one of two kinds, either – to shew that the thing which he did not do was a thing which was commonly done by other persons in like circumstances, or – to shew that it was a thing which was so obviously wanted that it would be folly in anyone not to provide it.'

While the determination whether the particular defender has fallen below the requisite standard is a question of fact, the standard of care demanded is that of the hypothetical reasonable person and is ultimately the standard which the court decides is appropriate in a particular situation. If, for example, an employer does not take certain precautions, the court may still take the view that he did not reach the standard of care of the reasonable person in that situation, even although he was following the usual practice in his trade or business in not taking the precautions. Thus in *Cavanagh v Ulster Weaving Co*[3] an employee who was wearing rubber boots slipped off a roof ladder when carrying cement. No handrail was provided on the ladder. There was evidence that it was not the practice in the building trade to provide a handrail in these circumstances. The House of Lords held that evidence of the practice, while important, was not conclusive in establishing the requisite standard of care: that remained the standard of the reasonable person in the defendant's position. Given the circumstances of this case, including the fact that the employee's boots

1 1909 SC 807.
2 1909 SC 807 at 809.
3 [1960] AC 145, [1959] 2 All ER 745, HL.

were two sizes larger than they should have been, a reasonable employer would have supplied a handrail and therefore the defendant was negligent. Lord Dunedin's formula, while important, was not 'intended to depart from or modify the fundamental principle that an employer is bound to take reasonable care for the safety of his workmen'.[1]

Conversely, where the defender has not followed the usual practice in his trade or profession, he may nevertheless have taken reasonable care. In *Brown v Rolls Royce Ltd*[2] it was common practice in the defenders' industry to supply workers in the position of the pursuer with a barrier cream. The defenders considered that barrier cream was ineffective and instead took other precautions advised by a medical officer. The pursuer contracted dermatitis. The House of Lords held that while the defenders' failure to follow the usual practice was prima facie evidence of negligence, it was not conclusive. Because the defenders had taken other precautions against the risk of their employees suffering dermatitis, the defenders had not failed to take reasonable care. In relation to Lord Dunedin's formula, Lord Keith of Avonholm observed:[3]

'As has been said before in this House, Lord Dunedin was laying down no proposition of law; nor did he say that, if a practice was averred and proved which might have avoided the accident, this was necessarily conclusive of negligence on the part of an employer who had not followed the practice. The ultimate test is lack of reasonable care for the safety of the workman in all the circumstances of the case.'

The standard of care required of professional men and women, for example, members of the medical and legal professions, is discussed later in the book.[4]

(4) Remoteness of injury

In some earlier Scottish cases, delictual liability has been rejected on the ground that the injury suffered by the pursuer was 'too remote'. In *Reavis v Clan Line Steamers*,[5] for example, the court denied Mrs Reavis compensation for the loss of her orchestra on the simple basis that this loss was 'too remote'. It is submitted that the better analysis

---

1 [1959] 2 All ER 745 at 751 per Lord Keith of Avonholm.
2 1960 SC (HL) 22, 1960 SLT 119.
3 1960 SC (HL) 22 at 26.
4 See Chapter 7 below.
5 1925 SC 725, discussed at pp 86 ff above.

is that the defender did not owe her a duty of care to prevent her suffering secondary economic loss. Similarly, in *Bourhill v Young*,[1] it was argued by some of the judges that the pursuer could not sue in delict because the nervous shock she sustained was too remote. Again it is submitted that Mrs Bourhill's claim failed because (a) Young did not owe her a duty of care in respect of inflicting nervous shock (ie the duty of care as a threshold device) and (b) while Young did owe her a duty of care to prevent physical harm to her as a road user, there was no breach of that duty because it was not foreseeable that a person 50 feet away from the accident would suffer harm as a reasonable and probable consequence of the defender's careless driving. Conversely, *Hughes v the Lord Advocate*[2] has been treated as a case where the pursuer's injuries were not regarded as too remote. But it is thought that the decision is better analysed as an example of how a breach of duty occurs: viz since injury to the pursuer was foreseeable as a reasonable and probable consequence of the defender's carelessness, there was a breach of duty even although the extent of the pursuer's injuries could not have been reasonably foreseen. Accordingly, it is thought that the concept of remoteness of injury has no part to play in determining the existence of a duty of care or the breach of such a duty in the modern Scots law of delict.

Remoteness of injury must not be confused with remoteness of damages. Where there has been a breach of a duty of care and the pursuer has suffered harm, the pursuer may not be able to recover for all the losses suffered as a result of the defender's negligence. Some losses may be considered by the court to be too remote. For example, if A injures B as a result of negligent driving, B is entitled to damages for pain and suffering and derivative economic loss viz loss of wages, loss of future earnings etc. But if as a result of the accident, B was unable to post his football coupon, could he recover damages from A if he would have won a fortune if the coupon had been sent? In other words, is the loss of the winnings too remote to be compensated by A? This is a question of remoteness of damages and is discussed later in the book.[3]

1 1942 SC (HL) 78, discussed at pp 63 ff above.
2 1963 SC (HL) 31, discussed at pp 99 ff above.
3 See pp 225 ff below.

C. CONCLUSION

In this chapter we have been discussing when a breach of a duty of care arises. The defender's act or omission must be voluntary; harm to the pursuer must be reasonably foreseeable as a reasonable and probable consequence of the defender's act or omission; and, finally, the act or omission must constitute negligence ie the defender must have failed to reach the standard of care of the hypothetical reasonable person in the position of the defender. Where these criteria are satisfied, there is a breach of the duty of care owed to the pursuer and a delict is committed when the pursuer sustains harm as a result of the defender's breach of the duty of care. Even although there has been a breach of the duty of care, it is important to appreciate that the delict is only completed and delictual liability is only incurred when harm is sustained by the pursuer.[1] There must be a concurrence of *damnum* (loss or harm sustained) and *injuria* (breach of the duty of care) before delictual liability arises (*damnum injuria datum*).[2] If there is no harm or loss to the pursuer as a result of the defender's breach of a duty of care which he owes to the pursuer, then there is no delictual liability.

However, before the pursuer can succeed, he must prove that the harm or loss suffered was caused by the defender's breach of a duty of care owed to him. It is to the difficulties inherent in the concept of causation that we now turn.

1 *Watson v Fram Reinforced Concrete Co (Scotland) Ltd* 1960 SC (HL) 92, 1960 SLT 321.
2 Thus, for example, the prescriptive period will only begin to run from the date that the pursuer suffers harm, not the date of the breach of duty: for example, when Mrs Donoghue became ill, not when Stevenson manufactured the ginger beer negligently. See *Watson v Fram Reinforced Concrete Co (Scotland) Ltd* above.

CHAPTER 6

Causation and related issues

Before there is liability in delict, the pursuer must prove that the defender's breach of his duty of care was the cause of the loss or harm suffered by the pursuer. The concept of causation is a complex and difficult subject raising fundamental philosophical as well as legal issues. In a work of the present compass, only an outline of the relevant issues is given.[1]

A. FACTUAL CAUSATION

The first essential is that the defender's acts or omissions are a cause of the pursuer's injury or loss. This is a question of fact. If the defender's conduct is not a factual cause of the pursuer's injury or loss, there is no liability even if the defender has broken a duty of care which he owed to the pursuer. To use Latin terminology, the defender's breach of duty must be a *causa sine qua non* of the pursuer's injury or loss. In other words, 'but for' the defender's conduct, the pursuer would not have suffered harm. If the pursuer would have suffered the same injury notwithstanding the defender's breach of duty, then the defender's conduct is not a factual cause of the harm, ie it is not a *causa sine qua non*. Accordingly, to determine whether the defender's breach of duty is a factual cause of the pursuer's injury, we must ask ourselves whether 'but for' the breach of duty, would the pursuer's injury not have occurred. If it would *not* have occurred, the defender's act or omission is a factual cause of the pursuer's injury:[2] if it would still have occurred, the defender's act or omission is *not* a factual cause of the

---

1 For a superb account of the subject, see Hart and Honoré *Causation and the Law* (2nd edn, 1985). The book is an excellent example of the constructive use to which linguistic philosophy can be put in the context of law.
2 It is enough if it can be shown that 'but for' the defender's act or omission it was probable that the injury would not have occurred: *Porter v Strathclyde Regional Council* 1991 SLT 446.

pursuer's injury. The onus of satisfying the 'but for' test rests on the pursuer.

Two cases illustrate the application of the 'but for' test. In *Barnett v Chelsea and Kensington Hospital Management Committee*[1] the plaintiff's husband drank a cup of tea and became violently ill as the tea had been poisoned. The hospital doctor refused to treat the husband, telling him to see his own doctor. The husband died. It was held that while the defendant may have been in breach of a duty of care, the hospital was not liable because the husband would still have died of the poison, even if he had been treated by the hospital doctor, ie the husband did not die 'but for' the hospital's negligence. Accordingly, the breach of duty was not a *causa sine qua non* of the husband's death and the plaintiff's action failed.

In *Kay v Ayrshire and Arran Health Board*[2] a child was brought into hospital suffering from meningitis. He was given a massive overdose of penicillin.[3] The child thereupon suffered severe convulsions but as a result of treatment recovered. However, the child was deaf. In an action against the hospital, the defenders admitted that they were in breach of their duty of care in administering the overdose of penicillin. But the hospital denied that this breach of duty had caused the child's deafness. The House of Lords held that the onus lay on the pursuer (the child's father) to prove that 'but for' the overdose, the child would not be deaf. In the absence of evidence to show that an overdose of penicillin caused deafness in a patient and, given that deafness is common in patients who suffered meningitis, the pursuer failed to establish that 'but for' the breach of duty, deafness would not have occurred. The breach was therefore not a *causa sine qua non* of the child's deafness and the pursuer's action failed.

Perhaps the most striking example of the 'but for' test is *McWilliams v Sir William Arrol*.[4] The pursuer's husband, a steel erector, was killed. It was held that the defenders were in breach of their duty of care towards McWilliams in failing to provide him with a safety belt. However, it was also established that even if they had provided him with a safety belt, McWilliams would not have worn it. In these circumstances, the pursuer failed to prove that 'but for' the defender's breach of duty, the accident would not have occurred. The defender's breach was not a *causa sine qua non* of McWilliam's death and the pursuer's action failed.

Where the pursuer suffers loss which he would have suffered

1 [1969] 1 QB 428, [1968] 1 All ER 1068.
2 1987 SLT 577, HL, affirming 1986 SLT 435.
3 30 times the prescribed amount.
4 1962 SC (HL) 70, 1962 SLT 121.

anyway, but, as a result of the defender's breach of duty, he suffers the loss at an earlier date, the Scottish courts have held that the 'but for' test is satisfied and an action will lie in delict.[1]

Where a pursuer is injured as a result of the defender's breach of duty but later suffers an accident or disease unrelated to the defender's conduct, the fact that he would have been debilitated by the later accident or disease, is taken into account in assessing the pursuer's loss. Thus in *Jobling v Associated Dairies*,[2] as a result of the defendant's breach of duty, the plaintiff was injured. It was established that because of his injuries, he could only do 'light work' in the future. Before his claim for damages was litigated, the plaintiff suffered an illness with the result that he was totally incapacitated. The House of Lords held that in assessing compensation for loss of future earnings the fact that the plaintiff was now totally incapacitated as a result of an illness unconnected with the defendant's breach of duty had to be taken into account. Accordingly, the period for assessing future loss of wages was between the date of the injury and the onset of the illness.[3] If, of course, the claim had been settled before the plaintiff became ill, he would have obtained a windfall because future loss of wages would have been calculated on the basis that he would not have become totally incapacitated through illness. *Jobling* is therefore an example of where the logic of the 'but for' test is overridden on the basis of 'common sense', although it does, of course, work in favour of the defender.

Difficulties arise where there is more than one potential cause of the pursuer's injuries, ie the defender's breach of a duty of care and another source of danger which is not the responsibility of the defender. The starting point of the discussion is *Wardlaw v Bonnington Castings*.[4] A workman contracted pneumoconiosis from breathing dust in the atmosphere of his workplace. Some of the dust was caused by a hammer for which there was no known or available precautions which could be taken to prevent the employee breathing contaminated air. Therefore, the defender was not in breach of the duty of care owed to the pursuer in respect of the dust caused by the hammer. However, there were other machines in the workshop which also produced dust for which adequate extraction plant was available: the employers were held responsible for not adequately maintaining the

---

1 *Sutherland v North British Steel Group* 1986 SLT (Sh Ct) 29 (accelerated hernia operation).
2 [1982] AC 794, [1981] 2 All ER 752, HL.
3 On future loss of earnings, see pp 232 ff below.
4 1956 SC (HL) 26, 1956 SLT 135.

extracting plant.[1] There were therefore two possible sources of the dust which had caused the pursuer's illness, only for one of which was the defender delictually liable, ie the dust from the other machines. The House of Lords held that the onus lay on the pursuer to show that on the balance of probabilities, the dust from the machines was a *causa sine qua non* of his illness. In the situation of two potential sources of danger, the pursuer would discharge the onus if he could show that the source for which the defender was responsible had materially contributed to his injury. Lord Reid observed:[2]

'It appears to me that the source of his [the pursuer's] disease was the dust from both sources, and the real question is whether the dust from the swing grinders [the other machines] materially contributed to the disease. What is a material contribution must be a question of degree. A contribution which comes within the exception *de minimis non curat lex* is not material but I think that any contribution which does not fall within that exception must be material.'

In this case, the dust from the machines did materially contribute to the pursuer's illness and the pursuer was successful. Thus, where there are two or more sources of harm to the pursuer which operate concurrently, the source for which the defender is responsible will be regarded as a *causa sine qua non* of the pursuer's injury if it materially contributed to the injury.

The concept of factual causation was taken a considerable step further in *McGhee v National Coal Board*.[3] The pursuer worked all day in a hot and dusty kiln. He had to cycle home unwashed because the defender failed to provide on-site washing facilities. After several days, the pursuer contracted dermatitis. It was admitted that the dermatitis was attributable to the work the pursuer did in the brick kiln, but the defender was not in breach of a duty of care in allowing the pursuer to work there. The breach of duty was the failure to provide on-site washing facilities. This omission only resulted in the pursuer cycling home unwashed as opposed to the hours he spent working in the kiln. Common sense would suggest that it was far more likely that the dermatitis was contracted when he was working in the kiln, for which the employer was not delictually liable, rather than during the short time he cycled home. But the expert evidence could not establish how dermatitis was actually contracted. *Wardlaw v*

---

1 This was a breach by the employers of their statutory duty under the Grinding of Metals (Miscellaneous Industries) Regulations 1925: on breach of statutory duty, see Chapter 11 below.
2 1956 SC (HL) 29 at 32.
3 1973 SC (HL) 37, 1973 SLT 14.

Bonnington Castings[1] could therefore not provide a solution as it could not be proven that the additional exposure to injury caused by cycling home unwashed had materially contributed to his injury. *Wardlaw v Bonnington Castings* is concerned with two sources of danger operating *concurrently*; but *McGhee v National Coal Board* is concerned with two sources of danger operating *consecutively*, for which the defender was responsible only for the later. Therefore, it can be argued that the pursuer in *McGhee* would have to prove – which on the evidence he could not – that the later source of danger had caused, or, at least, materially contributed, to his dermatitis.

However, the House of Lords was prepared to take a broader view of causation. The medical evidence suggested that the fact that the pursuer had to cycle home caked with grime and sweat added materially to *the risk* that the disease might develop, though it could not explain why this was so. In the view of the House, materially to increase the risk of the pursuer's injuries was to be regarded as a material contribution to the injury. Lord Reid opined:[2]

'But it has often been said that the legal concept of causation is not based on logic or philosophy. It is based on the practical way in which the ordinary man's mind works in the every-day affairs of life. From a broad and practical viewpoint I can see no substantial difference between saying that what the defender did materially increased the risk of injury to the pursuer and saying that what the defender did made a material contribution to his injury.'

Lord Salmon observed:[3]

'In the circumstances of the present case,[4] the possibility of a distinction existing between (a) having materially increased the risk of contracting the disease and (b) having materially contributed to causing the disease may no doubt be a fruitful source of interesting academic discussions between students of philosophy. Such a distinction is, however, far too unreal to be recognised by the common law'!

Thus, where there are two or more sources of danger, for only one of which the defender is delictually liable, factual causation will be established if the pursuer can prove on the balance of probabilities *either* that the defender's breach of duty materially contributed to his injury *or* that the defender's breach of duty materially increased the risk of the pursuer sustaining injury. It does not matter if the sources of danger operate concurrently or consecutively.

---

1 1956 SC (HL) 26.
2 1973 SC (HL) 37 at 53–54.
3 1973 SC (HL) 37 at 62.
4 Given the defender's admitted breach of a duty of care.

However, there is an important limitation on this principle. While the *sources* of danger may be different, it must be established that each source could have in fact been the cause of the pursuer's injuries. In both *Wardlaw* and *McGhee* it was clear that dust caused the pursuers' diseases; the only question was whether the defenders' breach of duty had materially contributed to, or increased the risk of, the pursuers' illnesses. In contrast, in *Kay v Ayrshire and Arran Health Board*,[1] there was no evidence that the defender's breach of duty in giving the overdose of penicillin could in fact have caused the child's deafness. In these circumstances, *Wardlaw* and *McGhee* are irrelevant. As Lord Griffiths explained:[2]

'The principle in *McGhee* would only fall for consideration if it was first proved that it was an accepted medical fact that penicillin in some cases caused or aggravated deafness. The question would then arise whether when there are two competing causes of deafness, namely meningitis and penicillin, the law should presume in favour of the plaintiff (sic) that the tortious (sic) [delictual] cause was responsible for the damage.'[3]

B. LEGAL CAUSATION

For the purpose of liability in delict, it is not enough that the defender's breach of duty is a factual cause or *causa sine qua non* of the pursuer's harm or loss. While factual causation is a necessary condition of delictual liability, it is not sufficient. In addition, the defender's breach of duty must be the legal cause of the pursuer's injury. To use Latin terminology, it must be the *causa causans*. Various terms are used to describe legal causation: these include, for example, the direct, decisive, proximate, real, dominant, efficient, effective or substantial cause of the pursuer's loss or harm.

For example, A drops a brick on B's foot, breaking his toe. B is taken to hospital in an ambulance. The ambulance is driven carelessly and B is killed in a road accident. A's breach of duty is a *causa sine qua non* of B's death since 'but for' dropping the brick on his toe, B would not have been in the ambulance in which he died. But should A be delictually liable for B's death which was caused by the ambulance driver's careless driving? The answer is no. A's breach of duty while a

---

1 1987 SLT 577. Discussed at p 113 above.
2 1987 SLT 577 at 581.
3 See also *Wilsher v Essex Area Health Authority* [1988] 1 All ER 871, HL, affirming [1987] QB 730.

causa sine qua non of B's death, is not treated as the legal cause, ie it is not the *causa causans*. The *causa causans* is the ambulance driver's careless driving. We can say that the chain of causation between A's breach of duty has been broken as a result of the careless act of the ambulance driver, which prevents A's breach of duty being the legal cause of B's death. To use legal terminology, the ambulance driver's conduct is a *novus actus interveniens* which breaks the chain of causation so that A is not delictually liable for B's death, though A remains liable for B's broken toe.

In this example, the *novus actus interveniens* was the conduct of a third party, the ambulance driver. But the conduct of the victim may also break the chain of causation. So, for example, if A drops a brick on B's foot, breaking his toe, whereupon B cuts his own throat to put himself out of pain, A will not be delictually liable for B's death as B's action will break the chain of causation and, as a result, A's breach of duty is not regarded as the legal cause, the *causa causans*, of B's death.

When, then, will an act of a third party or the act of the victim constitute a *novus actus interveniens*, breaking the chain of causation? Since we are concerned with determining legal causation, this is ultimately a question for the courts: the judges will *evaluate* whether or not in the circumstances it is fair to relieve the defender of his delictual liability. At one time, this was a crucial decision where the victim had contributed to his own injuries: for if the court decided that the pursuer's conduct was a *novus actus interveniens* so that the defender's breach of duty was not the *causa causans*, the pursuer was denied any compensation. However, as a result of the Law Reform (Contributory Negligence) Act 1945, the court has now the power to reduce the damages awarded to the pursuer in proportion to the pursuer's responsibility for his own injuries.[1] While the 1945 Act has, in so far as the pursuer's conduct is concerned, reduced the importance of determining a single cause or *causa causans*, nevertheless the court still retains the power of limiting a defender's delictual liability for breach of a duty of care, by deciding that the breach is not the legal cause of the pursuer's injuries, for example, because of the intervention of a third party. Therefore, the determination of legal causation remains important.

The decision whether or not a breach of duty constitutes the *causa causans* of the pursuer's injuries 'must be dealt with broadly and upon common sense principles as a jury would probably deal with it'.[2] Two factors are important:

---

1 On contributory negligence, see pp 125 ff below.
2 *Admiralty Commissioners v SS Volute* [1922] AC 120 at 144 per Birkenhead LC.

(1) Foreseeability

Where there has been a breach of duty by the defender, the act of a third party or the victim will not generally break the chain of causation if it was reasonably foreseeable that the subsequent act would take place. Thus, for example, in *Sayers v Harlow Urban District Council*[1] the plaintiff entered a cubicle in a public lavatory maintained by the defendant. Owing to a fault in the lock, she could not reopen the door. She banged on the door and put her hand out of the window in unsuccessful attempts to attract attention. After 15 minutes, she tried to escape through the space between the top of the door and the roof. She put her left foot on the lavatory seat, her right foot on the toilet roll holder, one hand on the lavatory cistern and the other hand on the top of the door. When she found it impossible to squeeze through the space, she proceeded to come down but because of her weight, the toilet roll holder rotated, she lost her balance and fell. The court held that it was reasonably foreseeable that a person in Mrs Sayer's position would try to escape and that this was not a hazardous enterprise. Accordingly, her attempted escape was not a *novus actus interveniens* and the defendant's breach of duty was the *causa causans* of the accident. However, when she found she could not escape, she was careless in putting so much weight on the toilet roll holder: while this did not break the chain of causation, it did consitute contributory negligence and her damages were reduced by 25 per cent.[2]

Even if the subsequent act of a third party or the pursuer is reasonably foreseeable, it may break the chain of causation if it was hazardous for the third party or the pursuer to undertake. In *McKew v Holland and Hannon and Cubitts (Scotland) Ltd*[3], the pursuer injured his ankle as a result of the defender's breach of duty. Because of the fracture, his leg was liable to 'give way' from time to time. After the accident, the pursuer went to see a flat. The stairway leading to the flat had no handrail. Although he knew that his leg was likely to give way at any time, after visiting the flat, the pursuer went down the stairs in a normal manner, ie he did not go down the stairs slowly so that he could sit on a step if his leg 'gave way'. His leg gave way and in a panic the pursuer jumped down 10 steps and was injured. The court held that the defender was not liable for the second injury. While it was reasonably foreseeable that the pursuer might climb stairs which had no handrail, he had acted in a hazardous manner in walking down the

---

1 [1958] 2 All ER 342, [1958] 1 WLR 623.
2 On contributory negligence, see pp 125 ff below.
3 1970 SLT 68.

stairs in the normal way without assistance. The defender's breach of duty which had caused the injury to the pursuer's ankle was not the *causa causans* of the pursuer's second injury since the pursuer's carelessness in walking down the stairs without assistance constituted hazardous conduct on the pursuer's part which broke the chain of causation between the defender's breach of duty and the pursuer's second injuries.

(2) The order of events

The order of events may be important in determining whether or not the defender's breach of duty is the *causa causans* of the pursuer's injuries. In *Donaghy v National Coal Board*,[1] the defender broke the duty of care which was owed to the pursuer, by leaving a detonator lying around the workplace. The pursuer took the detonator home and hit it with a hammer. As a result he was injured. The court held that the pursuer's conduct amounted to a *novus actus interveniens*: it was unforeseeable, unreasonable, ie hazardous, and was the last act which had led to the accident. On the other hand, in *Davidson v City of Glasgow Corporation*,[2] the second defender supplied the pursuer's employer, the first defender, with planks which were too short for a particular task. The employer rejected the planks but owing to the employer's alleged carelessness one of the short planks was not rejected. As a result of the plank being too short, there was an accident and the pursuer was injured. The pursuer sued the employer (first defender) and the supplier (the second defender). The second defender argued that the employer's failure to reject all the planks constituted a *novus actus interveniens*. The court held that merely because the employer's conduct was the 'last act' that led to the accident, this did not necessarily mean that it amounted to a *novus actus interveniens*:

'Even although there was in effect an intermediate inspection, and assuming in the alternative that the first defenders [the employer] failed to discover that one of the planks remained and was inadvertently used, it does not follow that that was negligence or that it broke the chain of causation and was the sole cause of the accident.'[3]

As we have seen,[4] before the Law Reform (Contributory Negligence) Act 1945, if the pursuer's conduct was held to be the *causa*

1 1957 SLT (Notes) 35.
2 1993 SLT 479.
3 1993 SLT 479 at 482 per Judge D B Robertson QC.
4 Page 118 above.

causans of the injury, the defender was completely exonerated even although his breach of duty was a *causa sine qua non* of the accident. To avoid this result, the courts developed the 'last opportunity rule'.[1] Thus, for example, in *McLean v Bell*[2] a young girl crossed the road in a careless manner. She was hit by a motor car which was being driven carelessly. The House of Lords held that if the driver had taken care, he would have been able to avoid the accident. As the driver had the 'last opportunity to avoid the accident', his breach of duty was the *causa causans* of the accident in spite of the fact that the girl (the pursuer) had not taken reasonable care for her own safety. Today, the court would not have had to resort to such artificial reasoning and could reach the common sense solution that both had caused the accident and that the pursuer's damages should be reduced to reflect her responsibility for the accident.[3] In the *Boy Andrew v St Rognvald*[4] the St Rognvald, a steamship, was overtaking the Boy Andrew, a drifter. Although 100 feet from the drifter, this was too close. Therefore the St Rognvald was in breach of her duty of care towards the Boy Andrew. Suddenly, the drifter turned starboard across the St Rognvald's course. The master of the St Rognvald attempted to avoid the collison, but failed to do so; the drifter was struck and all the crew lost. The question before the court was whether the *causa causans* was the defenders' initial breach of their duty of care by overtaking too closely, or the drifter's sudden turning off course or the master of the steamship's failure to avoid the collision. In these circumstances, the House of Lords held that the 'last opportunity rule' was of limited value and that, on a common sense view, both ships had caused the accident. A similar approach is now taken in respect of, for example, motorway pile-ups when more than one driver is at fault.[5]

Thus, where an accident is caused to A as a result of a breach of duty by B *and* a breach of duty by C, the mere fact that B's breach of duty arose after C's breach of duty, will not necessarily break the chain of causation to exonerate C from delictual liability. In *Grant v Sun Shipping Co*[6] ship repairers working on a ship left hatches uncovered, ic were in breach of a duty of care owed to dock labourers on the ship. The ship owners also failed to ensure that the hatches were covered and did not provide an adequate system of lighting: this constituted a breach of their duty of care to dock labourers on the ship. The

---

1 The classic English case is *Davies v Mann* (1842) 10 M & W 546.
2 1932 SC (HL) 21.
3 On contributory negligence, see pp 125 ff below.
4 1947 SC (HL) 70, 1948 SLT 83.
5 *Rouse v Squires* [1973] QB 889, [1973] 2 WLR 925.
6 1948 SC (HL) 73, 1949 SLT 25.

pursuer, a dock labourer, fell through an unlighted hatch. The House of Lords held that the shipowner's breach of duty did not constitute a *novus actus interveniens* breaking the chain of causation between the accident and the ship repairer's breach of duty of care towards the pursuer by leaving the hatches uncovered. Instead, both the ship-owners and the ship repairers were jointly liable in delict.[1] Where there is joint liability, under section 3 of the Law Reform (Miscellaneous Provisions) (Scotland) Act 1940, the court has the power to apportion the damages between the defenders.[2]

(3) Conclusion

Where A's breach of a duty of care is a *causa sine qua non* of B's injuries, the courts appear unwilling to be persuaded that a subsequent act – even if careless – constitutes a *novus actus interveniens* unless it is so unusual or unexpected that it could not have been reasonably foreseeable, or so hazardous on the part of B, that it would be unreasonable to hold A liable. Where the subsequent act is that of a third party, C, and constitutes a breach of duty owed by C to B, A and C will be held jointly liable in delict to B; where the subsequent act is that of B, A remains liable, ie B's act will not break the chain of causation, but instead will lead to a reduction of damages on the grounds of contributory negligence. While this will be the usual result, there can, of course, still be exceptional cases where the chain of causation is broken and A's breach of duty is not treated as the *causa causans* of B's injuries. So, for example, if A injured B's foot and B suffered an infection in hospital, the chain of causation would not be broken as it is reasonably foreseeable that B might get an infection in hospital; but if the surgeon in the hospital is careless and amputates B's uninjured foot, the chain of causation is broken as the surgeon's conduct is so unusual and unexpected that it is not reasonably foreseeable and therefore constitutes a *novus actus interveniens*, exonerating A from delictual liability in respect of the amputation, but not, of course, for the original injury to B's foot.

The chain of causation is not broken by an act of a third party where the defender's duty of care was to prevent the third party from causing injury or damage to the pursuer.[3] But as a general rule, A does not owe B a duty of care to prevent B being injured as a result of the deliberate

---

1 See also *Davidson v City of Glasgow Corporation* 1993 SLT (Notes) 35, discussed at p 120 above.
2 On joint liability, see p 127 below.
3 *Dorset Yacht Co Ltd v Home Office* [1970] AC 1004, discussed at p 102 above.

conduct of a third party, C: here, of course, it is the absence of a duty of care which prevents A being liable to B in delict.[1]

C. RELATED MATTERS

(1) *Volenti non fit injuria*

The chain of causation will, however, be broken if the pursuer has voluntarily undertaken the risk of harm created by the defender's breach of duty. This is the doctrine of *volenti non fit injuria*. Because the chain of causation is broken and the defender's breach of duty is no longer the *causa causans* of the pursuer's injuries, the doctrine of *volenti* provides the defender with a complete defence to an action in delict. The theoretical basis of *volenti* is that by knowing acceptance of the risk, the pursuer has absolved the defender of the consequences of the defender's breach of the duty of care owed to the pursuer. In other words, the defender still owes the pursuer a duty of care but the chain of causation is broken by the pursuer voluntarily undertaking the risk.[2]

Before the defender will succeed in the defence of *volenti non fit injuria* the defender must prove that the pursuer knowingly and willingly undertook the risk of danger created by the defender's breach of duty. In *Titchener v British Railways Board*[3] the defender failed to maintain a fence made of sleepers which was positioned along a railway track. A 15-year-old girl climbed through the fence and went up the embankment to take a short cut across the railway line to a piece of waste ground where she intended to have a kiss and cuddle with her boyfriend. She was injured by a train when she was crossing the line. As we shall see,[4] the House of Lords held that in the circumstances the defender did not owe the pursuer a duty of care. But the House indicated that even if a duty of care had been owed and there had been a breach of duty, the defender would have had the defence of *volenti* since the pursuer knew and accepted the risk of being injured by a train when she crossed the line.

Because the pursuer must have knowledge of, and be *willing*, to accept the risk, the courts are unlikely to accept a plea of *volenti* in an

---

1 See, also, pp 155 ff below.
2 *Winnick v Dick* 1984 SC 48, 1984 SLT 185.
3 1984 SC (HL) 34, 1984 SLT 192. See also *Devlin v Strathclyde Regional Council* 1993 SLT 699.
4 Page 165 below.

action between employee and employer. Nevertheless, the defence succeeded in *ICI v Shatwell*.[1] Contrary to their employers' instructions, the plaintiff and his brother, who were experienced shotfirers, agreed to test their detonators without first returning to a safety shelter. There was an explosion; the plaintiff was injured and his brother was killed. It was held that the employer had not been in breach of a duty of care towards the plaintiff.[2] However, the plaintiff sued the employer as vicariously liable for his brother's careless act in testing the detonator.[3] The House of Lords held that since the plaintiff had agreed with his brother to run the risk of injury by testing the detonators without first returning to a place of safety, the employer could successfully plead the defence of *volenti*.

The defence of *volenti* does not apply in the case of a rescuer. By section 149 of the Road Traffic Act 1988, it is provided that the defence of *volenti* does not apply to a claim by a passenger against the driver of a vehicle which has compulsory third party insurance.[4] Thus, if a passenger accepts a lift from a drunken driver, if the car has compulsory third party insurance, the driver cannot plead *volenti* if the passenger is injured as a result of the driver's breach of duty; the passenger's damages could, of course, be reduced on the grounds of contributory negligence.

It is sometimes argued that the reason why a spectator at a dangerous sport, for example, motor racing, cannot sue a participant who injures him by crashing into the crowd at high speed, is that the spectator is *volens* of the risk of harm inherent in the sport. However, it is thought that the better way to analyse the situation is to argue that in the circumstances the participant does not owe the spectator a duty of care to avoid the possibility of such an accident. The organiser of the event may owe the spectator a duty of care, if, for example, the circuit was not suitable for racing or the safety precautions were inadequate, and the spectator will not be *volens* of these risks simply by attending the event.[5] Where a participant in a dangerous sport is injured by another participant, again it is thought the reason an action in delict will not be successful is not that the pursuer was *volens* but that the defender does not owe a duty of care to the pursuer to protect him from injuries the risk of which are inherent in the sport, for example being bruised when tackled at rugby football. Where the

---

1   [1965] AC 656, [1964] 2 All ER 999.
2   Or in breach of any statutory duty.
3   On vicarious liability, see pp 178 ff below.
4   On compulsory third party insurance, see Chapter 14 below.
5   *Wooldridge v Sumner* [1963] 2 QB 43, [1962] 2 All ER 978, CA; *Lewis v Buckpool Golf Club* 1993 SLT (Sh Ct) 43.

injury arises from conduct which is contrary to the rules of the game, the pursuer's remedy lies in assault rather than a breach of the duty of care.

(2) Contributory negligence

As we have seen,[1] where the defender's breach of duty to the pursuer is a *causa sine qua non* of the pursuer's injuries, the courts are reluctant to accept that the pursuer's subsequent conduct is a *novus actus interveniens* or amounts to *volenti*, so that the defender is exonerated from delictual liability. This is particularly the case where the pursuer has acted in the 'agony of the moment', ie reacts carelessly in a situation caused by the defender's breach of duty, for example, jumps out of a window to escape a fire caused by the defender's breach of duty. Instead, the court will hold that the pursuer's conduct was a contributory cause of the injury. The effect of a finding of contributory negligence is to reduce the damages which would otherwise have been awarded to the pursuer, to reflect the pursuer's responsibility for the damage or injury sustained. Section 1(1) of the Law Reform (Contributory Negligence) Act 1945 provides:

'Where any person suffers *damage as the result partly of his own fault* and *partly due to the fault of any other person or persons*, a claim in respect of that damage shall not be defeated by reason of the fault of the person suffering the damage, but the *damages recoverable* in respect thereof *shall be reduced* to such an extent as the *court thinks just and equitable* having regard to the *claimant's share in the responsibility* for the damage.' [emphasis added]

Before the Act applies the pursuer must have suffered damage partly as a result of his own *fault*. The pursuer's act must therefore fall below the standard of the reasonable person in the pursuer's position. The onus rests on the defender to prove that the pursuer was at fault. While, for example, a passenger injured in a motor accident will usually be at fault if he or she fails to wear a seat belt, in *Mackay v Borthwick*[2] the pursuer was held not to be contributorily negligent for failing to wear a seat belt as it was uncomfortable for her to wear it, as she was suffering from a hiatus hernia. In *Pace v Culley*[3] the pursuer who was a taxi driver failed to wear a seat belt because he had been advised by the police not to do so, in the event that he might be attacked by his passengers. While accepting that failure to wear a seat

---

1 Page 122 above.
2 1982 SLT 265.
3 1992 SLT 1073.

belt could amount to contributory negligence, the Lord Ordinary (Weir) thought that the driver's conduct in this case was a misjudgment rather than a failure to take care for his own safety.[1] Moreover, the defender must also prove that the pursuer's fault contributed to the injuries sustained, ie 'but for' the pursuer's fault, the injuries or damage suffered would not have been as bad as actually occurred. In other words, the defender must establish that the pursuer's fault was a factual cause, a *causa sine qua non*, of the injuries or harm sustained. Thus, contributory negligence was established when the defender proved, on the balance of probabilities, that the pursuer would have suffered less severe neck injuries if she had worn a seat belt.[2]

When contributory negligence is established, the proportion to be deducted from the damages is a matter for the discretion of the judge ie what the judge considers just and equitable having regard to the pursuer's share in the responsibility for the damage. This can vary from as little as 5 per cent in 'agony of the moment' cases to as much as 80 per cent.[3] It is submitted that 100 per cent deduction is not possible under the Act since in those circumstances the pursuer would be solely responsible and not 'share in the responsibility for the damage'.[4] A drunken pedestrian run down by a careless driver, has had his damages reduced by 50 per cent as a result of contributory negligence.[5]

As a matter of public policy, if the pursuer is participating in a criminal activity at the time he is injured, he may be barred from obtaining reparation: for example, if A and B steal a car and A is injured as a result of B's careless driving.[6] However, the bar is not automatic and depends on the circumstances. In *Weir v Wyper*[7] the pursuer was not barred when she was injured in a car crash even though she knew that the driver had only a provisional licence. When the action is not barred, the pursuer's damages could, of course, be reduced on the ground of contributory negligence.

1 The contributory negligence, if any, would have been *de minimis* in respect of the total claim and could therefore be ignored.
2 *Hanlon v Cuthbertson* 1981 SLT (Notes) 57.
3 *Uddin v Associated Portland Cement Manufacturers Ltd* [1965] 2 QB 582, [1965] 1 All ER 213, CA.
4 If the pursuer is solely responsible, the defender will escape liability because either his breach of duty is not the *causa causans* or the pursuer is *volens*: see *ICI v Shatwell* [1965] AC 656.
5 *Malcolm v Fair* 1993 SLT 342. See also *Porter v Strathclyde Regional Council* 1991 SLT 446.
6 *Duncan v Ross Harper & Murphy* 1993 SLT 105.
7 1992 SCLR 483, 1992 SLT 579.

(3) Joint fault

Joint fault arises where harm is caused to the pursuer as a result of the conduct of more than one defender. This is known as joint liability, if the harm has been caused as a result of a breach by each defender of a duty of care owed to the pursuer; in case of other delicts, it is known as joint wrongdoing. Before there can be joint liability, each breach of duty must have materially contributed to, or materially increased the risk of, the *same* delict to the pursuer. Thus, for example, in *Anderson v St Andrews Ambulance Association*[1] a passenger in a bus was injured in a collision between the bus and an ambulance. The bus driver had failed to observe a 'slow' sign; the ambulance driver had failed to observe a 'halt' sign. The court held that this was a case of joint liability, for both drivers were responsible for the same wrong suffered by the pursuer. Conversely, in *Fleming v McGillivray*[2] the court held that it was not a case of joint liability where an injured pursuer sued a van driver for careless driving and the owner of the van for failing to have compulsory third party insurance: the driver was being sued for breach of his duty of care (delict 1), while the owner was being sued for breach of statutory duty in not having insurance (delict 2). As they were not responsible for the same delict, this was not a case of joint liability or joint wrongdoing.

If A and B are jointly liable, the pursuer may sue A or B or both. If the pursuer only sues A and obtains a decree, if A pays the damages, the pursuer cannot then sue B; but if A does not pay the damages, the pursuer can sue B. If the pursuer successfully sues both A and B, he will be awarded a joint and several decree. This entitles the pursuer to obtain all the damages from either A or B. Where A has paid all the damages, the court can apportion the damages between A and B; and if B was not sued in the original action, A can, nevertheless, recover from B the proportion of the damages which the court deems attributable to B's conduct.[3] Where the pursuer is contributorily negligent, the total damages to be paid by A or B will be reduced to reflect the pursuer's responsibility for the injury or harm suffered.[4]

1 1943 SC 248, 1943 SLT 258.
2 1946 SC 1, 1945 SLT 301.
3 Law Reform (Miscellaneous Provisions) (Scotland) Act 1945, s 3. The proportions *inter se* the defenders is what the court, or jury, considers just in the circumstances: see, for example, *BOC v Groves* 1993 SLT 360 (75 per cent and 25 per cent).
4 On contributory negligence, see pp 125 ff above.

Part III
DELICTUAL LIABILITY IN SPECIFIC SOCIAL AND ECONOMIC CONTEXTS

Introduction

Having discussed the general principles of delictual liability, it is now proposed to examine the law of delict as it operates in certain specific social and economic contexts. As we shall see, the general principle of delictual liability for harm caused to the pursuer as a result of the defender's *culpa* is often supplemented by other common law principles, for example, nuisance and vicarious liability; more importantly, perhaps, in certain areas common law delictual liability has been supplemented or supplanted by statutory liability. It is thought that these developments are better understood if discussed in the context of the particular social and economic relationships in which they occur.

CHAPTER 7

Professional liability

The general principles of the law of delict apply where a person causes harm to another in the course of his trade, business or profession. Often, of course, the person harmed will be a client or a customer of the defender; if this is so, the pursuer's primary remedy will be to sue the defender in contract. However, if there is no direct contractual relationship between the parties, liability may lie in delict.

Where the pursuer suffers physical injury or harm to his property, the defender will be liable in delict if the injury or harm was caused intentionally or as a result of a breach of a duty of care owed by the defender to the pursuer. The existence of such a duty of care will, of course, be determined by the *Donoghue v Stevenson* neighbourhood principle.[1] Where the pursuer has suffered pure economic loss, liability will lie in delict only if the defender intended to harm the pursuer[2] or if the case falls into one of the narrow categories where the courts have been prepared to recognise a duty of care to prevent pure economic loss to the pursuer.[3]

In determining whether or not there has been a breach of a duty of care, the defender's conduct is judged by the standard of care expected in his/her profession. In other words, in order to establish that the defender was negligent, the pursuer must prove that the defender's conduct fell below that of the reasonable accountant, architect, lawyer, medical practitioner or surveyor etc. Accordingly, while ultimately a question of law,[4] the usual practice of persons in the same trade, business or profession as the defender will be particularly significant in determining whether or not the defender was negligent.

It can, however, be particularly difficult to establish negligence where the defender's conduct involved an exercise of professional judgment. Often there will be several courses of action open to the

---

1 Discussed at pp 54 ff above.
2 For example, the economic delicts or fraud: see Chapter 2 above.
3 For example, liability for negligent misrepresentation or *Junior Books* liability: see pp 68 ff and 75 ff above.
4 *Cavanagh v Ulster Weaving Co* [1959] 2 All ER 745: discussed at p 108 above.

defender. In these circumstances, the defender will *not* be negligent if he adopted a course of action which resulted in harm to the pursuer unless no reasonable professional person in his position would have chosen that option. Nor does it matter that the course of action chosen was *not* the normal practice in the profession. In the leading case of *Hunter v Hanley*[1] the pursuer alleged that the defender, a doctor, was negligent in using a needle which was unsuitable for treating the patient. In discussing the standard of care appropriate to a doctor, the Lord President (Clyde) observed:[2]

'. . . in regard to deviation from ordinary professional practice . . . such deviation is not necessarily evidence of negligence. Indeed it would be disastrous if this were so, for all inducement to progress in medical science would then be destroyed. Even a substantial deviation from normal practice may be warranted by the particular circumstances. To establish liability by a doctor where deviation from normal practice is alleged, three facts require to be established. First of all it must be proved that there is a normal practice; secondly it must be proved that the defender has not adopted that practice; and thirdly (and this is of crucial importance) it must be established that the course which the doctor adopted is one which no professional man of ordinary skill would have taken if he had been acting with ordinary care.'

Thus it is not enough to establish professional negligence that the defender's conduct deviated from normal practice: it must be demonstrated that no professional man of ordinary skill would have followed the course taken by the defender. Even if the pursuer can establish that a responsible body of medical opinion regarded the defender's decision or conduct as wrong, the defender will not be regarded as having been negligent if there is also a responsible body of medical opinion which regarded the defender's decision or conduct as reasonable in the circumstances.[3] This test applies not only to medical treatment[4] but also to diagnosis.[5]

In *Sidaway v Bethlem Royal Hospital Board of Governors*[6] the House of Lords held that a doctor who failed to warn his patient about all the risks inherent in a medical procedure would not be negligent unless he failed to disclose the risks which a responsible body of medical opinion considered should have been disclosed. It

1 1955 SC 200, 1955 SLT 213.
2 1955 SC 200 at 206.
3 *Maynard v West Midlands Regional Health Authority* [1985] 1 All ER 635, [1984] 1 WLR 634, HL.
4 *Whitehouse v Jordan* [1981] 1 All ER 267, [1981] 1 WLR 246, HL.
5 *Maynard v West Midlands Regional Health Authority* above.
6 [1985] AC 871, [1985] 1 All ER 643, HL.

will be remembered[1] that even if the doctor failed to inform the patient of those risks which a reasonable doctor would have disclosed, the delict arises as a result of the doctor's breach of his duty of care, ie the pursuer sues in negligence not for assault. There is no doctrine of informed consent in English and, it is submitted, Scots law. If a patient asks about a particular risk, the doctor must give a full and truthful answer – even if he would not have been negligent in failing to disclose the risk if the patient had not raised the issue.[2] Finally, in *Gold v Haringey Health Authority*[3] it was held that the test of negligence where a doctor gave advice to a patient is the same as for negligent treatment or diagnosis, ie the doctor would not be negligent if a responsible body of medical opinion would regard the advice as reasonable in the particular circumstances of the case.

Gordon v Wilson[4] provides an illustration of the formidable difficulties facing a pursuer in an action of medical negligence. The pursuer argued that a doctor was negligent in delaying to refer a patient to a specialist. Although the pursuer established that there was a responsible body of medical opinion which took the view that a reasonable doctor would have referred the patient to a specialist at an earlier stage, the court held that the defender was not negligent because the defender could show that there was also a responsible body of medical opinion to the effect that a reasonable doctor would not have referred the patient to a specialist until the defender had done so. Accordingly, the pursuer's action failed. Professional negligence cannot be established by preferring one body of professional opinion to another; instead the pursuer must prove that no reasonable doctor exercising his ordinary clinical skills would have taken the defender's course of action in the circumstances of the particular case.

These cases were concerned with the medical profession. However, as indicated above, the tests for establishing the requisite standard of care are applicable in relation to other professions where an exercise of professional judgment is involved.

The position of the legal professions requires further treatment. Where a solicitor gives *advice* to a person who is not a client, ie who does not have a contractual relationship with the solicitor, the solicitor may be liable in delict provided the *Hedley Byrne v Heller* criteria for a

---

1 Page 13 above.
2 It is submitted that if the doctor did not answer the patient's question truthfully, the patient's consent would be vitiated and the doctor would be liable in assault, not negligence.
3 [1987] 2 QB 481, [1987] 2 All ER 888, CA.
4 1992 SLT 849.

duty of care exist.[1] In *Midland Bank v Cameron, Thom, Peterkin and Duncans*[2], the Lord Ordinary (Jauncey) observed:[3]

'. . . I have no hesitation in concluding . . . that situations can arise in which a solicitor owes a duty not only to his client but to a third party who relies upon what the solicitor tells him. In my opinion four factors are relevant to the determination of the question whether in a particular case a solicitor, while acting for a client, also owes a duty of care to a third party: (1) the solicitor must assume responsibility for the advice or information furnished to the third party; (2) the solicitor must let it be known to the third party expressly or impliedly that he claims, by reason of his calling, to have the requisite skill or knowledge to give the advice or furnish the information; (3) the third party must have relied upon that advice or information as a matter for which the solicitor has assumed personal responsibility, and (4) the solicitor must have been aware that the third party was likely so to rely.'

Where such a duty exists, the pursuer will, of course, succeed only if it can be established that the solicitor was negligent in giving the advice, ie that a reasonable solicitor would not have given that advice in the circumstances.[4]

Midland Bank is concerned with a duty of care in giving *advice* to a person who is not a client. It is not concerned with the situation where a solicitor acts on the instructions of a client but as a result of the solicitor's carelessness does not give effect to the client's instructions, with the result that a third party suffers loss. The classic situation is where A instructs a solicitor to draw up a will under which B is the principal beneficiary. As a result of the solicitor's carelessness the will is invalid and B does not obtain the legacy. There is no contractual relationship between B and the solicitor. Therefore B's remedy, if any, lies in delict against the solicitor. B has suffered pure economic loss and before there is delictual liability the solicitor must owe B a duty of care to prevent B suffering such loss. As the solicitor has not given advice to B, there is not a *Hedley Byrne v Heller* duty of care,[5] nor is there any contractual nexus between B and the solicitor to establish a *Junior Books* duty of care.[6] We have therefore a situation where the courts must be prepared on policy grounds to impose a duty of care in these circumstances before the solicitor will be liable in delict.[7]

---

1 See pp 68 ff above.
2 1988 SCLR 209, 1988 SLT 611.
3 1988 SLT 611 at 616.
4 On the standard of care for professional persons, see pp 131 ff above.
5 See pp 68 ff above.
6 See pp 75 ff above.
7 Ie the duty of care is being used as a threshold device: see Chapter 4 above.

Hitherto, the Scottish courts have refused to recognise such a duty of care. In *Robertson v Fleming*[1] Lord Campbell LC observed:[2]

'I never had any doubt of the unsoundness of the doctrine . . . that A employing B, a professional lawyer, to do any act for the benefit of C, A having to pay B, and there being no intercourse of any sort between B and C – if through the gross negligence or ignorance of B in transacting the business, C loses the benefit intended for him by A, C may maintain an action against B and recover damages for the loss sustained. If this were law a disappointed legatee might sue the solicitor employed by a testator to make a will in favour of a stranger, whom the solicitor never saw or before heard of, if the will were void for not being properly signed or attested. There must be privity of contract between the parties. I am clearly of opinion that this is not the law of Scotland, nor of England, and it can hardly be the law of any country where jurisprudence has been cultivated as a science.'

Robertson v Fleming was a decision of the House of Lords in a Scottish appeal. In *Weir v J M Hodge*[3] the Lord Ordinary (Weir) took the view that the case was authority that a duty of care did not exist between a solicitor and a disappointed legatee. Although he considered that the decision in *Robertson* was 'out of sympathy with the modern law of negligence',[4] Lord Weir felt he was bound to follow its ratio as it constituted a binding precedent.[5]

On the other hand, in England, the courts have refused to follow *Robertson*. In *Ross v Caunters*,[6] for example, a solicitor was held to owe a duty of care to the plaintiff who was a beneficiary under the testator's will: the duty of care arose because the solicitor knew the identity of the plaintiff and that she would suffer loss if the will was invalid as a result of the solicitor's negligence. The decision in Ross was unanimously approved by the Court of Appeal in *White v Jones*.[7] In these circumstances, the approach of the Scottish courts appears even more anomalous. Given that the potential pursuer falls into a

---

1 (1861) 23 D (HL) 8, 4 Macq 167.
2 (1861) 4 Macq 167 at 177
3 1990 SLT 266.
4 1990 SLT 266 at 270.
5 See also *MacDougall v Clydesdale Bank Trustees* 1993 SCLR 832, where the Lord Ordinary (Lord Cameron of Lochbroom) also denied the existence of a duty of care; but here the pursuer was not the disappointed legatee, but the legatee of the beneficiary who would have inherited under the invalid will. Even if there was a duty to a disappointed legatee, it is doubtful if it would extend to his legatees.
6 [1980] Ch 297, [1979] 3 All ER 580.
7 [1993] 3 All ER 481. The Court held that the decision in Ross had not been impliedly overruled by *Murphy v Brentwood District Council* [1991] 1 AC 398 or *Caparo Industries plc v Dickman* [1990] 1 AC 605, [1990] 1 All ER 568, HL: for discussion of these cases see pp 84 ff and 70 ff above.

restricted class, ie the legatee named in the will and therefore known to the solicitor, it is thought by the present writer that a duty of care should exist in these circumstances. In his *Short Commentary*[1] Professor Sir Thomas Smith advocated that *Robertson v Fleming* deserved a decent burial after more than a century of 'inglorious life'; however, it is clear since *Weir v J M Hodge*[2] that a decision of the House of Lords overruling *Robertson* is necessary before the obsequies can take place.

Where there has been a breach of a duty of care by a solicitor, there may be difficulties in quantifying the pursuer's loss. In *Kyle v P & J Stormonth Darling WS*[3] the defender failed to lodge the pursuer's appeal in time with the result that the pursuer lost the opportunity to appeal. In rejecting the defender's argument that the pursuer was entitled to damages only if it could be established on the balance of probabilities that the appeal would have been successful, the Lord Ordinary (Prosser) said:[4]

'where there has been deprivation of a legal right, that will in itself constitute a completed wrong, and one will be entitled, as a matter of valuation, to take into consideration all reasonable prospects of success, if they exceed nuisance value, even if they fall short of probability.'

Advocates are not liable in delict in respect of the conduct and management of a case in court or any preliminary work connected with conducting such a case.[5] However, an advocate can be liable for giving negligent advice, for example, an opinion on a point of law.[6] It has been suggested that the same immunity extends to solicitors in respect of court work,[6] but there is Scottish authority that solicitors could, nevertheless, be liable.[7] Given that an advocate's immunity is justified on grounds of public policy, it is thought that a similar immunity should apply to solicitors for court work.

The delictual liability of surveyors has been discussed in the context of liability for careless misrepresentation.[8]

1 *A Short Commentary on the Law of Scotland* (1962) p 683.
2 1990 SLT 266.
3 1993 SCLR 18 affirming 1992 SLT 264.
4 1992 SLT 264 at 268.
5 *Rondel v Worsley* [1969] 1 AC 191, [1967] 3 All ER 993, HL.
6 *Saif Ali v Sydney Mitchell & Co* [1980] AC 198, [1978] 3 All ER 1033, HL.
7 *Murray v Reilly* 1963 SLT (Notes) 49.
8 Pages 71 ff above.

CHAPTER 8

Product liability

A. INTRODUCTION

The basis of product liability in Scots law was, of course, laid down in *Donoghue v Stevenson*.[1] There it was held that the manufacturer of a product owes a duty of care to the ultimate consumer, when a product is manufactured which is intended to reach the ultimate consumer in the form in which it left the manufacturer, without the possibility of intermediate examination. If the product was manufactured carelessly, with the result that the ultimate consumer suffered injury or harm to his property, the manufacturer is liable in delict. However, the onus lies on the pursuer to prove that there was a breach of duty by the manufacturer, ie that the manufacturer was negligent.[2] If negligence cannot be established, the action fails.

Apart from the difficulty of establishing negligence, other factors could operate to prevent the pursuer from succeeding. Where, for example, a manufacturer has provided an adequate warning that a product is potentially dangerous and this is ignored by the ultimate consumer, then there will be no liability because the pursuer's failure to heed the warning will constitute a *novus actus interveniens* which breaks the chain of causation.[3] Similarly, where there is the opportunity of intermediate inspection and the defect in the product is patent, if the ultimate consumer nevertheless uses the product and is injured or his property is damaged, again the manufacturer will escape liability as the chain of causation is broken. Where the product is a complex structure made up of components manufactured by various persons, an action may fail if the pursuer is unable to identify the person who was responsible for the defect in the product. For example, in *Evans v Triplex Safety Glass*,[4] the plaintiff was injured when the windscreen of his motor car disintegrated. The manufac-

---

1 1932 SC (HL) 31. Discussed at pp 54 ff above.
2 On the general criteria for breach of duty, see Chapter 5 above.
3 *Kubach v Hollands* [1937] 3 All ER 907. On causation, generally, see Chapter 6 above.
4 [1936] 1 All ER 283.

turer of the car fitted a windscreen made by the defendant. Evans failed to establish whether the accident was the result of the windscreen being fitted carelessly by the manufacturer of the car or whether it was due to a defect in the windscreen caused by the negligence of the defendant. In those circumstances, his action was dismissed. Finally, there is no liability under *Donoghue v Stevenson* if the only loss suffered by the pursuer arises from the fact that the product itself is defective, ie the cost of repair or the difference in value between a defective and non-defective product. This is pure economic loss and is prima facie not recoverable in delict.[1]

B. STATUTORY REGULATION

Because of these difficulties, but particularly the fact that the onus of proof of negligence lies on the ultimate consumer, the law has now imposed a statutory regime of strict liability in respect of product liability. What this means is that provided the case falls within the statutory provisions, the defender is liable in delict to compensate the pursuer without the pursuer having to prove that the defender was negligent. The strict liability regime for defective products is to be found in Part I of the Consumer Protection Act 1987. This statute implements EC Directive No 85/374/EEC and it is expressly enacted that it should be interpreted to comply with the Directive.[2] The general idea of the Act is simple: it is to place the primary responsibility for injury or damage caused by a defective product on the producer and to enable the consumer who has been injured by the defective product or whose property has been damaged by the defective product to obtain compensation from the producer without having to prove fault. However, as we shall see, the provisions of the statute are hideously complex. Before considering them, however, it should be noted that where the statutory regime is not applicable, common law liability remains[3] and the pursuer may bring an action based on a breach of the *Donoghue v Stevenson* duty of care but will, of course, have to prove negligence if he is to be successful.

The 1987 Act imposes strict liability on the producer of a product

---

1 For full discussion, see pp 67 ff above.
2 Consumer Protection Act 1987, s 1(1). The Act came into force on 1 March 1988. It is not retrospective. References in this section are to the 1987 Act unless otherwise stated.
3 s 2(6).

'where any damage is caused wholly or partly by a defect in a product'.[1] Damage is defined as 'death or personal injury or any loss of or damage to property (including land)'.[2] Thus, if a person is killed by a defective product or injured by a defective product, or his land or other property is damaged by a defective product, the producer of the product is liable to pay compensation without proof of fault, ie the producer is strictly liable.

(1) Exceptions to strict liability

However, damage to certain types of property is excluded from the statutory regime viz:

(a) loss or damage to the defective product itself.[3] Thus, the cost of repair or the difference in value between a defective and non-defective product is not recoverable under the Act. Nor is it recoverable in delict at common law since it is pure economic loss. Where the product is a complex structure, loss or damage to the whole or part of the product caused by a defective component is also excluded. Thus, for example, if a motor car (complex product) is damaged as a result of a defective wheel (component), the damage to the car is excluded but, not of course, injury to the driver or damage to other property;[1]

(b) property damaged or lost as a result of a defective product, where the property *damaged or lost* is not for private use.[4] Property is not for private use, if it is not a description of property ordinarily intended for private use, occupation or consumption *and* intended by the person suffering the loss or damage mainly for his own private use, occupation or consumption. What this means is that before the Act applies and there is strict liability, the property damaged must be 'consumer' property, ie of a kind ordinarily intended for private use which the person suffering the loss or damage intended to be used for private use. For example, if A produces a defective vacuum cleaner, the Act will apply if it damages the carpet in B's home but not if it damages the carpet in B's office or factory. It is important to note that it is the property which is damaged which must be 'consumer' as opposed to 'business' property. If A produces a defective lorry which is used in B's

1 s 2(1).
2 s 5(1).
3 s 5(2).
4 s 5(3).

business, the Act *will* apply if the defective lorry damages C's family motor car but the Act will not apply if the defective lorry damages C's van which he uses for his business. When the Act is excluded because the property damaged is not 'consumer' property, resort will have to be made to delictual liability at common law when negligence will have to be established;

(c)   property damaged or lost as a result of a defective product, where the loss or damage does not exceed £275.[1] Where such loss or damage occurs, resort must again be made to delictual liability at common law when negligence will have to be established.[2] It should be noted that this exception only applies to damage to property. If, for example, A cuts his finger as a result of B's defective product, the Act still applies and B is strictly liable even if A's damages are less than £275.

(2) Definition of product

Strict liability applies where damage is caused wholly or partly by a defect in a product. A product is defined[3] as any goods or electricity. It includes – and this is important – components and raw materials which are parts of a complex product. So, for example, if there is a complex product such as a motor car and a component of the car, for example a windscreen, is defective, that component is regarded as a product for the purpose of the Act as well as the motor car. Thus the problem which arose in *Evans v Triplex Safety Glass*[4] will not arise under the Act. Goods also include 'substances, growing crops and things comprised in land by virtue of being attached to it and any ship, aircraft or vehicle'.[5] Substance means any natural or artificial substance, whether in solid, liquid or gaseous form or in the form of vapour and includes substances which are comprised in or mixed with other goods, for example, a cylinder of gas. Things comprised in land by virtue of being attached to it include, for example, window frames of a house, a garden shed or a swing. Ship includes any boat or vessel used for navigation; aircraft include gliders, balloons and hovercraft; vehicle is not defined. Game or agricultural produce do not constitute products for the purpose of the Act unless they have undergone an

1 s 5(4). This includes interest.
2 Such an action would be brought under the small claims procedure.
3 s 1(2).
4 [1936] All ER 283, discussed at pp 137 ff above.
5 s 45(1).

industrial process.[1] Thus, A will be strictly liable under the Act if he produces defective smoked salmon which causes illness to the consumer but he will not be strictly liable if he supplies contaminated 'fresh' salmon:[2] this is because smoked salmon has undergone an industrial process. The victim of the contaminated 'fresh' salmon must resort to delictual liability at common law and establish that A was negligent in supplying fish in that condition.

(3) Parties liable

As mentioned above, prima facie strict liability is imposed on the producer of the product. A producer is defined as the person who manufactured the product[3] or who won or abstracted the substance.[4] Where a product is not manufactured, won or abstracted but its essential characteristics are attributable to an industrial or other process, the producer is the person who carried out the process: for example, where the product is pasteurised milk, the producer is the person who carried out the pasteurisation process.[5] A person who merely packages goods is not a producer. Any person who puts his own name on a product, or uses a trade mark on a product, is liable under the Act if by so doing he holds himself out to be the producer.[6] This provision brings 'own branders' within the strict liability regime. Similarly, any person who imports products from abroad with a view to distributing them within the EC is liable under the Act.[7] This clearly is to protect ultimate consumers in EC member states from having to sue a producer outwith the EC; the importer may, of course, have a remedy, for example, in contract, against the non-EC producer. The producer of a component or raw materials used in a complex product is prima facie jointly and severally liable with the producer of the complex product if it is defective.

While strict liability falls on the producer, own brander or importer of a defective product, as a fall back position a supplier of the product may also be liable. Thus all parties in the distribution chain from the producer, own brander or importer are potentially liable under the Act viz:

1 s 2(4).
2 It does not matter if the salmon is farmed as opposed to wild as agricultural produce means any produce of the soil, of stock-farming or of fisheries: s 1(2).
3 s 1(2)(a).
4 s 1(2)(b).
5 s 1(2)(c).
6 s 2(2)(b).
7 s 2(2)(c).

Producer————Wholesaler————Retailer————Purchaser

In this example, the wholesaler and retailer are suppliers within the meaning of the Act. However, a supplier will be liable only if the person who suffered the damage asked the supplier within a reasonable time of the damage being sustained to identify the producer or a supplier further up the chain of distribution and the supplier failed to provide the information within a reasonable time, provided it was not reasonably practicable for the person suffering the damage to identify the producer. Thus, in order to escape potential strict liability under the Act, the supplier must keep records of his suppliers or producers.[1]

A supplier will not be strictly liable if the defective goods were not supplied in the course of business.[2] Thus, A will not be strictly liable if A sells his washing machine to his neighbour B in a private transaction or if A gives B the washing machine as a birthday present. Of course, A may be liable for breach of contract or in delict at common law if the washing machine is defective and injures B or damages B's property. Where we are dealing with a producer, own brander or importer, they will escape strict liability under the Act only if the goods were supplied otherwise than with a view to profit.[3] Thus if A makes lemon curd which is *donated* to the local church sale of work, A is not liable, although a producer, because the goods were not supplied with a view to A's profit. But if A *sells* the lemon curd to the sale of work, A will remain liable under the Act. In both cases, the church will not be liable under the Act, as the only potential liability is as a supplier and the lemon curd was not sold in the course of a business: the church could, of course, be liable at common law.[4]

(4) Meaning of defective product

In order to attract strict liability the damage must be caused 'wholly or partly' by a *defect* in the product.[5] What then is a defective product? A product is defective 'if the safety of the product is not such as persons are entitled to expect':[6] for these purposes, 'safety shall include safety in the context of risks of damage to property as well as in the context of

---

1 s 2(3).
2 s 4(1)(c)(i).
3 s 4(1)(c)(ii).
4 If A supplies a 'free gift' when selling another product, A will be strictly liable under the Act if the gift is given away in the course of A's business.
5 s 2(1).
6 s 3(1).

risks of death or personal injury'.[1] It will be noted that the test is what the *consumer* is entitled to expect in terms of the safety of the product: if it falls below the *consumer's* expectations then the product is defective. This, in theory at least, is in marked contrast to the concept of negligence at common law which is tested by the standards of the hypothetical reasonable person in the position of the manufacturer.[2]

However, in determining what the consumer is entitled to expect, the court must consider all the circumstances of the case.[3] These include:

(1) the purposes for which the product was marketed, its 'get up', any mark in relation to the product and any instructions or warnings.[4] Instructions or warnings are of particular importance where the product is inherently dangerous, for example, a poison. Obviously if no warning was given, the product would be defective; but if there is an adequate warning, for example, in respect of drug dosage, will that satisfy the consumer's expectation of safety or must the container of the drug be, for example, child proof?;
(2) what might reasonably be expected to be done with or in relation to the product.[5] Theoretically, this should be what the *consumer* might *reasonably* expect to be done with the product rather than what the producer expects it to be used for; ultimately, however, it will be the court's view of reasonable expectation which will prevail. The test is clearly objective. So, for example, it is unlikely that a freezer which cannot be opened from within would be held to be defective even though a child climbed into the freezer and could not get out: freezers cannot reasonably be expected to be the hiding places for toddlers!;
(3) the time when the product was supplied by its producer to another.[6] The relevant time for assessing the standard of safety of a product is the time at which it was supplied by the producer: the fact that products which are put on the market after that date have more safety features does not per se mean that the earlier product was defective at the time it was supplied.

At the end of the day, the test is sufficiently open that it will be left to the courts to determine the requisite standard of safety and in spite of the fact that it is the consumer's expectation of safety that is in

1 s 3(1).
2 For discussion, see pp 102 ff above.
3 s 3(2).
4 s 3(2)(a).
5 s 3(2)(b).
6 s 3(2)(c).

issue, the courts will no doubt consider the factors, for example, costs, with which they are familiar in establishing negligence at common law.[1]

Before there is strict liability under the Act, the pursuer has to show that the damage was '*caused* wholly or partly by a defect in a product'.[2] Therefore, as in the case of delictual liability at common law, the claim may fail unless there is a sufficient causative link between the damage and the defective product.[3] However, provided there are no causation problems, the pursuer who has suffered damage is entitled to compensation from the producer, own brander, importer or supplier without having to establish negligence ie it is strict liability.

(5) Defences to claim of strict liability

The Act does, however, provide the defender with the following defences to a claim based on *strict* liability:

(a) If the defect in the product is attributable to the defender's compliance with statutory or EC obligations.[4]
(b) If the defender did not at any time supply the product to another, for example, if the product was stolen.[5]
(c) If the defect did not exist in the product at the relevant times.[6] In the case of a producer, own brander or importer this will be the time he first supplied the product to another; in the case of a supplier, when the product was last supplied by a producer, an own brander or an importer into the EC. So in the case of the producer etc, he will escape strict liability if the product was not defective when it entered circulation, although it subsequently becomes defective; there can, of course, still be delictual liability at common law. The supplier will escape strict liability if the product was not defective when it was last supplied by a producer etc even though the defect was subsequently caused by the supplier himself: for example, if a retailer keeps food which was fresh when he obtained it from the producer but sells it when it has gone off. This is, to say the least, an odd result but, of course, the retailer will be liable in contract to the purchaser and at

---

1 See pp 102 ff above.
2 s 2(1) (emphasis added).
3 On causation generally see Chapter 6 above.
4 s 4(1)(a).
5 s 4(1)(b).
6 s 4(1)(d).

common law in delict to the ultimate consumer, when negligence will readily be inferred.

(d) If the state of scientific and technical knowledge at the relevant time[1] was not such that a producer of products of the same description as the product in question might be expected to have discovered the defect if it had existed in his products while they were under his control.[2] This is known as the 'state of the art' defence. It is controversial in that a producer can escape *strict* liability if the defect in his product would not have been known by manufacturers of a similar product, given the state of scientific and technical knowledge at the time. This defence is, of course, similar to the common law principle that a defender cannot be liable in delict, if as a result of the scientific knowledge available to the hypothetical reasonable person at the time, injury to the pursuer was not a reasonable and probable consequence of the defender's conduct.[3] Moreover, the defence expressly refers to the awareness of producers of similar products: this is similar to the important role that the practice of persons in the same trade, business or profession of the defender plays in establishing a breach of a duty of care at common law.[4] Thus, the state of the art defence re-introduces negligence into the regime of strict liability laid down in the 1987 Act.

In many cases, the defence will not be available to the producer, simply because, given the state of scientific and technical knowledge at the time, he[5] should have known the product was defective. Where the defence could be used is in the production of drugs whose side effects could not have been discovered given the state of scientific knowledge which existed at the time they were produced; it may take years before the side effects of certain drugs become apparent in patients. In these circumstances, the defence could be used by the defender. It is somewhat ironic that one of the reasons for the move towards a strict liability regime for defective products was to avoid the shortcomings of the law of negligence which became apparent in the thalidomide tragedy. However, the EC will consider whether member states can continue to have such a defence in 1995.

(e) If the defective product is a complex product, the producer of a component or raw materials comprised in the complex product

1 See discussion immediately above.
2 s 4(1)(e).
3 *Roe v Minister of Health* [1954] 2 QB 66, discussed at p 98 above.
4 See pp 108 ff above.
5 Or, technically, producers of similar products.

has a defence if the defect in the complex product was wholly attributable to the design of the complex product or the fact that he complied with the instructions of the producer of the complex product;[1] otherwise, of course, both the producer of the complex product and the producer of the component or raw materials are jointly and severally liable.[2]

(f) Contributory negligence.[3] Liability under the 1987 Act cannot be excluded by an exemption clause.[4]

This discussion of product liability is important as it illustrates how the common law of delictual liability based on the defender's *culpa* was thought to be inadequate to protect the interests of consumers who might be injured or whose property might be damaged by defective products. Accordingly, a regime of strict liability was introduced by statute so that the ultimate consumer would no longer have to prove fault before obtaining compensation. However, as we have seen, the 1987 Act is not comprehensive and it will still be necessary on occasions for a pursuer to resort to delictual liability at common law, when, of course, negligence will have to be established.[5]

1 s 2(4)(f).
2 See p 141 above.
3 s 6(4).
4 s 7.
5 For a full treatment of product liability, see A M Clark *Product Liability* (1989, Sweet & Maxwell).

CHAPTER 9

Delictual liability for animals

A. DELICTUAL LIABILITY AT COMMON LAW

Where the defender owes the pursuer a duty of care, the defender can be liable where the pursuer's injuries or damage to property is caused by an animal. In *Henderson v John Stuart (Farms) Ltd*[1] an employee was killed by a bull when cleaning out its box. The employer was held to be negligent in failing to fit the box with baffles or escape gaps, ie the employer had broken the duty of care he owed to his employee by failing to provide a safe working environment.[2] Similarly, in *Hill v Lovett*[3] an employee of the defenders, who were veterinary surgeons, was bitten by one of their West Highland terriers when she went into the garden to clean the windows of the surgery. As a result, the unfortunate pursuer eventually had to have her leg amputated. The Lord Ordinary (Weir) held that the defenders had broken the duty of care they owed to the pursuer both as employers and occupiers of the garden,[4] in failing to take reasonable care to ensure that the pugnacious dogs were not in the garden when the pursuer was there.

An unusual case is *Cameron v Hamilton's Auction Marts*.[5] The defenders were driving cattle along the highway. A cow escaped, climbed the stairway of a property adjoining the road, turned on a tap, and fell through the floor into the pursuer's shop causing flooding and damage. Clearly the defender owed a *Donoghue v Stevenson* duty of care to the pursuer as the owner of property adjacent to the highway. In these circumstances, the sheriff held that the defenders would be liable for breach of their duty of care if the cow had escaped because of their negligence.

These cases, then, are examples of breach of an existing duty of care as a result of the defender's carelessness: the fact that the injuries and

1 1963 SC 245, 1963 SLT 22, OH.
2 On employers' liability, see Chapter 12 below.
3 1992 SLT 994.
4 On occupiers' liability, see pp 162 ff below.
5 1955 SLT (Sh Ct) 74, (1955) Sh Ct Rep 285.

damage were caused by an animal is largely irrelevant. They are simply examples of common law delictual liability for negligence.

However, at common law, certain animals were regarded as *ferae naturae*, ie as having vicious propensities. These included, for example, lions, tigers and elephants. If such an animal caused injury or damage to a person, the person in charge of the animal was strictly liable, ie there was no need to prove fault. Strict liability applied even though the animal had not shown any vicious propensities before.[1] On the other hand, certain animals were regarded as *domitae naturae*, ie as having no vicious propensities. These included, for example, dogs, cats and cattle, including bulls. If such an animal had *in fact* shown vicious propensities before the pursuer suffered injury or damage, then strict liability would attach to the defender. But as in *Henderson v John Stuart (Farms) Ltd*[2] and *Hill v Lovett*,[3] where the bull and the dog had not hitherto shown vicious tendencies so that strict liability could not be imposed, the defenders were nevertheless successfully sued in negligence for breach of their duty of care.[4]

B. LIABILITY UNDER THE ANIMALS (SCOTLAND) ACT 1987

(a) Introduction

The common law on strict liability for injuries or damage caused by animals was regarded as unsatisfactory. For injury or damage caused by an animal after June 10 1987, the common law on *strict* liability has been replaced by the provisions of the Animals (Scotland) Act 1987.[5] The Act is not retrospective and the old common law on *strict* liability applies in relation to damage or injuries caused by an animal before that date.[6] However, common law liability for injury or damage caused by an animal as a result of the defender's *negligence* has *not* been

---

1 See the English case of *Behrens v Bertram Mills Circus* [1957] 2 QB 1, [1957] 1 All ER 583 where the defendants were held strictly liable for the injuries caused to a midget by an elephant which had hitherto appeared docile.
2 1963 SC 245, 1963 SLT 22.
3 1992 SLT 994.
4 Special rules applied to dogs under the Dogs Acts 1906-1928; damage done by straying cattle was governed by the Winter Herding Act 1686.
5 s 1(8). References in this section are to the Animals (Scotland) Act 1987 unless otherwise stated.
6 June 10 1987 was the date when the 1987 Act came into force: because it is not retrospective, the pursuer could not rely on the 1987 Act in *Hill v Lovett* 1992 SLT 994.

replaced by the provisions of the 1987 Act[1] and a pursuer is therefore able to sue on the general principles of *culpa* if his case does not fall within the strict liability regime imposed by the 1987 Act.

Where the 1987 Act applies, the defender's liability is strict, ie the defender is liable without the pursuer having to prove that the defender was negligent. The person who is liable is the *keeper* of the *animal* 'at the time of the injury or damage complained of'.[2] The keeper of an animal for the purposes of the Act is defined as follows:[3]

(a) the owner of the animal: remains the owner, even if the animal has been abandoned or has escaped, until someone else becomes the owner;[4]

(b) the person with possession of the animal:[5] remains in possession, even if the animal has been abandoned or has escaped, until someone else obtains possession.[6] However, a person is not a keeper of an animal by virtue of possession if he is detaining the animal to prevent it causing injury or damage on his land[7] or is 'temporarily detaining it for the purpose of protecting it or any other person or other animal or restoring it as soon as is reasonably practicable to its owner or a possessor of it';[8]

(c) a person with 'actual care and control of a child under the age of 16' who is the owner or has possession of the animal.[9] Thus, for example, a parent of a child under the age of 16 is regarded as the keeper of any animal owned by the child, provided the parent has actual care and control of the child.

Where an animal is owned by A but in the possession of B, A and B can be jointly and severally liable under the Act.

(b) Meaning of animal

What animals fall within the Act? For strict liability to apply, the animal must be of 'a species whose members generally are by virtue of their physical attributes or habits likely (unless controlled or restrained) to injure severely or kill persons or animals, or damage

---

1 s 1(8).
2 s 1(1).
3 s 5(1)(a).
4 s 5(2)(b): the Crown does not become the owner if an animal is abandoned, s 5(2)(c).
5 s 5(1)(a).
6 s 5(2)(b).
7 s 3.
8 s 5(2)(a).
9 s 5(1)(b).

property to a material extent'.[1] Read literally, this definition is potentially very wide indeed. While bulls clearly fall within the definition, it could, for example, include a domestic cat, since a cat by virtue of its physical attributes or habits is likely to injure severely or kill animals like birds or mice! It will ultimately be for the court to decide whether or not a certain species falls within the statutory criterion.

Certain animals are deemed to be likely (unless controlled or restrained) to injure severely or kill persons or animals for the purpose of section 1(1)(b). These are dogs and dangerous wild animals within the meaning of section 7(4) of the Dangerous Wild Animals Act 1976.[2] Therefore all types of dogs are regarded as animals for the purpose of the Act so that strict liability is imposed on their keepers, even if the dog concerned has never shown any vicious tendencies in the past. Where an animal is a dangerous wild animal within the meaning of the 1976 Act, it is regarded as an animal for the purpose of strict liability under the 1987 Act. Dangerous wild animals include wild dogs, wolves, jackals, coyotes, foxes (but not the common red fox), cassowaries, Old World monkeys, crocodiles and alligators, emus, poisonous snakes, lions and tigers, cheetahs and panthers, Gila monsters and Mexican beaded lizards, gibbons, orang-utans, gorillas and chimpanzees, ostriches and bears.[3] In addition, cattle, horses, asses, mules, hinnies, sheep, pigs, goats and deer *in the course of foraging*, are deemed to be likely (unless controlled or restrained) to damage to a material extent land or the produce of land for the purpose of section 1(1)(b).[4]

As a result of these provisions a wide range of species are deemed to be animals for the purpose of the Act. But if an animal is not deemed to fall within the definition in section 1(1)(b), it is, of course, possible to argue that it is nevertheless of a species which by virtue of the physical attributes or habits of the members is likely to injure severely or kill persons or other animals, or damage property to a material extent. In assessing whether this is so, the age and sex of the animal is relevant:[5] thus, a non-foraging cow is unlikely to fall within the definition in section 1(1)(b), while a non-foraging bull would. The Act expressly *excludes* from the definition of animal, viruses, bacteria, algae, fungi and protoza.[6]

1 s 1(1)(b).
2 s 1(3)(a).
3 Dangerous Wild Animals Act 1976, s 7(4) and Sch 3.
4 s 1(3)(b).
5 s 1(2)(a).
6 s 7.

Where the animal falls within the definition in section 1(1)(b) or is deemed to do so by virtue of section 1(3)(a) or (b), its keeper is strictly liable, ie liable without establishing *culpa*, for any damage or injury suffered by the pursuer which is directly referable to the animal's dangerous attributes or habits.[1] In other words, the damage or injury sustained must arise from the particular attributes or habits of the species which bring the animal within the definition in section 1(1)(b). So, for example, the keeper of a red setter dog is strictly liable under the Act if the dog bites the pursuer since the injury is directly referable to a dog's attribute or habit to bite;[2] but if the pursuer's injury is sustained as a result of falling over the red setter dog, the keeper is not strictly liable under the Act, though the keeper could be liable if he owed a duty of care to the pursuer and negligence could be established.[3] Strict liability does not apply to injury or damage caused by the mere fact that the animal was present on a road or in any other place.[4] Thus, if the pursuer was injured as a result of being harassed by a dog when cycling, the keeper is not strictly liable under the Act, but may, of course, be liable at common law if a breach of a duty of care towards the pursuer can be established. The Act does not apply if the injury caused by the animal consists of a disease which was transmitted by means which were unlikely to cause severe injury other than disease.[5] So, for example, if A is savaged by a rabid dog and contracts rabies, the keeper is strictly liable under the Act as the disease was transmitted by means which were likely to cause severe injury, ie the dog's bites; but if the animal had merely licked the pursuer thereby transmitting the disease, the keeper is not strictly liable under the Act as the means, ie the licking was unlikely to cause severe injury other than the disease. In the latter situation, of course, the keeper could still be liable at common law provided there was a breach of a duty of care owed to the pursuer ie that negligence could be established.

(c) Defences to liability under the Act

Even where the Act applies and the keeper is prima facie strictly liable, there are several possible defences viz:

---

1 s 1(1)(c).
2 So if a domestic cat was a dangerous animal, its keeper would only be liable if, for example, it killed the pursuer's pet bird ie the injury must be referable to the attributes or habits of a domestic cat which bring the cat under the statutory definition.
3 For discussion, see pp 147 ff above.
4 s 1(5).
5 s 1(4).

(1) if the injury or damage was due wholly to the fault of the person sustaining it or in the case of an injury sustained to another animal, the keeper of that animal.[1] This will cover the situation where, for example, the pursuer has goaded a docile animal which attacks the pursuer in defence;

(2) if the person sustaining the injury or damage, or a keeper of the animal sustaining the injury, willingly accepted the risk of it as his.[2] The classic example is a person who willingly puts his head in a lion's mouth. This defence is, of course, a statutory form of *volens non fit injuria*.[3]

(3) if the person who was injured or suffered damage was a trespasser ie was not authorised to be on the keeper's property.[4] The effect of this provision is only to remove *strict* liability from the keeper. As we shall see,[5] the keeper of the animal as occupier of property owes a duty of care to any person who enters on to the property, including a trespasser. Thus, although the keeper is not *strictly* liable under the Act to the trespasser who has been injured by an animal, the keeper may be liable as occupier of the property if negligence can be established.

Strict liability in relation to a trespasser is *not* removed by section 2(1)(c), if the animal which caused the injury or damage was there for the purpose of protecting persons or property; but the keeper will get the benefit of section 2(1)(c) if it is shown that it was reasonable to keep such an animal there and that the use made of the animal was reasonable.[6]

Consider the following example:

If A, a trespasser, is injured by B's goose,[7] prima facie section 2(1)(c) applies and B is not strictly liable. But if the goose was on the land to protect B's warehouse, then section 2(1)(c) is disapplied and B is strictly liable. But if B can show it is reasonable to have a goose as a 'guardbird' section 2(1)(c) is reapplied and B is not strictly liable. It is thought that B would succeed in this case since it is reasonable to have a goose as opposed to a tiger as a 'watch animal'.[8]

---

1 s 2(1)(a).
2 s 2(1)(b).
3 For discussion of the *volens* doctrine, see pp 123 ff above.
4 s 2(1)(c). In the case of injury to another animal, if the keeper of that animal was not entitled to have the animal on the land.
5 On occupiers' liability, see pp 162 ff below.
6 s 2(2).
7 Assuming, of course, that a goose is an animal for the purpose of s 1(2)(b).
8 s 2(2).

Where the animal concerned is a guard-dog, the keeper remains strictly liable to a trespasser ie section 2(1)(c) is disapplied, unless the keeper can show that he has complied with the provisions of section 1 of the Guard Dogs Act 1975.[1] Under this section, *either* the dog's handler must be present and have the dog under his control *or* the dog is secured so that it is not at liberty to go freely about the premises; in addition, notices of the dog's presence must be displayed at every entrance to the property.

Consider the following example:

If A, a trespasser, is injured by B's guard dog, prima facie section 2(1)(c) does not apply and B remains strictly liable. But if B can show that he complied with the provisions of section 1 of the Guard Dogs Act 1975 then section 2(1)(c) is reapplied and B is not strictly liable.

In both examples, B could be liable if he was in breach of the duty of care he owed to A as occupier of the property. To be successful, A would have to prove that B did not take reasonable care to protect him from the danger arising from having the animal on the land.[2]

Where the Act applies, there is no defence on the ground of *damnum fatale* or, for example, intervention by a third party which caused the animal to escape: this is because liability is strict. However, the pursuer's damages may be reduced on the grounds of contributory negligence.[3]

In this chapter we have seen how the general principles of delictual liability for negligence apply where damage or injury has been caused by an animal. However, even at common law it was thought to be in the interests of society that the owner of a dangerous animal should be liable without proof of fault. These rules were, however, unclear and, in so far as strict liability is concerned, have been replaced by the regime imposed by the 1987 Act. But where a case does not fall within the statutory regime of strict liability, the keeper may still be liable if he was in breach of a duty of care which he owed to the pursuer, but in these circumstances the onus rests on the pursuer to prove that the keeper was negligent.

---

1 s 2(2).
2 On occupiers' liability, see pp 162 ff below.
3 The keeper's statutory liability is treated as fault for the purposes of the Law Reform (Contributory Negligence) Act 1945: Animals (Scotland) Act 1987, s 1(6). On contributory negligence, see pp 125 ff above.

CHAPTER 10

Delictual liability arising from ownership or occupation of property

A. DELICTUAL LIABILITY AT COMMON LAW

The owner or occupier of property may be liable under general principles of *culpa* if a person is injured or property is damaged as a result of the state of the defender's property. In a case of unintentional acts or omissions, it will be necessary for the pursuer to show that the owner or occupier owed him a *Donoghue v Stevenson* duty of care[1] and that the defender was in breach of that duty.[2] In order to establish a breach of duty, it will, of course, be necessary to show that the defender was negligent. So, for example, if a slate falls off the defender's roof and injures a pedestrian who is using the highway or damages a motor car, the defender may be liable for breach of a duty of care owed to the pedestrian or the owner of the car[3] if the pursuer can establish negligence.[4]

While it is clear that the owner of property does not act at his peril, ie is not strictly liable,[5] if the defender has built a structure on his land which if unsafe would cause serious damage, the court will readily infer negligence. In *Kerr v Earl of Orkney*[6] the defender built a dam on his land across a stream on which the pursuer had a mill about half a mile lower down. Four months later, after several days of heavy rain, the dam burst and the pursuer's house and his mill were swept away. The court held that the defender was liable unless he could show that the dam had collapsed as a result of a *damnum fatale*, for example, an earthquake as opposed to several days of heavy rain: the fact that the dam had burst shortly after it had been built, inferred that the defender was at fault. Liability arises either because the *opus manufactum* could not be constructed so as to avoid harm to the neighbouring

1 See Chapter 3 above.
2 See Chapter 5.
3 It is thought that as a general principle the owner or occupier of property adjoining the highway would owe a duty of care to a pedestrian or motorist.
4 *MacColl v Hoo* 1983 SLT (Sh Ct) 23.
5 *McLaughlan v Craig* 1948 SC 599, 1948 SLT 483.
6 (1857) 20 D 298, 30 SJ 158.

property, in which case there was fault in building the structure at all, or the work was built negligently.[1] While achieving a similar result in cases such as *Kerr*, Scots law does not accept the English doctrine laid down in *Rylands v Fletcher*[2] that the owner of land is strictly liable for damage caused by the escape of dangerous things brought on to his property as a consequence of the defendant's non-natural use of his land.[3] In *RHM Bakeries (Scotland) Ltd v Strathclyde Regional Council*[4] Lord Fraser of Tullybelton was adamant that *Rylands v Fletcher* 'has no place in Scots law, and the suggestion that it has, is a heresy which ought to be extirpated'.[5]

While reasonable foreseeability of injury to the pursuer or harm to his property is the usual criterion for the imposition of a duty of care on the owner or occupier of property, in one situation at least the duty of care has been used as a threshold device to restrict the potential delictual liability of proprietors.[6] The question is whether the owner or occupier of property owes a duty of care to owners or occupiers of adjacent property, to prevent damage to their property as a result of the acts of third parties. For example, does the owner of derelict property owe a duty of care to adjacent proprietors, to prevent vandals entering the derelict property, starting a fire which spreads and damages the adjacent properties; or does the owner of a flat owe a duty of care to the owner of the shop below the flat, to prevent a thief entering the flat in order to gain access and steal from the shop?

These difficult issues were explored by the House of Lords in *Smith v Littlewoods; Maloco v Littlewoods*.[7] It was accepted by the court that the owner or occupier of property owed a duty to proprietors of adjacent property to take reasonable care of his property so that it did not cause them physical injury or damage to their property. But there was no general duty to take reasonable care of property to prevent a *third party* from using the premises to cause physical injury or damage to neighbouring proprietors. Using the duty of care as a threshold device, the House of Lords held that no such duty arose even if it was reasonably foreseeable that a third party could enter the defender's property and cause harm to the adjacent proprietor. Thus, while it is

1 *GA Estates Ltd v Caviapen Trs Ltd (No 1)* 1993 SLT 1037 at 1041 per the Lord Ordinary (Coulsfield) at 1041.
2 (1868) LR 3 HL 330. The scope of *Rylands v Fletcher* liability has recently been re-examined by the House of Lords in *Cambridge Water Co v Eastern Counties Leather* [1994] 1 All ER 53.
3 In Scots Law liability does not arise simply because a dangerous thing escapes but from the construction of the *opus manufactum*; *GA Estates Ltd* above.
4 1985 SLT 214, HL.
5 1985 SLT 214 at 217.
6 On the duty of care as a threshold device, see Chapter 5 above.
7 1987 SCLR 489, 1987 SLT 425, HL; for facts, see discussion at p 101 above.

reasonably foreseeable that if a person leaves his flat unlocked a thief may enter the premises and gain access to an adjacent flat or shop, the owner of the flat does not owe a duty to take reasonable care to prevent this occurrence. In these circumstances, the owner of the adjacent flat or shop must seek redress against the thief, ie against the third party.

However, Lord Mackay was prepared to accept that a duty of care could be imposed on the owner or occupier of property if in the circumstances it was highly probable – as opposed to reasonably foreseeable – that a third party would cause harm to an adjacent proprietor.[1] Lord Goff took the view that this could arise if the owner 'negligently causes or permits a source of danger to be created on his land, and can reasonably foresee that third parties may trespass on his land and, if interfering with the source of danger, may spark it off, thereby causing damage to the person or property'.[2] For example, a duty of care would arise if A kept explosives in his house, told persons that the explosives were there, but took no precautions to prevent trespassers from having access to the premises. Similarly, a duty of care would arise if the owner had allowed his property to become a fire hazard, knew persons had been trespassing on the premises and had already started fires, but did not take reasonable precautions to prevent access.[3] As we have seen[4], no duty arose in the *Littlewoods* case, since the defenders did not know that the derelict cinema had, in fact, become a fire hazard: derelict buildings are not, per se, fire hazards.

Lord Goff doubted[5] whether the owner or occupier of property ever owes a duty of care to adjacent proprietors to prevent a thief gaining access to their premises:

'. . . I do not think that liability can be imposed on an occupier of property in negligence simply because it can be said that it is reasonably foreseeable, or even (having regard, for example, to some particular temptation to thieves in adjacent premises) that it is highly likely that, if he fails to keep his property lockfast, a thief may gain access to his property and thence to the adjacent premises. So to hold must presuppose that the occupier of property is under a general duty to prevent thieves from entering his property to gain access to neighbouring property, where there is a sufficient degree of foresight that this may occur. But there is no general duty to prevent third parties from causing damage to others, even though there is a high degree of foresight that they may do so. The practical effect is that everybody has to take such steps as he

---

1 1987 SLT 425 at 429.
2 1987 SLT 425 at 439.
3 *Thomas Graham & Co v Church of Scotland General Trustees* 1982 SLT (Sh Ct) 26.
4 Page 101 above.
5 *Smith v Littlewoods; Maloco v Littlewoods* 1987 SLT 425 at 441.

thinks fit to protect his own property, whether house or flat or shop, against thieves.'

While obiter, this dictum is a remarkable example of the duty of care being used as a threshold device to deny delictual liability for reasons of policy.[1] As a result, the decision of the Inner House in *Squires v Perth and Kinross District Council*[2] must be regarded as unsound. There the pursuers who were jewellers successfully sued building contractors who were working on a flat above their shop for not adequately securing the flat against entry by a thief who gained access to their shop and stole jewellery. However, in the light of Lord Goff's dictum, the case should have been dismissed *in limine* because of the absence of a duty of care.[3]

The occupier of property owes the owner a duty of care to prevent damage to the premises. As there will usually be a contract between them, this duty will be contractual. However, it was held in *Fry's Metals Ltd v Durastic Ltd*[4] that the defenders were liable in *delict* for failing to maintain an alarm system after their lease with the pursuer had expired: their duty of care arose because they had retained the keys and were the only persons who had access to the building to operate the alarm. Moreover, they were liable for the damage caused by vandals who had broken into the premises because, in the circumstances, it was highly probable that this would occur if the alarm system was not working.

B. THE *ACTIO DE EFFUSIS VEL DEJECTIS* AND THE *ACTIO DE POSITIS VEL SUSPENSIS*

As we have seen,[5] the owner or occupier of property may be liable in delict for injury or damage caused by the defective state of the property on general principles of *culpa*. To be successful the pursuer must establish fault on the part of the defender. In Roman law,

---

1 For full discussion, see Chapter 5 above.
2 1986 SLT 30.
3 Even if there was a duty of care it is doubtful whether the defender should have been liable. In his evidence, the burglar claimed that while he got the idea of gaining access to the shop via the flat when he saw the defender's scaffolding and the open windows, he in fact entered the flat from the back by going up a drain pipe and entering an open door. The chain of causation between the defender's carelessness and the theft is therefore very fragile – provided, of course, we believe the thief.
4 1991 SLT 689.
5 Pages 154 ff above.

however, in two situations actions were available in which an owner or occupier was strictly liable, ie where there was no need to establish *culpa*. These were the *actio de effusis vel dejectis* where something was poured or thrown out of a building causing harm to the victim, and the *actio de positis vel suspensis* where something placed on or suspended from a building fell, causing harm to the victim. Under these *actiones* the owner or occupier was strictly liable for personal injuries or damage to property. Given its civilian background, it has been argued that these *actiones* are part of Scots law.[1]

While there is no authoritative decision of the Court of Session or House of Lords, attempts to rely on the *actiones* have not been successful. In *Gray v Dunlop*[2] the pursuer's son had the contents of a pot of urine poured over him from a window of a hostel for the indigent. In an action against the occupier of the premises, it was argued that the *actio de effusis vel dejectis* was applicable and the defender was strictly liable. But the court held that the *actio* did not apply and the pursuer's case failed because fault could not be established. Similarly, in *MacColl v Hoo*[3] the *actio de positis vel suspensis* was held not to apply when the pursuer's car was damaged by a slate which fell off the defender's roof. The defender was therefore not strictly liable and in order to succeed the pursuer would have to establish that the slate fell off the roof because the defender had failed to take reasonable care in respect of the maintenance of the property, ie that the defender was negligent.

C. *AEMULATIO VICINI*

If the proprietor uses his land in such a way as to interfere with his neighbour's use or enjoyment of his property, then the conduct may be actionable *in aemulationem vicini*. Before there is liability, it must be shown that the defender's use of his property was done with the intention of interfering with the neighbour's use or enjoyment of his land. A single incident is sufficient to establish liability. This delict has been fully discussed in the context of the intentional delicts.[4]

---

1 For example, D M Walker, *The Law of Delict in Scotland* (2nd edn, 1981, Greens) p 284.
2 1954 SLT (Sh Ct) 75.
3 1983 SLT (Sh Ct) 23.
4 See p 20 above.

D. NUISANCE

The owner of property must not use his land in such a way as to disturb or cause inconvenience to his neighbour or damage his neighbour's property.[1] If a person does so, he may be liable in nuisance. Unlike conduct *in aemulationem vicini*, nuisance is a continuing wrong, ie there must be more than one act; but delictual liability for nuisance arises even although the defender did not intend to disturb or cause inconvenience to the pursuer or harm the pursuer's property or person. The delict can be summarised in the brocard, *sic utere tuo ut alienum non laedas*, ie use your own property in such a way that you do not do harm to others.

Common examples of nuisance are noise, smells, the emission of fumes and burst pipes. The essence of the delict is that as a result of the defender's actions on his property, the pursuer has suffered more than he could reasonably be expected to tolerate: *plus quam tolerabile*. Whether this has been established is a matter of fact and degree in the particular circumstances of the case. For instance, the smell of dung may be acceptable in the countryside but not in the confines of a city tenement: regularly to play CDs of Wagner at full blast may be acceptable in a large detached house, but not in a two-bedroomed semi-detached. Even if the defender is a professional musician who has to practise 12 hours a day, if the noise disturbs his neighbour more than the neighbour can be expected to tolerate, it is a nuisance and the fact that it is a normal and familiar use of a musician's home is no defence. Nor can it be argued that the pursuer came to the nuisance. So if in our example, the musician's previous neighbour enjoyed hearing him practise, this is no defence to an action of nuisance brought by the new proprietor of the neighbour's house, if the continual practising is driving the pursuer mad!

Moreover, even if the use of the defender's property is in the public interest, this is still no defence if it would otherwise constitute nuisance. In *Webster v Lord Advocate*[2] the pursuer had bought a flat in Edinburgh near the Castle. As the Edinburgh Festival approached, the enjoyment of her flat was disturbed by the noise of erecting the grandstand for the military tattoo. The court held that this was a prima facie case of nuisance: it was irrelevant that the noise could be reduced if the pursuer closed her windows or installed double glazing. While accepting that the tattoo was a valuable and profitable part of

1 *Watt v Jamieson* 1954 SC 56 at 58 per the Lord President (Cooper).
2 1984 SLT 13.

the Festival, this 'greater good' argument was not sufficient to prevent the court ordering that the nuisance should cease. Accordingly, the court granted declarator that a nuisance was established and that the defender should take steps to ensure that the grandstand was constructed by using less noisy techniques. It is a defence, however, to an action that the conduct constituting the nuisance was carried out with statutory authority.

Because nuisance involves *continuing* acts or omissions, the primary remedy is interdict, ie an order that the defender's act or omission should cease. In determining whether or not to grant interdict, the court is concerned with the position of the pursuer, ie whether the pursuer should have to continue to suffer the nuisance. Whether or not the nuisance was caused by conduct which amounted to *culpa* on the part of the defender is largely irrelevant. Thus, in the context of granting interdict, the defender's liability for nuisance is strict, ie there is no need to aver or prove fault.

However, where the nuisance has caused injury to the pursuer or damage to the pursuer's property, no claim for damages will be successful unless the pursuer avers and proves that the nuisance arose as a result of the defender's *culpa*, ie intentional or negligent conduct. This was settled by the House of Lords in *RHM Bakeries (Scotland) Ltd v Strathclyde Regional Council*.[1] The pursuer's premises were flooded as a result of the collapse of a sewer, the maintenance of which was the responsibility of the defender. Food and packing materials stored in the bakery were damaged. Even if the failure to maintain the sewer adequately amounted to nuisance, the House of Lords held that the pursuer's action in damages failed because they had not averred, let alone proved, that the collapse of the sewer was due to the negligence of the defender. Thus, before the pursuer can obtain damages for harm caused by nuisance, *culpa* on the part of the defender must be established.

Because of the difficulty of proving fault, Lord Fraser expressed the view in the *RHM Bakeries (Scotland)* case that the court would readily infer *culpa* from the fact that the sewer had collapsed causing serious damage.[2] While, as we have seen,[3] this may be the case where the defender has built a dangerous *opus manufactum* on his property, it is doubtful that negligence will be inferred from the mere fact that the pursuer has sustained harm. In *Argyll and Clyde Health Board v*

---

1 1985 SLT 214, HL.
2 1985 SLT 214 at 219.
3 Pages 154 ff above.

Strathclyde Regional Council[1] the Lord Ordinary (McCluskey) held that in an action for damages it was not sufficient for the pursuers simply to aver that a pipe running below their field had burst causing damage. Instead the pursuers had to have specific averments showing why the defenders were at fault: for example, that they were negligent in failing to inspect the pipe and carry out regular maintenance. The fact that the pipe had burst causing damage to the pursuers did not have the effect that the onus automatically shifted to the defenders to show that they were not negligent in maintaining the pipe.

In the *RHM Bakeries (Scotland)* case the House of Lords did not over-rule its earlier decision in *Caledonian Rly Co v Greenock Magistrates*.[2] In that case, Greenock Corporation altered the channel of a burn to make a paddling pool: after heavy rainfall, the pursuer's property was flooded. The House of Lords awarded the pursuer damages without the need to prove fault ie the defender was held to be strictly liable. This decision was distinguished in the *RHM Bakeries (Scotland)* case on the ground that it was concerned with the alteration of the natural direction of a stream not with damage caused by 'unnatural' use of property. It is submitted that the distinction is tenuous and that, at the very least, the decision in the *Caledonian Rly* case rests uneasily with the ratio in *RHM Bakeries (Scotland)* viz that damages are available only where harm has been caused by nuisance if *culpa* on the part of the defender can be established.[3]

It is now clear that if nuisance is established an interdict can be granted without proof of fault while damages are awarded only on proof of *culpa*. The question arises whether this distinction is sensible. Where, for example, the nuisance is fumes emanating from the defender's factory, the effect of an interdict may mean that the defender has to close the factory while extensive – and expensive – repairs are carried out; yet, in theory at least, the defender may not have been negligent. But given that nuisance is a continuing wrong, even where the nuisance has caused damage, the defender still remains obliged to ensure that the nuisance stops, ie the defender could be interdicted if it were to continue. It is therefore submitted that the defender should not have to meet the *additional* obligation of compensating the pursuer unless *culpa* is established; *culpa* is, after all, the basic tenet of the obligation to make reparation in Scots law.[4]

1 1988 SCLR 120, 1988 SLT 381, OH.
2 1917 SC (HL) 56, 1917 2 SLT 67.
3 The exception in relation to altering the natural flow of a stream was accepted by the Lord Ordinary (Coulsfield) in *GA Estates Ltd v Caviapen Trs Ltd (No 1)* 1993 SLT 1037 at 1041.
4 For an authoritative statement of the law of nuisance see 14 *Stair Memorial Encyclopaedia* paras 2001–2168.

E. OCCUPIERS' LIABILITY

We have been considering cases where, as a result of acts or omissions on his property, the owner/occupier of property causes harm to persons who are not on his property, for example, adjacent proprietors, neighbouring proprietors, pedestrians or motorists on the highway who pass the defender's property. In this section, we shall consider the delictual liability of the occupier of property towards persons who *enter* upon the property.

Scots common law was strongly influenced by English law. As a result of the decision of the House of Lords in *Dumbreck v Robert Addie & Sons*,[1] the duty of care towards a person entering on to property depended on the status of the person who was injured, ie whether he was a licensee, for example, a lodger or member of the occupier's family; an invitee, for example, a guest or a lodger; or a trespasser. In the case of a trespasser, liability was restricted to intentional, as opposed to negligently caused, injury. However, as a matter of law, these classifications were swept away by the Occupiers' Liability (Scotland) Act 1960.[2] As we shall see, the 1960 Act places a general duty on the occupier to take such care of persons who enter his property as is reasonable in all the circumstances. How the pursuer came to be on the land is, of course, an important circumstance in determining whether or not the defender has taken reasonable care: what may constitute reasonable care in respect of a burglar may not be reasonable in respect of a guest.

The law on occupiers' liability is now laid down in the Occupiers' Liability (Scotland) Act 1960. The general thrust of the Act is that occupiers of property owe a duty to take care in respect of persons entering their land or premises as is reasonable in all the circumstances of the case. The statutory obligation rests on the person 'occupying or having control of land or other premises' who is referred to in the Act as the 'occupier of premises'.[3] Where the owner of the property is also the occupier of the premises, the statutory obligation lies with him. If, however, the owner is not the occupier, he will not be liable under the 1960 Act, but may incur liability under the general duty of care incumbent on owners of property, provided *culpa* is established.[4] A

---

1 1929 SC (HL) 51, 1929 SLT 242. See T B Smith 'Full Circle: The Law of Occupiers' Liability in Scotland' in *Studies Critical and Comparative* (Greens) p 154.
2 In this section, references are to the 1960 Act unless otherwise stated.
3 s 1(1). The common law rules for determining whether or not a person is an occupier for these purposes is expressly reserved in the Act: s 1(2).
4 See pp 154 ff above.

person occupies the land or other premises if he is in possession of the property, for example, a tenant. But he will also be treated as the occupier if he has control of the land or other premises. A person has 'control' if he is entitled to take the steps in relation to the land or property which the statute requires in order to fulfil the duty of taking reasonable care of the premises. So, for example, the owner of derelict property who is not *in fact* in possession is nevertheless the occupier as he has control of the premises. The determination whether a defender has sufficient possession or control as to be an occupier is one of fact and degree in the light of the circumstances of the particular case.[1]

While land is self-explanatory, 'premises' are not defined in the Act. They would include houses, flats, sheds, garages, shops etc; land would include gardens. Moreover, the statutory obligation to take such care as is reasonable in all the circumstances expressly applies to occupiers of 'any fixed or moveable structure, including any vessel, vehicle or aircraft'.[2] Thus, the Act applies to a wide range of property: for example, ships, barges, oil rigs, buses, caravans, cars, tractors, helicopters, planes and hovercraft. It is *not* therefore restricted to heritable property.

Section 2(1) of the Act lays down the nature and extent of the statutory duty:

'The care which an occupier of premises is required, by reason of his occupation or control of the premises, to show towards a person entering thereon in respect of dangers which are due to the state of the premises or to anything done or omitted to be done on them and for which the occupier is in law responsible shall . . . be such care as in all the circumstances of the case is reasonable to see that that person will not suffer injury or damage by reason of any such danger.'

It will be noted that the Act imposes a positive duty on the occupier to take such care as is reasonable in all the circumstances to ensure that a person entering the premises will not suffer injury or damage by reason of any danger on the premises. Nevertheless, the onus lies on the pursuer to show that the occupier did not take the care that was reasonable in the circumstances: it is not enough simply to aver that there was a danger and that the pursuer suffered injury or damage as a result.[3] In *McGuffie v Forth Valley Health Board*,[4] for example, the pursuer slipped on snow on the defender's premises which had not been removed by the defender. The pursuer's action failed because

1 *Feely v Co-operative Wholesale Society* 1990 SCLR 356, 1990 SLT 547.
2 s 1(3)(a).
3 *Wallace v City of Glasgow District Council* 1985 SLT 23.
4 1991 SLT 231.

she had not specified the period in which it would have been reasonable for the defender to have removed the snow or instructed its employees to do so. On the other hand, in *Porter v Strathclyde Regional Council*,[1] the pursuer slipped on food which had been spilled on the floor of a nursery under the control of the defender. She was able to establish that the defender did not have a system of working whereby an employee would mop up the mess soon after it was spilled. The failure to have such a system was held to be a breach of the occupier's statutory duty to take reasonable care to prevent the pursuer slipping on the floor as it was probable that the accident would not have occurred if such a system had been in operation.[2]

The Act applies where the injury or damage arose from dangers 'which are due to the state of the premises *or* to anything done or omitted to be done on them'.[3] Dangers due to the state of the premises clearly covers dangers arising from dilapidated buildings, for example, dry rot. It would also include slippery floors or unsafe furniture or plenishings. In *Taylor v Glasgow Corporation*,[4] where a child died as a result of eating poisonous berries which were growing in the Glasgow Botanic Gardens, the poisonous berries constituted a danger due to the state of the premises. But the statutory duty also applies to dangers which are due to anything done or omitted to be done on the premises. Thus, the Act would apply to dangers caused by the occupier's failure to provide adequate lighting or to secure a fence, as well as by positively creating a hazard. As we have seen, the failure to ensure that a pursuer would not enter a garden to clean windows while pugnacious West Highland terriers were also there, has been held to be a breach of the Act.[5]

It is important to appreciate that the occupier's statutory obligation is only to take such care as is reasonable in all the circumstances to prevent injury or damage from such dangers: it is not to eliminate the risk that an accident might happen. Accordingly, in determining whether or not the occupier has taken reasonable care, the calculus of risk is relevant.[6] The court will therefore consider such factors as the nature of the danger, the occupier's knowledge of the danger, the extent of the injury or harm, the probability of the injury or harm

---

1 1991 SLT 446.
2 However, the pursuer's damages were reduced by 50 per cent as a result of her contributory negligence.
3 s 2(1) (italics added).
4 1922 SC (HL) 1, 1921 2 SLT 254. This was, of course, a case before the 1960 Act.
5 *Hill v Lovett* 1992 SLT 994, discussed in the context of liability for animals, p 147 above.
6 On the calculus of risk generally, see pp 102 ff above.

arising, the age of the person injured, whether or not the pursuer was permitted on to the premises and the cost of eliminating the danger. Thus, in *McGlone v British Railways Board*,[1] the defender was held to have taken reasonable care in respect of the danger of a 12-year-old child being burnt by a transformer: it had put up warnings and surrounded the transformer with a barbed wire fence which had proved not to be impenetrable. Nevertheless, the House of Lords held that to provide an impenetrable and unclimbable fence went beyond what was reasonable in the circumstances given that a 12-year-old child should have realised the danger he would incur if he climbed through the barbed wire. In the circumstances, the defender had discharged its duty of reasonable care by erecting an obstacle which a 12-year-old would take some trouble to overcome before he would be in danger. If the fence could have been penetrated by a 3-year-old, then there might well have been a breach of the duty to take reasonable care in respect of a child of that age. The fact that the pursuer was a trespasser was also held to be a relevant factor in assessing whether or not reasonable care had been taken.

A similar approach can be discerned in *Titchiner v British Railways Board*.[2] A young man was killed by a train and his 15-year-old girlfriend was seriously injured. The couple had taken a short cut over the line to have a 'kiss and a cuddle' in a derelict brickworks. The defender had provided a fence made of sleepers but there were gaps in the fence through which it was possible for persons to reach the railway line. It was argued that the Board had been in breach of its duty of reasonable care in failing to maintain the fence and thus ensure that there were no gaps in providing access to the railway. The House of Lords held that the statutory duty was owed to the particular pursuer ie a 15-year-old girl who knew the danger involved in crossing a railway line. Accordingly, in determining whether or not the defender had taken reasonable care, the pursuer's age and knowledge were relevant factors. In these circumstances, the fence – even with gaps – gave adequate warning to a girl of 15 who knew the danger of crossing the line. Indeed, Lord Fraser thought[3] that the defender would have taken reasonable care in respect of the pursuer if there had been no fence at all! It would therefore appear that the more obvious and greater the danger, the *less* by way of warning is required for the average person; conversely *more* is required if the pursuer is, for example, a young child.

---

1 1966 SC (HL) 1, 1966 SLT 2.
2 1984 SC (HL) 34, 1984 SLT 192. See also *Devlin v Strathclyde Regional Council* 1993 SLT 699. (No breach of duty in respect of injuries to a 14-year-old child deliberately jumping on a skylight cover on a roof: the child was also a trespasser.)
3 1984 SLT 192 at 195.

The defence of *volenti non fit injuria* can be used by the defender.[1] Thus, if there had been a breach of duty in *Titchiner*, the House of Lords indicated that *volenti* would have been a defence.[2] Damages may be reduced on the ground of contributory negligence. The parties are free to vary the statutory duty by *agreement*.[3] This enables the occupier to undertake a more onerous or less onerous obligation. Where, however, the premises are used for business, any exemption clause excluding or limiting the occupier's liability for death or personal injuries is void and any clause restricting liability for other kinds of damage is unenforceable unless it satisfies the requirement of reasonableness.[4]

The Occupiers' Liability (Scotland) Act 1960 was necessary to sweep away the common law rules which were based on the artificial distinctions between licensee, invitee and trespasser. In their place, the Act imposes on an occupier a statutory duty to take reasonable care that a person entering the premises does not suffer injury or damage from any dangers thereon. This is a statutory duty but the wording of the provision is not without its difficulties. Given the way in which it has been interpreted, perhaps the time has come to repeal the Act, so that the delictual liability of an occupier of property towards a person entering his premises will be determined by the general principles of intentional and unintentional delictual liability.

---

1 s 2(3). On *volenti* see pp 123 ff above.
2 *Volenti* would also have been a defence in *Devlin v Strathclyde Regional Council* 1993 SLT 699.
3 s 2(1). A non-contractual notice is therefore ineffective.
4 Unfair Contract Terms Act 1977, s 16.

CHAPTER 11

Breach of statutory duty and public law issues

A. BREACH OF STATUTORY DUTY

The common law principle of delictual liability may be supplemented or supplanted by delictual liability for breach of a statutory duty. Provided the pursuer can establish that he was injured or suffered damage to his property as a result of the defender's breach of statutory duty, the pursuer will obtain reparation: it is not necessary for the pursuer to establish delictual liability at common law. The statutory duty may be similar to the common law standard of reasonable care as, for example, in the case of the Occupiers' Liability (Scotland) Act 1960.[1] More often, however, the statute may impose a standard which is higher than that expected of the reasonable person at common law, ie the statute imposes strict liability on the defender. We have seen examples of this in Part I of the Consumer Protection Act 1987[2] and the Animals (Scotland) Act 1987.[3]

These statutes expressly stipulate that breach of the statutory duty gives rise to a civil remedy in delict for reparation. Conversely, some statutes expressly stipulate that a breach of statutory duty does not give rise to a civil remedy for reparation even if a person is injured as a result.[4] But there are many statutes which are silent on whether or not a person is entitled to seek reparation in a civil action if he or she suffers injury or loss as a result of a breach of statutory duty. Yet it has long been recognised that even where a statute is silent on the matter, a person who has suffered loss may still be able to seek reparation in a delictual action for breach of statutory duty. Thus, for example, where an employee was injured at work and the injury arose as a result of a breach of the employer's statutory duty to maintain machinery, the court held that the employer was liable to compensate the

1 Discussed in Chapter 10 above.
2 Discussed in Chapter 8 above.
3 Discussed in Chapter 9 above.
4 For example, the Health and Safety at Work etc Act 1974.

employee for breach of statutory duty, even though the statute provided criminal sanctions for breach.[1]

What criteria are used by the courts to determine whether or not a breach of statutory duty gives rise to a civil action in delict where the statute is silent on the matter? The answer appears to be that it is a question of construction of the particular statute to discover whether Parliament intended to confer on the pursuer the right to obtain reparation for breach of statutory duty. This gives the courts considerable discretion, albeit within the confines of the language of the statute; and, like the use of the duty of care as a threshold device[2], the decision whether or not to allow the pursuer an action for breach of statutory duty will ultimately turn on policy considerations, ie whether or not such an action makes social or economic sense. That said, there are certain presumptions which are used by the courts when construing a statute in order to determine whether a civil remedy lies for breach of statutory duty and these will now be briefly considered.

As a general principle, where a statute provides a specific mode of enforcement of the statutory duties, the presumption is that Parliament did not intend that a civil action for damages in delict was necessary as an *additional* sanction if the statutory obligation is breached; conversely, if the statute does not provide a specific mode of enforcement of the statutory duties, then there is a presumption that Parliament did intend that a civil action for damages would lie. So, for example, in *Dawson v Bingley UDC*[3] the defendant's breach of statutory duty in failing to provide a notice indicating the position of a fire plug, with the result that there was a delay in putting out a fire at the plaintiff's premises, was held to be actionable by the plaintiff in a civil action. The statute did not provide a penalty or other remedy for breach of the statutory obligations. Where, however, the pursuer would already have a private law remedy against the defender if the statute was broken, for example, for breach of contract, it is presumed that Parliament did not intend that the pursuer should have the additional remedy of suing in delict for breach of statutory duty. While the position is not clear, it is submitted that the existence of a right to seek judicial review should not be presumed to exclude the possibility of a civil remedy for breach of statutory duty: judicial review is simply a procedure and damages are available only if the pursuer has a private law remedy. Accordingly, the right to seek

---

1 *Groves v Lord Winborne* [1898] 2 QB 402.
2 For further discussion, see Chapter 4 above.
3 [1911] 2 KB 438.

judicial review, while a factor to be taken into consideration by the courts, should not be conclusive in deciding whether or not Parliament intended that the pursuer should also have the private law remedy of suing in delict for breach of statutory duty.[1]

While the general presumption where a statute provides a penalty for breach of statutory duty is that Parliament did not intend that there should be the additional sanction of delictual liability for breach of statutory duty, there are two exceptions to this rule.[2] First, if it is apparent that the statutory obligations were passed for the protection of a particular class of individuals, then a delictual action for breach of statutory duty may lie if the pursuer belongs to that class and has suffered injury or loss. This explains how employees have been able to sue for breach, for example, of the Factories Acts, even although this legislation imposed criminal penalties on employers who were in breach. Similarly, performers whose work was recorded by record companies without their permission in breach of the Dramatic and Musical Performers' Protection Act 1958 were held to have been intended by Parliament to be able to pursue private law remedies for breach of statutory duty, in spite of the fact that the statute also provided criminal sanctions.[3] But it must be clear that the pursuer falls within the class. So, for example, in *RCA Corporation v Pollard*[4] it was held that companies who had exclusive recording contracts with performers could not sue for breach of statutory duty under the 1958 Act.

If the statute is not designed to protect a particular class and provides penalties for breach, no action for breach of statutory duty will lie. But it may be difficult to determine whether or not the legislation was designed to protect a particular class. In *Cutler v Wandsworth Stadium Ltd (in liquidation)*,[5] for example, the appellant brought proceedings against a licensed dog track to compel it to allow him space at the track to carry on his profession as a bookmaker. Statute provided that the occupier of a licensed track 'shall take such steps as are necessary to secure that . . . there is available for the bookmakers space on the track where they can conveniently carry on bookmaking in connection with dog races run on the track'. The House of Lords held that the purpose of the legislation was to protect those members of the public who wished to place bets by ensuring that

1 *Hague v Deputy Governor of Parkhurst Prison* [1992] 1 AC 58, [1991] 3 All ER 733 at 752 per Lord Jauncey.
2 *Lonrho v Shell Petroleum Co Ltd (No 2)* [1981] 2 All ER 456 at 461 per Lord Diplock.
3 *Ex parte Island Records Ltd* [1978] Ch 122, [1978] 3 All ER 824.
4 [1983] Ch 135, [1982] 3 All ER 771.
5 [1949] AC 398, [1949] 1 All ER 544, HL.

there was a choice of bookmakers at the track: it was not to give bookmakers the right of a place at the track. Accordingly, the appellant was not entitled to a remedy for breach of statutory duty. But it could equally be argued that it was Parliament's intention to protect the rights of bookmakers to earn their living. The decision in *Cutler* was ultimately a matter of policy. It is interesting to note that the courts are more prepared to construe statutes as giving a delictual remedy for breach of statutory duty where the pursuer has been physically injured[1] than, as in *Cutler*, where the pursuer has only suffered pure economic loss as a result of the breach of the statutory obligations.

In *Lonrho v Shell Petroleum Co Ltd (No 2)*[2] Lord Diplock maintained that there was a second exception where a private law remedy could arise for breach of statutory duty, even although the statute provided criminal penalties for its breach:

'The second exception is where the statute creates a public right (ie a right to be enjoyed by all those of Her Majesty's subjects who wish to avail themselves of it) and a particular member of the public suffers . . . "particular, direct and substantial" damage other and different from that which was common to all the rest of the public.'[3]

However, the extent of this exception is not as yet developed and need not be discussed further.

Once it has been decided as a matter of construction that Parliament intended that a delictual action should lie for breach of statutory duty, a person who has suffered harm must show that the statute was intended to protect a person in his position, ie that the pursuer fell within the class to be protected[4] and that the damage sustained was of the kind that the statute was designed to prevent. In *Gorris v Scott*,[5] for example, statutory regulations required that sheep or cattle being shipped from a foreign country to the United Kingdom had to be put in pens. The defendant failed to provide the pens and, as a result, the plaintiff's sheep were washed overboard in a storm. The plaintiff's action for breach of statutory duty failed because the court held that the purpose of the pens was to prevent animals from being infected by contagious diseases, not to prevent them being swept overboard. If the sheep had died as a result of such a disease, a delictual claim for breach of statutory duty would have been successful.

---

1 As in the case of the Factories Acts.
2 [1981] 2 All ER 456.
3 [1981] 2 All ER 456 at 461.
4 See discussion at pp 169 ff above.
5 (1874) LR 9 Exch 125.

The defender must, of course, have broken a statutory duty which was incumbent upon him. Whether or not the defender's conduct constitutes a breach will depend on the interpretation of the particular provision. Statutes may impose absolute liability, strict liability, or reasonable practicability. If a breach of the statutory duty is established, ie the defender has broken the duty,[1] there is no need for the pursuer to prove *culpa*. The pursuer must establish that the breach of statutory duty caused the injury or harm.[2] Unless, as in the case of the Occupiers' Liability (Scotland) Act 1960,[3] the defence is expressly stated to be available, *volentia non fit injuria* cannot be pleaded.[4] This is because a person cannot agree to take a risk of injury or harm which Parliament has legislated to prevent arising. However, the pursuer's damages may be substantially reduced as a result of contributory negligence.[5]

B. PUBLIC LAW ISSUES

Ministers of the Crown, local authorities and other governmental agencies are often given statutory powers to implement policy. This will often involve the exercise of discretion. Consider the following examples:

(1) A minister is given the power to send some criminals to an open prison: if such a criminal should escape, steal and damage a person's motor car, is the minister liable in delict?[6]

(2) A local authority is given the power to inspect and approve the plans of buildings: if the local authority approves the plans for the foundations of a house, is the local authority liable to the owner of the house if the foundations were unsuitable and have to be repaired?

(3) A minister is empowered to give information to the public on the risks of HIV infection: is the minister liable to a person who contracts HIV through injecting heroin if the information only

---

1 For examples see discussion of Part I of the Consumer Protection Act 1987, the Animals (Scotland) Act 1987 and the Occupiers' Liability (Scotland) Act 1960, above.
2 On causation generally, see Chapter 6 above.
3 s 2(3).
4 See, for example, *Wheeler v New Merton Board Mills* [1933] 2 KB 669.
5 For discussion, see pp 125 ff above.
6 Of course, the criminal will be liable in delict.

disclosed the risk of infection from sexual contact and omitted the danger of infection from drug abuse?

Before the pursuer can succeed in these examples, two formidable hurdles must be crossed. The first we shall call the 'public law' hurdle. The defender's act or omission must go beyond the errors of judgment which are inevitable in the exercise of discretionary powers: in other words, the discretion must have been exercised improperly. This means that the defender's act or omission was ultra vires of the statutory powers, or was made in bad faith, or was so wholly unreasonable that it was no real exercise of discretion at all: it is not enough that the defender did not take reasonable care. If, and only if, the pursuer can cross this 'public law' hurdle and establish that the defender's act or omission was an improper exercise of the statutory powers or duties, ie that it was outside the ambit or scope of the defender's discretion, can an action in delict lie.

So, for example, if in the exercise of his statutory powers, a minister sends A to an open prison, having considered A's case and taken the view that A is suitable for such treatment; A then absconds and damages B's motor car which A stole when he escaped. Before B can sue the minister in delict, B must establish that the minister's selection of A was an improper exercise of the minister's discretion. This will be established only if (a) the choice of A was ultra vires of the minister's powers, for example, if A was a category of prisoner who was not eligible to be sent to an open prison; or (b) the choice of A was not made in good faith, for example, if A was selected because A was a relative or friend of the minister; or (c) the decision to select A was so totally unreasonable that it was not an exercise of discretion at all, for example, if A was selected merely because of his sex or colour. If the selection of A was merely an error of judgment which fell within the scope or ambit of the minister's powers, B's action will fail *in limine*.

In *Bonthorne v Secretary of State for Scotland*[1] parents of a child brought an action against the Secretary of State for an alleged failure to provide sufficient information in respect of the risks inherent in vaccinating a child against whooping cough. The Lord Ordinary (Grieve) held that under the national health legislation the amount of information to be disseminated during a campaign to encourage parents to have their children vaccinated was a matter for the discretion of the defender. In the absence of evidence that the Secretary of State had acted ultra vires of his statutory powers, or had acted in bad faith or that his decision was totally unreasonable, the pursuer

1 1987 SLT 34, OH; see also *Hallet v Nicholson* 1979 SC 1, OH.

had failed to show that the defender had exercised his discretion improperly. Accordingly, the pursuer had failed to cross the 'public law' hurdle and the action was dismissed.

Where the pursuer has successfully crossed the 'public law' hurdle, a formidable second hurdle remains. Before there is liability in delict, the pursuer must show that the defender owed him a duty of care. As we have seen,[1] the court using the duty of care as a threshold device may deny the existence of such a duty. There is, for example, no duty of care owed by the police to a member of the public to prevent injury as a result of the act of an unidentified criminal who has not been apprehended.[2] Nor, it is submitted, is there a duty of care to prevent harm to the public when a criminal escapes. Thus, even if B, in the example above, could establish that the selection of A was an improper exercise of the minister's discretion, it is doubtful that the minister owed him a duty of care as an ordinary member of the public to prevent damage to B's car by the escapee. The plaintiffs in *Dorset Yacht Co v Home Office*[3] only succeeded in establishing the existence of a duty of care because the only method of escape from the island was by sea and it was therefore reasonably foreseeable as a probable consequence of the defendants' omissions that the yacht would be damaged. As Lord Diplock observed:[4]

'In the present appeal the place from which the trainees escaped was an island from which the only means of escape would presumably be a boat accessible from the shore of the island. There is thus material . . . for holding that the respondents, as the owners of a boat moored off the island, fell within the category of persons to whom a duty of care to prevent the escape of the trainees was owed by the officers responsible for their custody.'

Similarly, even if a government agency or a local authority exercises its powers improperly, the pursuer may fail if the only loss is economic as there is generally no 'threshold' duty of care to prevent a person suffering pure economic loss.[5]

In addition, even if a duty of care exists, the usual criteria for breach of duty must be established viz the act or omission must be voluntary, have as its reasonable and probable consequence injury or loss to the

---

1 Chapter 4 above.
2 *Hill v Chief Constable of West Yorkshire* [1988] 2 All ER 238.
3 [1970] 2 All ER 294. Discussed at p 102 above.
4 [1970] 2 All ER 294 at 334.
5 *Yuen Kun Yeu v Attorney-General of Hong Kong* [1988] AC 175, [1987] 2 All ER 705, PC; *Murphy v Brentwood District Council* [1990] 3 WLR 414; cf *Anns v Merton London Borough Council* [1978] AC 728, [1977] 2 All ER 492, HL. See generally, pp 67 ff above.

pursuer, constitute negligent conduct and be the cause of the pursuer's injury or loss.[1]

It is important to appreciate that in this section we have been concerned with the possibility of delictual liability arising from the exercise of a discretionary power by a minister of the Crown, a local authority or another governmental agency. Where, however, there is no degree of discretion involved, then the 'public law' hurdle withers away. The driver of a ministerial motor car or a local authority bus, for example, owes the same *Donoghue v Stevenson* duty of care to a fellow road user as an ordinary driver and will be liable in delict if the duty of care is breached.

1 See Chapters 5 and 6 above.

CHAPTER 12

Employers' liability and vicarious liability

A. EMPLOYERS' LIABILITY

It is an implied term of the contract of employment that an employer will take reasonable care for the safety of his employees. If an employer does not take reasonable care, he will be in material breach of contract. In these circumstances, an employee may withdraw his labour and sue for damages. An employer may be in breach of his contractual obligations even if the employer has not suffered any injury. However, in addition to his contractual obligations, an employer owes a *Donoghue v Stevenson* duty of care[1] to his employees to prevent them suffering physical injury or harm as a result of the employer's negligent conduct. Accordingly, an employee who is injured may sue his employer in delict as well as for breach of contract: but the employee cannot be compensated twice for the same loss.

The obligation to take reasonable care for the safety of his employees is personal to the employer ie it cannot be delegated by the employer to senior employees or a third party.[2] However, in a modern industrial context, in order to *fulfil* the obligation of reasonable care, an employer may have to appoint a safety officer and/or safety committee. The scope of the duty incumbent on an employer includes taking reasonable care to supply the employee with proper plant and equipment, to select competent fellow workers and to provide a safe system of working; however, it is a *general* duty to take reasonable care. Moreover, it cannot be overemphasised that at common law the employer is only expected to maintain the standards of the reasonable person in his position ie it is only to take reasonable care. An employer is not expected to ensure that an employee is never injured. In assessing whether or not a particular employer has taken reasonable

---

1 On *Donoghue v Stevenson*, see Chapter 3 above. The existence of a contract between the employer and employee is an important factor in establishing the 'foreseeability of injury or harm' criterion.
2 *Hislop v Durham* (1842) 4 D 1168.

175

care, the calculus of risk will be relevant.[1] The court will therefore consider such factors as the nature of the danger, the employer's knowledge of the danger, the extent of the injury or harm, the probability of the injury or harm arising and the cost of eliminating the risk.

In *Davie v New Merton Board Mills*,[2] for example, an employee was injured when a piece of a chisel he was using broke and a splinter entered into his eye. The defect in the chisel was latent and arose as a result of the metal used for the chisel not having been tempered properly by the manufacturer. The employer had bought the chisel from a reputable retailer who had in turn bought it from a reputable wholesaler who had purchased it from the manufacturer. In these circumstances, the House of Lords held that the employer had taken reasonable care and the employee's action againt the *employer* failed. The employee could, of course, have sued the manufacturer in delict for breach of the manufacturer's *Donoghue v Stevenson* duty of care which he owed to the ultimate consumer of the product.[3] However, the view was taken that this was placing too heavy an onus on an employee. Accordingly, under the Employers' Liability (Defective Equipment) Act 1969,[4] if an employee suffers personal injury as a result of a defect in equipment provided by the employer and the defect is attributable wholly or partly to the fault of a third party, for example, the manufacturer, then the defect is deemed to be also attributable to negligence on the part of the employer. In other words, the employee can sue the employer without the need to prove that the employer was negligent. The *employer* will then seek redress against the third party either in contract or, theoretically at least, in delict.[5]

The employer has to take reasonable care in selecting competent workers who will not cause injury or harm to the other employees; if the employer fails to do so and an employee is injured as a result, the employee can sue the employer for breach of the duty of care. Again it must be emphasised that the employer is only expected to take reasonable care. Before the employer can be negligent, he must know that the employee he has appointed could be a danger to fellow workers.[6] The contract of employment is not a contract *uberrimae fidei*; the

---

1 On the calculus of risk, generally, see pp 102 ff above.
2 [1959] AC 604.
3 On product liability, generally, see Chapter 8 above.
4 s 1(1).
5 The difficulty in suing in delict is, of course, that the employer is seeking reparation for pure economic loss: on economic loss, see pp 67 ff above.
6 See, for example, *Hudson v Ridge Manufacturing* [1957] 2 QB 348, [1957] 2 All ER 348.

employer must therefore make reasonable enquiries to determine whether or not an aspirant employee would be a source of danger to fellow employees if he were to be engaged. For example, the employer should ask whether or not an applicant for a job as a van driver has a clean driving licence and whether or not he has been convicted of careless or reckless driving.[1]

The duty to provide a safe system of working is owed to the particular employee. Thus, for example, if an employer knows that an employee is an epileptic or has only one eye, the standards required to constitute reasonable care may be greater in respect of that employee than the other workers: accordingly, the employer may be negligent vis à vis that employee even if his conduct would not amount to negligence if the employee was not epileptic or had two eyes.[2] It is always important to remember that the cost of eliminating the risk of danger is a very important factor in determining whether or not an employer is negligent.[3]

At common law the onus lay on the employee to prove that the injury or harm sustained was a breach of the employer's duty of care ie that the employer was negligent. Since the nineteenth century, safety at work has been the subject of statutory regulations. These provided detailed safety requirements for machinery, particular processes and operations. While these statutes provided criminal sanctions in cases of breach, as we have seen,[4] the courts allowed an employee who was injured as a result to sue the employer in delict for breach of statutory duty. Moreover, as the statutes often imposed strict liability, an employee who sued for breach of statutory duty did not have to establish negligence. But, of course, the employee had to show that the employer was in breach of the statutory obligations and this could involve complex issues of statutory construction.[5] The Health and Safety at Work etc Act 1974 lays down the minimum standards required of employers for safety at the work place; it is, however, a criminal statute and it is expressly enacted that its breach does not give rise to a private law remedy for breach of statutory duty. However, the morass of safety legislation, in particular the Factories Act 1961, continued in force and breach of these provisions did give rise to an action for breach of statutory duty. However, much of this legislation has been repealed and replaced by statutory regulations implementing

1 Subject to the offences being spent under the Rehabilitation of Offenders Act 1974.
2 *Paris v Stepney Borough Council* [1951] AC 367, [1951] 1 All ER 42, HL, discussed at p 104 above.
3 *Latimer v AEC Ltd* [1953] AC 643, discussed at p 107 above.
4 Pages 167 ff above.
5 See, for example, *Hunter v British Steel Corpn* 1980 SLT 31.

EC directives. Breach of these detailed regulations will in general, continue to give rise to delictual liability. Discussion of these regulations is outside the compass of this current work.[1] Nevertheless, where an employer is injured as a result of a breach of these regulations, it is important to remember that he will still be able to sue for breach of statutory duty and plead the employer's negligence at common law in the alternative. As in all cases of breach of statutory duty, *volens* is not a defence unless expressly allowed in the statutory regulations, but the employee's damages may be reduced on the grounds of contributory negligence.[2]

An employer may owe the employee a duty of care under the Occupiers' Liability (Scotland) Act 1960[3] as well as the general duty of care owed to employees at common law.[4]

B. VICARIOUS LIABILITY

(1) Introduction

In certain circumstances a person may be liable for the delicts committed by another. This is known as vicarious liability. While the doctrine arises out of several relationships,[5] the most common by far is that of employer and employee. An employer is vicariously liable for the delicts committed by the employee in the course of his employment. This arises when the employee concerned injures or harms a third party or another employee, provided the delict was committed in the course of employment. While the employer and employee are jointly and severally liable,[6] in practice the pursuer will sue the employer, who is more likely to have funds or be insured. Where it is an employee who has been injured, the employer is obliged by statute to have insurance so that funds are available if he is found to be vicariously liable.[7] Where an employee has been negligent, if the employer is found vicariously liable, the employer can, in theory at least, recover the damages he has paid from the employee, since the employee's delictual conduct constitutes a breach by the employee of

---

1 For an excellent introduction to the law, see W J Stewart *Delict* (2nd edn, 1993, Greens) p 145.
2 On contributory negligence, see pp 125 ff above.
3 On occupiers' liability, see pp 162 ff above.
4 *Hill v Lovett* 1992 SLT 994.
5 See pp 186 ff below.
6 On joint and several liability, see p 127 above.
7 Employers' Liability (Compulsory Insurance) Act 1969.

the contract of employment.[1] In practice, an employer – or his insurers – do not exercise this right to sue the employee for breach of contract.

(2) Delicts of an employee

The first issue is to determine whether the relationship of employer and employee exists between the person who committed the delict and the person alleged to be vicariously liable: whether the person who committed the delict is working under a contract of employment (*locatio operarum*) or is an independent contractor, working under a contract for services (*locatio operis faciendi*). The traditional test for distinguishing between a contract of employment and a contract for services is that of 'control':[2] an employer has the power to control not only what the employee should do but also *how* he should do it. If A has a cleaner who regularly cleans A's house, there is a contract of employment since A can tell the cleaner not only what to do but the manner in which the work is to be done. On the other hand, if A wishes to have a suit dry cleaned, while he may tell the cleaners what to do, A does not have the power to tell them how to carry out the dry-cleaning process: here A is simply entering into a contract for the services of the dry cleaner and not a contract of employment.

The 'control' test remains a useful criterion where the work involved is relatively unskilled. But it is of less value where the alleged employer is a company or large organisation and the work involved is specialist and sophisticated. The courts have therefore had to develop other criteria. Where a person works as an integral part of an organisation, he is likely to be working under a contract of employment, particularly if there is some element of control.[3] While the parties' expressed intention in their contract is an important factor, the 'label' they have used to describe their relationship is not decisive. As Lord Denning MR observed,[4] 'if the true relationship of the parties is that of master and servant under a contract of service [a contract of employment], the parties cannot alter the truth of that relationship by putting a different label upon it'. On the other hand, if the relationship between the parties is ambiguous, the 'label' in the contract may be a very important factor in determining the true relationship

---

1 *Lister v Romford Ice and Cold Storage Co Ltd* [1957] AC 555, [1957] 1 All ER 125.
2 *Yewans v Nokes* (1880) 6 QBD 530.
3 *Stevenson, Jordan and Harrison Ltd v MacDonald and Evans* (1952) 69 RPC 10, [1952] 1 TLR at 103.
4 *Massey v Crown Life Insurance* [1978] ICR 590 at 594, [1978] 2 All ER 576, CA.

between them.[1] An important factor is the economic reality of the situation. If, for example, the worker supplies his own equipment and materials and takes the 'economic risk' inherent in the enterprise, it is more likely that he is an independent contractor than an employee.[2] On the other hand, where the worker purchases equipment using money lent to him by the other party to the contract who has an option to purchase the equipment for a nominal sum at the end of the contract, then the court would be likely to hold that this is a contract of employment, although technically the worker owns the equipment. Other important factors include the payment of national insurance contributions, the pension position, the payment of Schedule D or Schedule E taxation, whether or not the worker is paid a fee or a sum on a regular basis and the arrangements for termination of the contract.

The courts can therefore consider a wide range of factors. This has long been recognised as the proper approach in Scots law.[3] It should be emphasised that in the vast majority of cases, it will be clear whether the contract between the parties is one of employment or for services. However, in hard cases, ie where the nature of the contract is ambiguous, the multiple tests approach gives the courts considerable discretion in determining whether or not a contract of employment exists. Where the issue is whether a worker is an employee for the purpose of the doctrine of vicarious liability, it is thought that the courts would be reluctant to find that a worker was not an employee if this would mean that the pursuer would not obtain reparation because the defender was without requisite funds or insurance.

Having established that a contract of employment exists between the parties, the employer will be vicariously liable for the delicts committed by the employee 'in the course of the employment'. In other words, before an employer is vicariously liable, the employee's acts or omissions which constitute the delict must fall within the scope of his employment. In short, the delict must be a mode or method – albeit wrongful – of the kind of work the employee is engaged to do. The classic exposition of the doctrine in Scots law is to be found in the judgment of the Lord President (Clyde) in *Kirby v National Coal Board*:[4]

'But, in the decisions, four different types of situation have been envisaged as guides to the solution of this problem. In the first place, if the master actually

---

1 *Massey v Crown Life Insurance* [1978] ICR 590 at 594, [1978] 2 All ER 576, CA.
2 See, for example, *Ready Mixed Concrete (South East) Ltd v Minister of Pensions and National Insurance* [1968] 2 QB 497, [1968] 1 All ER 433.
3 See, for example, *Short v J & W Henderson* 1946 SC (HL) 24; *United Wholesale Grocers Ltd v Sher* 1993 SLT 284.
4 1958 SC 514 at 532–533, 1959 SLT 7.

authorised the particular act, he is clearly [vicariously] liable for it. Secondly, where the workman does some work which he is appointed to do, but does it in a way which his master has not authorised and would not have authorised had he known of it, the master is nevertheless still responsible, for the servant's act is still within the scope of his employment. On the other hand, in the third place, if the servant is employed only to do a particular work or a particular class of work, and he does something outside the scope of that work, the master is not responsible for any mischief the servant may do to a third party. Lastly, if the servant uses his master's time or his master's tools for his own purposes, the master is not responsible.'

Taking these four situations in turn:

(1) If an employer has expressly or impliedly authorised the delictual conduct, the employee is acting within the scope of the employment and the employer is vicariously liable for the delict. In *Neville v C & A Modes*,[1] for example, the pursuer was suspected of shoplifting by employees of the defender. She was forcibly taken from the street back into the shop and there accused of theft. She argued that the defender was vicariously liable for defamation of her character. The Inner House held that the defender's employees had a duty under their contracts of employment to protect the defender's property and take action to prevent theft. The employees' action had therefore been authorised by the defender ie was within the scope of their employment, albeit that it may have been defamatory in the circumstances of this case.[2]

(2) If the employee does work which he was authorised to do, but does it in a way which the employer has not authorised and would not have authorised, nevertheless the employer is vicariously liable as the employee's act is still within the scope of his employment ie the delictual act or omission is a mode – albeit a wrongful mode – of carrying out the work the employee was authorised to do. An example will illustrate the point. A is employed by B as a van driver. A drives the van carelessly or over the speed limit. As a result of his negligent driving, A injures C. In an action for reparation, B is vicariously liable for A's negligent driving. The careless driving is a mode – albeit a wrongful mode – of carrying out the work A was authorised to do. B would still be vicariously liable even if he instructed A not to drive carelessly or over the speed limit.

1 1945 SC 175, 1945 SLT 189.
2 On defamation, see Chapter 15.

(3) If the employee is employed to do a particular work or particular class of work, and does something outside the scope of his work, then the employer is not vicariously liable as the employee was not acting within the scope of his employment. For example, A is employed by B to pack goods at B's warehouse. A decides to deliver goods to a customer and drives B's van. If A injures C as a result of A's careless driving, prima facie B is not vicariously liable as A was not employed as a driver and was not therefore authorised to drive B's van. A's driving of the van is outside the scope of his employment and B is not therefore vicariously liable.

It may be difficult to determine what is the scope of a worker's employment. Obviously the terms of the contract are important, but the courts are not prepared to accept that for the purpose of vicarious liability, the scope of employment is limited to the employee's express contractual duties. In the example above, if to B's knowledge, A had delivered goods to a customer in the van on previous occasions, driving the van could well fall within A's employment, even although A's job description in his contract is that of a packer. Moreover, given that the pursuer has *ex hypothesi* been injured or suffered harm, courts will be reluctant to allow an employer to escape vicarious liability by arguing that the employee's failure to follow the employer's detailed instructions resulted in the employee acting outside the scope of employment (no vicarious liability) as opposed to engaging in a wrongful mode of carrying out the work the employee was authorised to do (vicarious liability). Thus, in *Rose v Plenty*,[1] a milkman was expressly instructed by his employer not to use boys to help him deliver milk or to give boys lifts in his milk float. In breach of this order, a milkman continued to use a 13-year-old boy to help him. The lad was injured as a result of the milkman's negligent driving of the float. The employers argued that they were not vicariously liable as the employee was acting outside the scope of his employment. In other words, his particular work was delivering milk without the help of young boys and therefore he was acting outside the scope of his employment when he delivered milk with the help of a 13-year-old lad. However, the Court of Appeal held,[2] that the express prohibition did not change the scope of the milkman's employment. As Lord Denning MR explained:

'In considering whether a prohibited act was within the course of the employment it depends very much on the purpose for which it is done. If it is done for his employer's business, it is usually done in the course of his employment,

---

1 [1975] ICR 430, [1976] 1 All ER 97.
2 Lord Denning MR, Scarman LJ; Lawton LJ dissenting.

even though it is a prohibited act. . . But if it is done for some purpose other than his master's business, as, for instance, giving a lift to a hitchhiker, such an act, if prohibited, may not be in the course of his employment. . . In the present case it seems to me that the course of Mr Plenty's [the milkman's] employment was to distribute the milk, collect the money and to bring back the bottles to the van. He got, or allowed this young boy, Leslie Rose, to do part of that business which was the employer's business. It seems to me that although prohibited, it was conduct which was within the course of employment . . . I agree it is a nice point in these cases on which side of the line the case falls.'[1]

In certain situations it will be a question of degree whether the employee's conduct is or is not within the scope of his employment. In *Williams v Hemphill*,[2] members of the Boys' Brigade were at a camp at Benderlock. A company of Girl Guildry was also at the camp. The girls were to return to Dollar by train. A lorry driver was instructed by his employer to take the boys back to Glasgow. He was persuaded by some of the boys to return to Glasgow via Connell, Stirling and Dollar railway stations, so that the boys could catch a glimpse of the girls. The shortest route back to Glasgow was via Loch Lomond. There was an accident and one of the boys, who had not instigated the change of route, was injured. The employers would not have authorised the route the driver had taken. The question was whether by deviating from the authorised route, the driver was no longer acting within the scope of his employment, with the result that the employer would not have been vicariously liable. The House of Lords held that it was ultimately a question of degree whether, as a result of the deviation, the employee was no longer engaged on the employer's business. In this case, the dominant purpose of the journey was to transport the boys to Glasgow and the driver was still engaged on that task when the accident occurred in spite of not having taken the most direct route. As Lord Pearce explained:[3]

'In weighing up, therefore, the question of degree whether the admittedly substantial deviation of the vehicle with its passengers and baggage was such as to make the lorry's progress a frolic of the servant unconnected with or in substitution for the master's business, the presence of the passengers is a decisive factor against regarding it as a mere frolic of the servant. In the present case the defenders remained liable, in spite of the deviation, for their driver's negligence.'[4]

---

1 [1976] 1 All ER 97 at 100–101.
2 1966 SC (HL) 31, 1966 SLT 33.
3 1966 SC (HL) 31 at 46.
4 Lord Pearce did indicate, however, that there must be limits set by common sense: for example, if the deviation involved going to Glasgow via Inverness!

(4) If an employee uses his master's time or his master's equipment for the employee's own purpose, the employer is no longer vicariously liable as the employee is no longer acting within the scope of his employment. As Lord Pearce indicated, in these circumstances the employee is acting on a 'frolic' of his own. So, for example, if during the time he is supposed to be working, an employee goes shopping, the employer will not be vicariously liable for any delict the employee may commit as shopping is clearly outside the scope of the employment. Similarly, if a van driver, without authorisation, uses his employer's van to help a friend move house, the employer is not vicariously liable if an accident occurs during the move as that is outside the scope of the employment.

Difficulties may arise, however, if the employee's delictual act or omission occurs at the workplace. In *Kirby v National Coal Board*,[1] a miner during a temporary break went to a prohibited place in order to smoke. When he struck a match, there was an explosion and the pursuer was injured. The court held that by going to the prohibited area in order to smoke, he was no longer acting within the scope of his employment – mining – and consequently the defender was not vicariously liable. On the other hand, in *Century Insurance Co v Northern Ireland Transport Board*[2] an explosion took place when an employee lit a cigarette while transferring petrol. The House of Lords held that this was an unauthorised mode of doing his job which was to transfer petrol and that the employer therefore remained vicariously liable.

Where a person is injured at work as a result of horseplay by other employees, the employer may escape vicarious liability if the horseplay constitutes 'a frolic of their own'. In *Smith v Crossley Bros Ltd*,[3] an apprentice was injured by fellow employees during initiation rites.[4] It was held that the employer was not in breach of the general duty of care to provide competent fellow workers.[5] Nor was the defendant vicariously liable as the actings constituted a frolic and were outside the scope of the workers' employment. On the other hand, in *Harrison v Michelin Tyre Co*[6] the employer was held to be vicariously liable when an employee who was standing on a duckboard was injured as a result of a fellow employee jumping on the other end of the

1 1958 SC 514, 1959 SLT 7.
2 [1942] AC 509.
3 (1951) 95 So Jo 655, CA.
4 The unfortunate lad had a compressed-air pipe placed in close proximity to his rectum.
5 See pp 176 ff above.
6 [1985] ICR 696, [1985] 1 All ER 918.

duckboard for a lark. The court took the view that a reasonable person would consider that, even although the act was unauthorised, it was nevertheless 'part and parcel' of the job and accordingly not outside the scope of employment.

It is generally accepted that travel to and from work is outside the scope of employment and that the employer is not vicariously liable for an employee's delicts at that time. However, where the employer retains an element of control, vicarious liability may continue before or after work. Thus in *Bell v Blackwood, Morton & Sons*[1] an employer was held to be vicariously liable when the pursuer was injured by a fellow employee when leaving work. The employers had attempted to prevent employees rushing downstairs to catch their buses and had supervised the descent of the stairway from time to time. In these circumstances, the employees were still within the scope of their employment when on the stairway where the accident occurred. Where an employee works at two places, it has been held that he is within the scope of his employment when travelling between them.[2]

In certain situations, an employee may be hired out to work under the instructions of another employer. For example A, a general contractor, may hire equipment from B to be operated by an employee of B, but under A's instruction. If the 'borrowed' employee is negligent and injures one of A's employees or a third party, who is vicariously liable, A or B? The general rule is that the employer with whom the borrowed employee has a contract of employment remains vicariously liable, even although the employee works under the general instructions of another. Thus, in our example, B remains vicariously liable. B will only escape vicarious liability if he has delegated to A, not only the power to control what B's employee does but also *how* the employee should do the job. The onus rests on B to establish that the full plethora of control has passed from B to A. This will be almost impossible to establish where B's employee operates sophisticated equipment.

This principle was settled by the House of Lords in the leading case of *Mersey Docks and Harbour Board v Coggins and Griffith (Liverpool) Ltd*.[3] The plaintiff hired a mobile crane to the defendant which was to be operated by an employee of the plaintiff. It was agreed in the contract of hire that the operator of the crane was to be treated as an employee of Coggins. The craneman injured a worker while operating the crane negligently. The question arose whether the plaintiff or the

1 1960 SC 11, 1959 SLT (Notes) 54, OH.
2 *Thomson v British Steel Corporation* 1977 SLT 26.
3 [1947] AC 1, [1946] 2 All ER 345.

defendant should be vicariously liable. The House of Lords held that *in a question with the injured third party*, vicarious liability could not be determined by the contractual arrangements made between the plaintiff and defendant to which the injured person had not been a party. Prima facie, the plaintiff was the employer and was vicariously liable unless it could be established that full control of the craneman had passed to Coggins. While Coggins could tell the craneman what to do, since he was a highly skilled worker, they could *not* tell him *how* to do his job. Accordingly, Mersey Docks had failed to discharge the onus which lay upon them to prove that their employee had been transferred *pro hac vice* to Coggins. Therefore, as far as the injured person was concerned, he could sue Mersey Docks as vicariously liable for the negligence of their employee, the crane man. But, because of the terms of their contract of hire with Coggins, Mersey Docks could recover the damages from Coggins since they had agreed to treat the crane man as their employee.[1]

(3) Vicarious liability for independent contractors

As a general rule, a person is not vicariously liable for the delicts of an independent contractor whom he hires to undertake a particular job, for example, a taxi driver, a plumber, a builder etc. If, for example, A, a general contractor, hires the services of B, an independent contractor, and through his negligence B causes injury to C, an employee of A, A is not vicariously liable for B's delicts. If C is injured by the negligence of an employee of B, B will, of course, be vicariously liable to C. However, A may be liable in delict to his employee, C, if A's act in hiring B is a breach of A's general duty to take reasonable care for the safety of his employees.[2] But this is a breach of A's personal duty of care towards his employees – it is not *vicarious* liability for B's delictual act. To succeed against A, C must show that A did not take reasonable care in hiring B's services, for example, if A knows that B is incompetent or unqualified; the duty is analogous with that of taking reasonable care to provide an employee with competent fellow workers. However, in *Marshall v William Sharp & Sons*,[3] the defender hired the services of a worker who was paid an hourly rate for work done. The defender had full control over the actings of the worker concerned. The pursuer, an employee of the defender, was injured as

---

1 This principle has been accepted as part of Scots law: see *Park v Tractor Shovels* 1980 SLT 94.
2 On an employer's duty to take reasonable care, see pp 175 ff above.
3 1991 SCLR 104, 1991 SLT 114.

a result of the worker's negligence. The Inner House held that the defender was *not* in breach of his personal duty to the pursuer to provide a competent independent contractor to work with him. Nevertheless, the court found that the defender was vicariously liable, in spite of the fact that the person who had injured the pursuer was an independent contractor. It is submitted that this decision can be supported on the ground that the defender had the power to control not only what the independent contractor could do but how he should do it. This is not usually the case when a person hires an independent contractor, for example, a taxi driver or a plumber. Thus, unless the hirer has the full plethora of control over an independent contractor, he will not be vicariously liable for the delicts of an independent contractor in carrying out a job.

(4) Principal and agent

A principal can be vicariously liable for the delicts of his agent. This will arise if (i) the acts of the agent were expressly authorised by the principal; or (ii) the principal ratified the agent's acts after they were done; or (iii) the delict is within the actual or ostensible authority of the agent. For vicarious liability to arise it is not enough that X permits Y to do a particular act, for example, drive X's car: instead, X must have delegated a task or duty to Y.[1] The principle is important in the context of employment where an employer prima facie escapes vicarious liability because the employee is working outside the scope of his employment: the employer may still be vicariously liable as principal if in the circumstances the employee is acting within his actual or ostensible authority as the employer's agent at the time of the delictual act.

C. CONCLUSION

The discussion of vicarious liability is important as it illustrates how the common law developed an exception to the principle that a person is not obliged to make reparation unless he has caused injury or harm as a result of his own *culpa* or fault. As a result of industrialisation, it became apparent that those who were injured by the delicts of workers would, in practice, have little likelihood of obtaining compensation

1 *Launchbury v Morgans* [1973] AC 127, [1972] 2 All ER 606.

from the worker himself. Accordingly, the doctrine of vicarious liability arose to enable the pursuer to sue the employer, in addition to the employee, since the employer was more likely to have funds or be insured.

CHAPTER 13

Delict and the family

It is now proposed to consider delictual liability in the context of family relationships. We will be concerned with delictual liability *between* members of the family and the rights of members of the family to seek reparation if a relative is injured or killed.

A. TITLE TO SUE

At common law, spouses could not sue each other in delict. Thus, if a woman was injured as a result of her husband's negligent driving, she could not obtain reparation. This rule was clearly anachronistic especially as the loss would ultimately fall on her husband's insurance company. The position was changed by section 2(1) of the Law Reform (Husband and Wife) Act 1962 which provides that each of the spouses has 'the like rights' to bring proceedings against the other in respect of a delict 'as if they were not married'. Where the action is brought during the subsistence of the marriage, the court has a discretion to dismiss the proceedings if it appears that no substantial benefit would arrive to either party if the action continued.[1] The court's discretion is unlikely to be invoked as the action will proceed if any benefit accrues to the pursuer, even although the couple, as a family unit, will be no better off. Since the discretion in section 2(2) is both anomalous and unnecessary, the Scottish Law Commission has proposed that it should be repealed.[2]

A spouse is not liable for the delicts of the other spouse unless liability is established on a basis other than marriage itself; so, for example, a wife could be vicariously liable for a delict committed by her husband if she was his employer and the delict arose in the course of his employment.

As a general rule, a child or young person under the age of 16 has no

---

1 Law Reform (Husband and Wife) Act 1962, s 2(2).
2 Report on Family Law (Scot Law Com No 135) Rec 54.

active legal capacity.[1] Thus, where a child under the age of 16 is injured or suffers damage, an action in delict must be brought on behalf of the child or young person by the child's guardian who will usually be the child's parent.[2] Where the guardian is the defender in the action, for example if the child was injured as a result of a parent's negligent driving, the court will appoint a *curator ad litem* to represent the child. However, the Age of Legal Capacity (Scotland) Act 1991 does not affect the delictual responsibility of children and young persons under the age of 16.[3] Thus, a child under the age of 16 can, theoretically at least, be sued if the child has committed a delict. Guardians are not vicariously liable for the delicts committed by their children. But where a child causes injury or damage as a result of a guardian's negligence, the guardian may be liable for a breach of a duty of care which the guardian owed to the pursuer; for example, if a child runs in front of a car and the driver is injured trying to avoid the child, the guardian may be liable in delict if the guardian had not taken reasonable care to ensure that the child was not on the road.[4] Because the 1991 Act does not affect the age of delictual responsibility, a child who has been injured may have any damages awarded reduced on the ground of contributory negligence.[5] Thus, in *McKinnell v White*[6] a child of five was held to be 50 per cent contributorily negligent because he ran in front of a speeding motorist: the Lord Ordinary (Fraser) took the view that by the age of five, a child brought up in an urban environment should have been aware of the danger of road traffic. It has always been competent for a child to sue his or her parent in delict.[7]

Where a foetus sustains injury *in utero*, the unborn baby has no right to sue in delict unless and until it has been born alive. Only on birth does a child obtain legal personality. However, provided the defender owed a duty of care towards the foetus, if the baby is born alive, an action in delict can be brought on the child's behalf in respect of the injuries sustained *in utero*. This is sometimes said to be a consequence of the civil law principle *nasciturus pro iam nato habetur quotiens de eius agitur*, ie that in a matter affecting its interests, an unborn child *in utero* should be deemed to be born (the *nasciturus* doctrine).[8] However, it is

---

1 Age of Legal Capacity (Scotland) Act 1991, s 1(1)(a).
2 Law Reform (Parent and Child) (Scotland) Act 1976, s 2(1)(a) and (b); s 8 as amended by para 43 of Sch 1 to the Age of Legal Capacity (Scotland) Act 1991.
3 Age of Legal Capacity (Scotland) Act 1991, s 1(3)(c).
4 *Hardie v Sneddon* 1917 SC 1, 1916 2 SLT 197.
5 On contributory negligence, see pp 125 ff above.
6 1971 SLT (Notes) 61, OH.
7 *Young v Rankin* 1934 SC 499, 1934 SLT 445.
8 *Cohen v Shaw* 1992 SCLR 182, 1992 SLT 1022, discussed at p 197 below.

submitted that there is no need to rely on the *nasciturus* doctrine to achieve this result. Given that the defender owes a *Donoghue v Stevenson* duty of care to the foetus, based on reasonable foreseeability of injury *in utero*, then if there is breach of the duty which causes injury to the foetus, a delict will be committed when the baby is born. It is at that stage, ie when the baby is born alive, that the delict is completed because, while the breach of duty took place during the pregnancy, damage for the purpose of delictual liability is not sustained by the child until the child is born.[1] It is only then that the damage arises as a result of the breach of the duty of care: *damnum injuria datum*.[2]

Because it is competent for a child to sue a parent, a mother who injures her foetus during the pregnancy can, in theory at least, be sued by her child in delict provided the child is born alive. A mother clearly owes a duty of care to the foetus. If during her pregnancy she fails to take reasonable care, for example if she abuses drugs or falls down the stair when drunk, then she can be liable in delict if her breach of duty of care results in damage to the child when born alive. It would therefore appear that a mother carries a potential litigant in her womb for nine months! Similarly, a father who injures his wife's foetus through, for example, negligent driving, may be liable in delict if the child is born alive suffering from harm as a result of the injuries sustained *in utero*.

In practice, it is likely that where a foetus is injured *in utero* the mother will also have sustained injury. If the defender owed her a duty of care which has been broken, the mother may sue for the injuries she has suffered. Where the mother miscarries as a result of the defender's breach of duty, she may obtain damages for the loss of her baby. Of course, in these circumstances, the unborn child has no title to sue as the child has not been born alive.

B. INJURY TO A RELATIVE

In *Robertson v Turnbull*,[3] it was held that where a person was injured, the defender did not owe a threshold duty of care to the victim's spouse or relatives who had suffered economic loss as a result of the injuries sustained; so, for example, members of the injured person's family could not sue in delict for loss of support.[4] The victim can, of course, sue

---

1 *Hamilton v Fife Health Board* 1993 SLT 624, discussed at p 196 below.
2 For further discussion, see p 196 below.
3 1980 SC 108, 1982 SLT 96, HL.
4 This is an example of secondary economic loss: on non-recoverability of secondary economic loss, see pp 86 ff above.

for loss of future earnings as derivative economic loss.[1] Moreover, at common law, a pursuer who was injured could not recover damages for the economic loss suffered by a relative as a result of the pursuer's injuries, for example, where a spouse had given up work in order to nurse her injured husband.[2] The common law on this point has now been superceded by section 8 of the Administration of Justice Act 1982.[3] This provides that where a person has sustained personal injuries, the injured person can recover damages which amount to reasonable remuneration for necessary services rendered to the pursuer by a relative.[4] The pursuer, ie the injured person, then accounts to the relative for any damages recovered under this provision.[5] Originally damages could only be awarded in respect of necessary services rendered by the relative up to the date of the action;[6] but it is now provided that damages will be awarded for reasonable remuneration of necessary services likely to be rendered by a relative to the injured person in the future.[7] Damages are not available under section 8 if the relative expressly agreed that no payment should be made in respect of the services rendered or to be rendered.[8] Where the injured person has died before the action is concluded, the deceased's executor may recover damages for necessary services rendered by a relative before the victim died.

When a person who was not in employment was injured, at common law he had no right to sue for loss of earnings as *ex hypothesi* the person was not earning. This was particularly unfair to wives who had given up their jobs to look after the home or children. Section 9(1) of the Administration of Justice Act 1982 gives an injured person who has been providing unpaid personal services to a relative,[9] the right to sue for damages if the pursuer is unable to continue to do so as a result

---

1 On loss of future earnings, see pp 232 ff below; on derivative economic loss, see pp 67 ff above.
2 *Edgar v Lord Advocate* 1965 SC 67, 1965 SLT 158.
3 As amended by the Law Reform (Miscellaneous Provisions) (Scotland) Act 1990, s 69.
4 Relative includes the injured person's spouse or divorced spouse, heterosexual cohabitee, any ascendant or descendant, any brother, sister, uncle or aunt or their issue and any person accepted by the injured party as a child of the family: illegitimacy is irrelevant: Administration of Justice Act 1982, s 13.
5 Administration of Justice Act 1982, s 8(2).
6 *Forsyth's Curator Bonis v Govan Shipbuilders* 1989 SCLR 78, 1989 SLT 91.
7 Administration of Justice Act 1982, s 8(3) added by s 69 of the Law Reform (Miscellaneous Provisions) (Scotland) Act 1990. However there is no equivalent to s 8(2) imposing an obligation on the injured person to account to the relatives for the damages obtained under s 8(3).
8 s 8(1) and (3): *Denheen v British Rail Board* 1988 SLT 320, 1986 SLT 249.
9 For the definition of relative, see above, note 4.

of the injuries sustained. The personal services must be services which (a) were or might have been expected to have been rendered by the pursuer before the injuries; (b) were of a kind which when rendered by a person other than a relative would ordinarily have been obtainable on payment; and (c) the injured person but for the injuries in question might have been expected to render gratuitously to a relative.[1] In *Ingham v John G Russell (Transport) Ltd*[2] the Inner House refused to restrict the concept of personal services to services which were rendered to the person of the relative, for example, nursing, as opposed to the relative's property, for example, cleaning the relative's house. It was enough that the services had been rendered *in person* by the injured person and therefore included maintenance or DIY services rendered by the injured person to his spouse. It is therefore clear that an injured woman, for example, can recover damages if she is unable to provide unpaid housekeeping and child rearing services for her spouse, cohabitee or children. Because the personal services must have been rendered gratuitously before section 9 applies, the 1982 Act recognises the fact that work in the home is still prima facie unpaid, but that its economic value is such that justice demands that the injured person should receive compensation for the inability to continue to do so, though technically the pursuer has not suffered any patrimonial loss, ie loss of earnings.

Where the injured person has died, a relative may claim as a head of loss a reasonable sum in respect of the loss of gratuitous personal services rendered to the relative by the deceased.[3] Before he can do so, the pursuer must be a relative who has the right to claim damages for loss of support by the deceased under the Damages (Scotland) Act 1976. Accordingly, it is to the provisions of the 1976 Act that we shall now turn.

C. DEATH OF A RELATIVE

If a person dies as a result of another's delict, two potential claims arise. First, the deceased's own claim, which can transmit to the deceased's executor who can pursue the action for the benefit of the deceased's estate. Second, a dependent claim by the deceased's relatives.

---

1 Administration of Justice Act 1982, s 9(3).
2 1991 SCLR 596, 1991 SLT 739.
3 Administration of Justice Act 1982, s 9(2); *Ingham v John G Russell (Transport) Ltd* above.

(1) The deceased's claim

Where a person is killed outright as a result of the defender's delict, the deceased's executor cannot raise an action in delict in respect of the death. In these circumstances, the only claims are those of the deceased's relatives.[1] However, if a person is injured and subsequently dies as a result of the injuries, the deceased's right to sue in delict in respect of personal injuries transmits to the executor, who can sue on behalf of the deceased's estate. This complex area of the law is now regulated by the Damages (Scotland) Act 1976.[2]

Where a person dies on or after 16 July 1992, the rights which vested in the deceased immediately before his death to sue for damages in respect of personal injuries transmit to the executor.[3] As a result, the executor can raise an action or, if an action has been raised by the deceased before he died, continue the action on behalf of the deceased's estate.[4] The executor may sue in respect of patrimonial loss, for example, loss of earnings sustained by the deceased, but only up to the date of death.[5] In other words, patrimonial loss attributable to any period after the deceased's death, for example, loss of future earnings, is non-transmissible to the executor. This is necessary to prevent double compensation given that the defender may have to meet claims for loss of support brought by the deceased's relatives. The deceased's right to damages by way of *solatium* is also transmissible to the executor,[6] but again in assessing damages for *solatium*, the court is to have regard only to the period ending immediately before the deceased's death.[7] *Solatium* is damages for pain and suffering arising from the personal injuries. In assessing damages for *solatium*, the court is entitled to have regard to the extent to which the deceased suffered because he was aware that his expectation of life had been reduced as a result of the injuries.[8]

1 See pp 195 ff below.
2 This Act has been amended by *inter alia* the Administration of Justice Act 1982, the Law Reform (Parent and Child) Act 1986, the Consumer Protection Act 1987 and the Damages (Scotland) Act 1993; it now bears little resemblance to the original act. References in this chapter are to the Damages (Scotland) Act 1976 as amended unless otherwise stated. For text of the amended Act see Appendix.
3 s 2(1).
4 s 2A.
5 s 2(3).
6 s 2(1).
7 s 2(3).
8 s 9A(1). Damages can also be awarded in respect of patrimonial loss arising from the fact that the injured person's expectation of life has been reduced: s 9(1) and 9(2). Where the action is brought by the executor, however, only patrimonial loss arising before the date of death can be recovered: s 2(2).

The effect of these provisions can be illustrated by the following example. A is seriously injured as a result of the negligent driving of B. A dies two years after the accident.[1] If A had begun an action against B, A's executor can continue the action provided it has not been concluded.[2] If A had not begun proceedings, A's executor can bring an action against B.[3] However, the executor's claims for patrimonial loss and *solatium* are restricted to losses incurred by the deceased at the date of death: any patrimonial loss referable to a period after the date of death cannot be recovered by the executor.[4] If the action is successful,[5] the damages awarded become part of the deceased's estate. This means that they will be distributed to the deceased's legatees if there is a will or to a surviving spouse and the deceased's heirs according to the rules of intestate succession where the deceased died without a will. If A has relatives, they may have a claim against B if A's death *was* as a result of the personal injuries A has sustained. It is to the relative's dependent claim that we now turn.

(2) The dependent claims

Where a person dies in consequence of personal injuries sustained by him[6] as a result of the defender's conduct, then if the defender would have been liable to pay damages to the deceased if he had lived, he is also liable to pay damages to a certain class of the deceased's relatives.[6] It will be seen that a relative's right to sue is *dependent* on the defender being liable to pay damages if an action had been brought by the deceased in respect of the personal injuries sustained. Accordingly, the relative's claim can be defeated if the deceased would not have succeeded against the defender, for example, if the defender did not owe a duty of care to the deceased or had not broken the duty or the deceased was *volens*. The relative's damages can also be reduced on the grounds of the deceased's contributory negligence.

Before a relative's claim is triggered, the deceased must have died 'in consequence of *personal injuries* sustained by *him*'. The Scottish

---

1 It is irrelevant whether or not the death was a result of A's injuries.
2 s 2A(1)(b). An action is not concluded while any appeal is competent or before any appeal taken has been disposed of: s 2A(2).
3 s 2A(1)(a).
4 For the position for deaths before 16 July 1976, see W J Stewart *Delict* (2nd edn, 1993, Greens) pp 216 ff.
5 Any defences, for example, *volens*, which B could use in an action by A are good against an action brought by A's executor. Similarly, damages can be reduced as a result of A's contributory negligence.
6 s 1(1).

courts have experienced difficulties where a child dies shortly after birth as a result of injuries sustained while in *utero*. In *Hamilton v Fife Health Board*[1] the Lord Ordinary (Prosser) held that parents of a child had no title to sue on the ground that before section 1(1) was applicable the death had to have been as a result of personal injuries sustained when the deceased had legal personality: accordingly, since their baby had died shortly after birth as a result of injuries sustained while *in utero*, section 1(1) was not triggered as a foetus has no legal personality until born alive. This narrow construction of section 1(1) was, however, rejected by the Lord Ordinary (Lord Morton of Shuna) in *McWilliams v Lord Advocate*[2] decided seven months later. The conflict has now been resolved as a result of the decision of the Inner House in an appeal from Lord Prosser's decision in the *Hamilton* case.[3] There the court held that while the injuries were sustained by the foetus while *in utero*, the delict was completed only when the baby was born alive and suffered damage as a result of the defender's breach of duty of care: *damnum injuria datum*. At that stage, ie when born alive, the child could have sued the defender for damages for personal injuries; consequently, when the child died as a result of these injuries, the parents' dependent action in respect of the death arose, ie section 1(1) was triggered. For the reasons discussed above, it is thought that the decision of the Inner House is correct. But it should be noted that if the baby is not born alive, the parents do not have a dependent claim under section 1(1); for the defender is not under any obligation to pay damages to the child as the delict was never completed, since the child never had legal personality. In this situation, the mother may well have her own individual right of action if the defender's acts which injured the foetus *in utero*, amounted to a breach of the duty of care which was owed to the mother herself.

The nature of the dependent claim turns on whether the pursuer is a member of the deceased's immediate family or a wider class of relatives specified in the 1976 Act.

(a) The immediate family

The deceased's immediate family consists of the following relatives:[4]

---

1 1992 SCLR 288, 1992 SLT 1026.
2 1992 SCCR 954, 1992 SLT 1045.
3 *Hamilton v Fife Health Board* 1993 SLT 624.
4 s 10(2) and Sch 1 to the Act.

(a) the deceased's spouse;
(b) the deceased's cohabitee, ie any person not being the spouse of the deceased who immediately before the death was living with the deceased as husband or wife: it will be noted that this is restricted to heterosexual cohabitation;
(c) the deceased's children: this includes step-children and children accepted by the deceased as a child of the family. Relationships by affinity are covered, ie the deceased's daughter-in-law or son-in-law. Illegitimacy is irrelevant. In *Cohen v Shaw*1 the Lord Ordinary (Cullen) held that a child *in utero* at the time of his father's death had title to sue as a child, provided the child was born alive, ie a posthumous child is included;[2]
(d) the deceased's parents: it is irrelevant that the deceased was illegitimate. Relationships by affinity are covered and consequently the deceased's mother-in-law or father-in-law are included.

Members of the deceased's immediate family may claim damages for the following:

(1) Damages for loss of the financial support they would have obtained if the deceased had not died as a result of the injuries. This covers both loss of support up until the date of death and loss of support in the future. These claims can be substantial.[3] Where a woman married her husband knowing that he was dying as a result of personal injuries, her action for loss of support was still relevant.[4] As the Lord Ordinary (Clyde) observed:[5] 'The proposition appeared to be that a widow could claim no loss if the death was one which could have been reasonably expected. I find no precedent or principle to justify such an approach and no warrant for it in the simple wording of the statute'.

No account is taken of a widow's remarriage prospects[6] and her entitlement to a widow's pension. If the deceased had obtained a provisional award of damages before his death, in assessing the relative's loss of support the court takes into account such part of the

---

1 1992 SLT 1022.
2 In this case Lord Cullen relied on the *nasciturus* principle: discussed at p 190 above.
3 For an example of the complex calculations involved, see, for example, *Wotherspoon v Strathclyde Regional Council* 1992 SCLR 806, 1992 SLT 1090.
4 *Phillips v Grampian Health Board* 1992 SLT 659, 1989 SLT 538.
5 1992 SLT 659 at 660.
6 Law Reform (Miscellaneous Provisions) Act 1971, s 4.

provisional award as was intended to compensate the deceased for any period beyond the date when he died.[1]

(2) Such sum of damages, if any, as the court thinks just by way of compensation for all or any of the following:
(a) distress and anxiety endured by the relative in contemplation of the suffering of the deceased before he or she died;
(b) the grief and sorrow of the relative caused by the deceased's death;
(c) the loss of such non-patrimonial benefit as the relative might be expected to derive from the deceased's society and guidance if the deceased had not died.

These heads of loss replace the former loss of society award and were introduced by the Damages (Scotland) Act 1993[2] which amended section 1(4) of the 1976 Act. In making such an award, the court is not obliged to ascribe any of the award to any of the heads of damage. Given the nature of the losses, the amount awarded will depend very much on the impression made by the relative on the judge in the particular case.[3]

(3) Reasonable funeral expenses.

(b) Specified relatives

The specified relatives include the deceased's divorced spouse, but not former cohabitee, grandparents, grandchildren, brothers and sisters, uncles and aunts, nephews and nieces and cousins: such relatives include the appropriate 'in-laws'. Specified relatives are entitled to claim only for loss of the deceased's support and reasonable funeral expenses. The fact that the deceased had no legal obligation to support the specified relative is irrelevant: reparation is made for the loss of de facto financial support both before the date of death and in the future.

The right of a relative of the deceased to a dependent claim under section 1 of the 1976 Act can transmit to the executor of the relative if the relative dies before an award of damages is made.[4] Thus, for example, if A dies leaving his wife, B, B's right to sue as a member of A's immediate family transmits to her executor if she dies before an

---

1 s 1(5A). On provisional damages, see pp 237 ff below.
2 s 1(1).
3 For an example of the calculation of the former 'loss of society' award, see Wother-spoon v Strathclyde Regional Council 1992 SCLR 806, 1992 SLT 1090.
4 s 1A.

award of damages has been made to her. This applies where B, ie the deceased's relative, dies on or after 16 July 1992. In determining the amount of damages payable to the relative's executor, the court can only have regard to the period ending immediately before the relative's death.[1] This proviso while obviously important in respect of the relative's claim for loss of support, could also affect a claim under section 1(4) if the relative died shortly after the deceased person.

Both the deceased's immediate family and the specified relatives can also seek compensation for the loss of the deceased's gratuitous personal services to them by virtue of section 9 of the Administration of Justice Act 1982.[2] Otherwise,[3] no person is entitled by reason of relationship, to damages in respect of the death of another person except by virtue of the provisions of the Damages (Scotland) Act 1976.[4]

---

1 s 1A.
2 *Ingham v John G Russell (Transport) Ltd* 1991 SCLR 596, discussed at p 193 above.
3 An exception is also made for claims under s 1 of the International Transport Convention Act 1983.
4 s 1(7).

CHAPTER 14

Delict and road traffic

A. INTRODUCTION

In modern society, motor vehicles which are driven carelessly are a major cause of accidents. Accidents involving vehicles are probably the area of the law of delict with which ordinary people are most likely to be involved. Where a person suffers personal injuries or damage to property as a result of a road accident, the general principles of delictual liability apply. Indeed, the paradigm of a duty of care based on reasonable foreseeability of harm,[1] is the duty of care which a driver owes to other road users. The pursuer must establish a breach of duty on the part of the defender, causation and damage as in any other action for reparation.[2] However, because of the frequency of such accidents, the common law has been supplemented by statutory provisions designed to ensure that victims of road accidents receive compensation. Moreover, the practices of insurance companies are of particular importance in this area. The 'peculiarities' of delictual liability for careless driving are discussed in this section.

B. THE STANDARD OF CARE

As stated above, before a driver is liable in delict the pursuer must establish that he was in breach of duty; in other words, that the defender did not reach the standard of care of the reasonable driver in his situation and was therefore negligent.[3] In road traffic cases, considerable assistance in establishing that the defender did not exercise reasonable care is provided by the Highway Code, an HMSO publication. The Road Traffic Act 1988 provides:[4]

---

1 On duty of care generally, see Chapter 3 above.
2 See Chapters 5 and 6 above.
3 On negligence, see pp 102 ff above.
4 s 78(7).

200

'A failure on the part of a person to observe the provisions of the Highway Code shall not in itself render that person liable to criminal proceedings of any kind but any such failure may in any proceedings (whether civil or criminal . . .) be relied upon by any party to the proceedings as tending to establish or negative any liability which is in question in those proceedings.'

While a breach of the terms of the Highway Code will not per se establish negligence,[1] if the conduct averred is in fact in breach of the Code then this will be highly persuasive in establishing that the defender did not take reasonable care.[2]

Under the Road Traffic Act 1988, it is a criminal offence to cause death by careless driving,[3] to drive dangerously[4] and to drive without due care and attention.[5] Moreover, statutory regulations, designed to protect road users, provide offences where vehicles are (1) constructed in such a manner as to create a hazard[6] and (2) used in such a way as causes danger to other road users.[7] While breach of these statutory provisions and regulations does not give rise to delictual liability for breach of statutory duty,[8] a conviction will be important evidence in establishing negligence on the part of the defender.

C. OBTAINING COMPENSATION

It is obvious that cars and other motor vehicles create considerable hazards to road users, whether they be pedestrians, cyclists or other drivers. To ensure that there is a fund available to provide compensation in the event of delictual liability as a result of a road accident, the owner of a vehicle is obliged to take out insurance. A motor vehicle

---

1 For example, merely because the defender was driving above the speed limit does not in itself establish that he was not taking reasonable care: speed is not per se the cause of an accident. See *Colborne v Wallace* 1993 GWD 17–1121 per the Sheriff Principal (Nicholson).

2 While the Highway Code is within judicial knowledge, its provisions cannot be used in place of evidence: *Cavin v Kinnaird* 1994 SLT 111.

3 s 1.

4 s 2.

5 s 3.

6 For example, it is an offence to drive a vehicle which exceeds the maximum length stipulated in the Road Vehicles (Construction and Use) Regulations 1986, SI 1986/1078.

7 For example, it is an offence to carry an object on a vehicle which overhangs that vehicle in excess of a distance prescribed in the regulations, without the leading edge being suitably marked.

8 On breach of statutory duty, see Chapter 11 above.

must be insured in respect of 'third party liability', ie it must be insured in respect of delictual liability for a person other than the owner himself. This compulsory third party insurance covers liability for causing death, or personal injuries, or property damage to the victim. It is a criminal offence to drive a vehicle which does not have a valid third party liability policy of insurance[1] or to allow a vehicle to be driven without such insurance.[2]

While it is only third party liability insurance which is compulsory, many drivers purchase additional insurance to cover their own losses which are incurred in an accident for which they are wholly or partly responsible. These losses include, for example, the cost of repair of the insured's own vehicle and the cost of hiring an alternative vehicle for a limited period while the insured's vehicle is being repaired. These are known as insured losses. Where a driver purchases additional insurance as well as third party liability insurance, this is known as a comprehensive policy of insurance. Comprehensive insurance does not usually cover death or personal injuries sustained by the driver as a result of his own negligence. It is common practice for the insurer to require the holder of a comprehensive policy to meet the first part of a claim made under that policy. This is typically between the first £50 and £300 of the claim. This sum of money is known as uninsured loss. Moreover, any loss not covered by the comprehensive policy, such as a claim in respect of death or personal injury of the driver, is an uninsured loss.

To summarise the position. If, as a result of negligent driving, A causes physical harm or damage to B, B can sue A in delict and his compensation will be covered by A's compulsory third party insurance. If B has a comprehensive insurance policy, he may elect to claim for his insured losses under the policy, but he is not obliged to do so; he must, of course, sue A for any uninsured losses. If the accident was not the result of A's negligence, B cannot sue A; but if B has a comprehensive policy of insurance, he can claim under the policy for insured losses, even though the accident was the result of B's negligence.

Where a person suffers damage as a result of another driver's negligence, if he elects to claim for insured losses under his comprehensive policy of insurance, then the principles of subrogation apply. This means that the insurer 'steps into the shoes' of the insured and is entitled to sue the negligent driver to recover the monies paid out under the comprehensive policy of insurance. In these circumstances,

---

1 Road Traffic Act 1988, s 143(a).
2 Ibid, s 143(b).

the action is raised in the name of the insured rather than in the name of the insurance company. The defender is cited personally, but again under principles of subrogation, the defender's compulsory third party insurance company will in effect take over the defence if the action has been intimated to them. In practice, insurers may have inter-office agreements whereby actions do not have to be raised, even if delictual liability is disputed. The insurers accept that they will meet their own outlays under the appropriate insurance policies without attempting to recover these from each other in defended civil proceedings. However, such agreements, often known as 'knock for knock' agreements, are becoming far less common since insurers are battling to minimise losses. Insurers who previously would have 'confirmed' a knock for knock agreement with the third party insurers are resorting to litigation to recover their outlays under their comprehensive insurance policy in full.

It should be emphasised that whether or not a comprehensive insurer confirms a 'knock for knock' agreement with a negligent driver's third party insurer, this does not affect the insured driver's right to sue the negligent driver personally in delict to recover his uninsured losses. If he is successful, he is entitled to look to the defender's compulsory third party insurer for any sums not recovered from the defender which are due under the decree, provided appropriate intimation of the action has been made to the insurance company.

An insurance company may be entitled under general principles of contract to refuse to indemnify the insured losses. This could arise, for example, if the insured was in material breach of the terms of the policy of insurance by not paying the premiums or if the policy could be rescinded by the insurance company on the ground of misrepresentation. However, where a pursuer successfully obtains decree against a negligent driver and seeks to recover his compensation from the defender's compulsory third party insurer, under the Road Traffic Act 1988 the insurance company cannot refuse payment on the ground that under general principles of contract it is not bound to indemnify the insured defender, unless the insurance company had already rescinded the contract prior to the accident. Similarly, should a driver cancel a compulsory third party liability policy of insurance, the insurer remains liable for any losses suffered by a third party in a subsequent accident caused by negligence of the driver, provided the contract has not been rescinded. The insurance company can then recover its outlays from the 'former' insured driver. In these circumstances, the insurer is known as a 'Road Traffic Act insurer'. However, the Road Traffic Act insurer will escape liability if the company does not retain an insurable interest in the vehicle: this would occur, for example, if the 'former' insured driver sold the car with the actual policy document in the glove compartment!

Motor Insurers Bureau

The legislation requiring owners of vehicles to have third party liability insurance was clearly designed to protect third parties. Such protection is not afforded where an individual flouts the law and drives a vehicle without appropriate insurance cover, although, of course, it is possible in these circumstances that the defender will have sufficient assets to meet a successful action for reparation.

In order to protect third parties in this situation, a body called the Motor Insurers Bureau (MIB) entered into an agreement with the Ministry of Transport on 17 June 1946 to provide from 1 July 1946 compensation for victims of road accidents where the injured parties were unable to obtain compensation due to the defender's lack of appropriate third party insurance. There have been various revised agreements since then, but the present text covering accidents on or after 31 December 1988 provides compensation for victims of those accidents in respect of both death and personal injuries, and property damage. Where the accident occurred before 31 December 1988, the MIB is only obliged to meet claims for death and personal injuries.

Clause 2 of the agreement provides that the MIB will 'pay or satisfy or cause to be satisfied to or to the satisfaction of the person or persons in whose favour the judgment was given' any sum due under the decree or judgment which remains unsatisfied for a period of seven days from the time at which the decree or judgment should have been in force. The MIB's liability includes any element of interest or expenses included in the decree. This obligation is, however, subject to certain conditions, the most important being that notification of the commencement of the proceedings must be given to the MIB before, or within seven days after, the commencement of the proceedings. The MIB's liability in respect of these claims is limited by the fact that there is currently a £175 excess payable, ie the first £175 is not paid. The MIB is only required to compensate for damage which is required to be insured against by law, ie under compulsory third party insurance.

Where an offending driver cannot be traced, this agreement is of no effect. However, a sister agreement, referred to as the MIB untraced drivers agreement then comes into play. This scheme differs from the foregoing by excluding claims for property damage and covers only claims for death or personal injuries as a result of accidents on or after May 1969. Ironically, perhaps, no excess is payable on these claims.

CHAPTER 15

Defamation and verbal injury

A. INTRODUCTION

The law has long recognised a person's interest in his honour and reputation. Accordingly, where A makes a false statement about B with the intention of harming B's honour or reputation, then B has a delictual action against A. In Roman law, there was a specific remedy, the *actio injuriarum*, which provided compensation (*solatium*) for insult (*contumelia*). In order to succeed, it had to be established that a false statement was made with the intention of insulting the victim. It followed, therefore, that the action lay even if the statement had only been made to the victim himself, ie where the statement had not been made to a third party. If the statement had been published to a third party and, as a result, the victim suffered economic (patrimonial) loss, in the later Roman Empire such loss could, in theory at least, be recovered under general principles of *culpa: damnum injuria datum*. Accordingly, where intention to insult could not be established, but the statement was made carelessly to a third party, the only damages that could be obtained were for patrimonial loss: but, if intention to insult could be established, *solatium* would also be available under the *actio injuriarum*.

Given the influence of Roman law, Scots law could have developed a simple set of principles viz:

(1) if A makes an untrue statement about B to B, with the intention of insulting B, then B can sue A for *solatium* even if the statement is not published to a third party, provided intention to insult can be proved;

(2) if A makes an untrue statement about B to C, then B could recover damages for patrimonial loss on the basis of *culpa* but only obtain *solatium* if intention to insult could also be established.

But as *culpa* covers both intentional and unintentional, but careless, conduct, the fact that the remedies were originally based on two separate, if related, principles, ie *culpa* and the *actio injuriarum*, was

205

overlooked.[1] Moreover, the law in this area was influenced by the English law of libel and slander, with its emphasis on the defendant's malice. As a result, the Scots law of defamation and verbal injury is complex and contentious, and it is difficult to reconcile all the authorities.

The modern law appears to proceed on two major delicts, defamation and verbal injury. These will be considered in turn.

B. DEFAMATION

Defamation is the delict which is committed when a person makes an injurious and false imputation against the character or reputation of another person. The victim is usually a natural person but could be a trading company,[2] partnership or voluntary association; however, as legal persons such as a company have no feelings, they can only recover for patrimonial loss and not *solatium*. Because, by statute, it does not have corporate status, a trade union cannot sue.[3] A local authority also cannot sue[4] but if individuals are defamed by attacks on a council (for example, councillors) then they can sue in their own right. Where a person has died, the executor can continue any action raised by the deceased before his death and recover both *solatium* and patrimonial loss; if no action has been raised by the deceased, the executor can raise an action but can only recover any patrimonial loss to the estate before the death.[5] These rules are not affected by the Damages (Scotland) Act 1976.[6]

For an action to be successful, it must be shown that the defender made a false statement which was defamatory of the pursuer, with the

---

1 For discussion of the confusion, see T B Smith *A Short Commentary on the Law of Scotland* (1962, Greens) pp 724–732.

2 *Incorporation of Fleshers of Dumfries v Rankine* Dec 10 1816 FC. If the individual board members are also defamed, they can sue in their own right. If the defamation is actually of the individuals, the company cannot sue.

3 Trade Union and Labour Relations (Consolidation) Act 1992, s 10(1); *EETPU v Times Newspapers Ltd* [1980] QB 585, [1980] 1 All ER 1097.

4 *Derbyshire CC v Times Newspapers Ltd* [1992] 1 QB 770, [1993] 1 All ER 1011. Similarly, the government cannot sue qua government; cf individual ministers.

5 Ie the executor cannot recover *solatium*. See generally *Neilson v Rodger* (1853) 16 D 325; *Auld v Shairp* (1874) 2 R 191; *Smith v Stewart & Co (No 2)* 1961 SC 91, 1961 SLT 67.

6 s 2 as substituted by s 3 of the Damages (Scotland) Act 1993; on the 1976 Act generally, see pp 193 ff above.

intention to harm the pursuer's character or reputation. However, and this is very important, if the pursuer proves that the statement concerned the pursuer (a question of fact) and is defamatory (a question of law), then the court presumes that the statement is false and was made with the intention to harm him. The onus thereafter lies on the *defender* to prove either that the statement was true (*veritas*) or that it was made without the intention to harm the pursuer. Moreover, the law will also presume that a person will be upset if defamed and it is therefore not necessary for the pursuer to prove loss in respect of insult (*solatium*); but if patrimonial loss is also claimed, such loss has to be established by the pursuer.

(1) The false statement

The pursuer must establish that the defender made a statement about the pursuer: this is a question of fact. The statement will usually take the form of words, written or spoken. Scots law does not make a distinction betweeen oral and written communication for the purpose of the law of defamation.[1] However, any form of communication can amount to a statement so that it could consist of a television or radio broadcast, a picture, cartoon or effigy.[2] In Scots law, the statement does not have to be communicated to a third party: it is enough if it is communicated only to the victim himself.[3] In these circumstances, however, only damages for insult (*solatium*) can be awarded. Before damages for patrimonial loss can be awarded, the statement must have been published to third parties.[4] If a defamatory statement is repeated, every person who repeats the statement commits a separate delict. So, for example, if A makes a defamatory statement about B to a newspaper reporter, who repeats it to his editor, who publishes it in his newspaper, then the editor and the reporter, as well as A, are liable to B in delict.

It should be emphasised that once the pursuer has established that a defamatory statement was made by the defender, the law *presumes* that

---

1 In English law such a distinction is made: oral communication constitutes slander – written communication constitutes libel.
2 In *Monson v Tussauds* [1894] 1 QB 671, placing a waxworks effigy of the plaintiff who had been acquitted of murder in the Chamber of Horrors along with convicted murderers constituted a slanderous statement.
3 *Ramsay v Mackay* (1890) 18 R 130.
4 If the pursuer published the statement to a third party, he is personally barred from claiming patrimonial loss: *Will v Sneddon, Campbell & Munro* 1931 SC 164.

the statement is false. The onus then lies on the defender to show that the facts in the statement were true (*veritas*). But before the pursuer has the benefit of this presumption, the statement must be defamatory. It is to that concept that we now turn.

(2) Defamatory nature of the statement

A defamatory statement is one which 'tends to lower [the pursuer] in the estimation of right thinking members of society generally'.[1] While it is settled that some types of statement are clearly defamatory, the categories of defamation – like the categories of negligence[2] – are never closed. The question whether or not a statement is defamatory is one of law, to be decided by the court.[3] The test is objective, ie whether the reasonable man would decide that this type of statement was defamatory. It is the general view of society as a whole which is important, not the views of the section of society in which the pursuer moves. However, as the mores of society change, what might once have been regarded as derogatory by right-thinking members of society in the past, may not be so regarded by them today. Thus, for example, in 1934 it was thought to be defamatory falsely to state that a woman had been the victim of rape:[4] that might not be regarded as defamatory today when victims of rape are treated with sympathy rather than shunned.

The following are examples of defamatory statements, but it must always be remembered that these are only examples and that other types of defamatory statements may arise.

(a) Imputations on moral character

It is defamatory to undermine a person's moral character. Thus it is defamatory to call a woman a prostitute or an adulteress or even suggest that she lacks 'proper womanly delicacy'.[5] It is defamatory to state that a person is homosexual.[6] Defamatory statements are not restricted to imputations on sexual morality. Thus, it is defamatory to

---

1 *Sim v Stretch* [1936] 2 All ER 1237 at 1240 per Lord Atkin.
2 *Donoghue v Stevenson* 1932 SC (HL) 31 at 70 per Lord MacMillan; see p 58 above.
3 Accordingly, the defence can make a plea to the relevancy of the issue.
4 *Youssoupoff v MGM Pictures Ltd* (1934) 50 TLR 581.
5 *Cuthbert v Linklater* 1935 SLT 94. But would this be regarded as defamatory today?
6 *AB v XY* 1917 SC 15; *Kerr v Kennedy* [1942] 1 KB 409. The increasing tolerance of homosexuality may result in such statements ceasing to be defamatory; *sed quare*.

call a person a liar[1] or a hypocrite.[2] To state that a woman whose child had died was a heartless and uncaring mother is defamatory.[3]

(b) Imputations of criminality

It is defamatory to accuse a person of a serious crime which ordinary people do not commit or condone, such as murder[4] or theft.[5] It would not perhaps be defamatory to accuse a person of careless driving (or tax evasion?). If the defender pleads *veritas*,[6] he can rely on the fact that the pursuer committed such a crime even if the offence is 'spent' under the Rehabilitation of Offenders Act 1974.[7] Similarly, it is defamatory to say that a person should be in jail since this implies that he is guilty of a crime.

(c) Imputations against competence or conduct

Statements which disparage a person's professional competence or conduct are defamatory, for example, to accuse a doctor of gross professional negligence[8] or a professor of his inability to teach[9] (or write textbooks on delict?). Allegations of conduct which is unprofessional in the circumstances are also defamatory, for example, to accuse a solicitor of conducting a case for his own – as opposed to his client's – interests[10] or that a prison warden had sexual relations with a prisoner.[11]

(d) Imputations of financial unsoundness

It is defamatory falsely to allege that a person is insolvent[12] or is unwilling[13] or unable to pay his debts.[14]

1 *Watson v Duncan* (1890) 17 R 404.
2 *Stein v Beaverbrook Newspapers Ltd* 1968 SC 272, 1968 SLT 401.
3 *McCabe v News Group Newspapers Ltd* 1992 SLT 707.
4 *Waddell v BBC* 1973 SLT 246.
5 *Sutherland v British Telecommunications Ltd* 1989 SLT 531.
6 See p 213 below.
7 s 4.
8 *Simmons v Morton* (1900) 8 SLT 230.
9 *Auld v Sharp* (1875) 2 R 940.
10 *McRostie v Ironside* (1849) 11 D 74.
11 *Winter v News Scotland Ltd* 1991 SLT 828.
12 *AB v CD* (1904) 7 F 22.
13 *Outram v Reid* (1852) 14 D 577.
14 *Mazure v Stubbs Ltd* 1919 SC (HL) 112, 1919 2 SLT 160.

(e) Disparaging public character

Persons who enter public life are expected to be able to withstand a degree of criticism[1] – or even ridicule[2] – in respect of the way in which they carry out their public duties. However, while the test may be stricter, allegations of, for example, dishonesty in carrying out a public office would, it is thought, constitute defamation. Statements undermining a public figure's sexual morality, ie concerned with his private as opposed to public life, are, of course, defamatory.

(f) Imputations on health

It is defamatory falsely to allege that a person is insane or has obnoxious physical defects or is suffering from certain illnesses such as venereal disease or AIDS.

A statement or action may appear to be harmless, yet when taken in the context of the facts and circumstances in which it was made, a defamatory meaning may be inferred. For example, it is not prima facie defamatory to display a wax effigy of a person in a waxworks: but to put it in the Chamber of Horrors along with those of convicted murderers implies that the person concerned is also a murderer.[3] Similarly, to announce the birth of twins to a married couple in a newspaper appears innocuous until it is appreciated that they married only a month before, thus implying pre-marital sexual intercourse.[4] In this situation, Scots law allows a pursuer to plead the facts and circumstances from which the defamatory meaning of the statement or act can be drawn. This is known as the doctrine of innuendo.

The onus rests on the pursuer to state the meaning of the acts or statement in the light of the relevant facts and circumstances. Thus, in *Cuthbert v Linklater*[5] the pursuer argued that the defender, an author, had defamed her when a female character in his novel took a Union Jack from Edinburgh Castle and placed it in a men's public urinal. An ardent Scottish nationalist, the pursuer had in fact taken a Union Jack from Stirling Castle and had tossed it at a guard. Consequently, by innuendo, a reasonable reader would assume that the character in the

---

1 *Mutch v Robertson* 1981 SLT 217.
2 *McLaughlan v Orr Pollock & Co* (1894) 22 R 38 at 42 per Lord McLaren.
3 *Monson v Tussauds* [1894] 1 QB 671.
4 *Morrison v Ritchie* (1902) 4 F 645.
5 1935 SLT 94.

novel was meant to be her and that she was capable of acting indelicately. The court accepted the argument.[1]

The test on whether an unnuendo can be inferred is that of the ordinary reasonable person,[2] ie whether a reasonable person would regard the words as offensive if placed in the same position as the pursuer. The question whether the statement or act *plus* the innuendo placed upon them by the reasonable person amount to defamation is a matter of law to be decided by the court. It is a question of fact whether the statement or act was taken as having a defamatory meaning by those to whom it was actually communicated.

(3) Intention to harm the pursuer

Once it has been established that a statement is defamatory, not only is it presumed to be false but it is also presumed that the statement was made with the intention of harming the particular pursuer (malice). A defender can rebut the presumption of falsehood by pleading *veritas*, ie that the statement was in fact true.[3] The question then arises whether or not the defender can rebut the presumption of malice by proving that he did not intend to harm the particular pursuer.

Authority suggests that the presumption of intention to harm cannot be rebutted. In *Hulton v Jones*[4] a newspaper published an article about an apparently fictitious character, Artemus Jones. This article contained material which would have been defamatory if Artemus Jones was an actual person. However, there was a 'real' Artemus Jones who sued the newspaper. The defence was that since the newspaper did not know of the existence of the plaintiff, it could not have intended to defame him. The House of Lords rejected this defence.

Although *Hulton v Jones* was an English case, Scots law appears to be similar. In *Outram v Reid*[5] a newspaper published a list of bankruptcies including 'John Reid, wine and spirit merchant, Glasgow'. There were two John Reids who were wine and spirit merchants in Glasgow, one of whom was, indeed, bankrupt while the other was

---

1 See also *Wragg v DC Thomson* 1909 2 SLT 315 where a newspaper published an article that a certain George Reeves had shot his wife twice and then had killed himself. The paper omitted to mention that the incident took place in the USA. At the time it was published, George Reeves, a famous music hall artiste, was appearing in Glasgow. The court held that there was an innuendo that the incident referred to him.
2 *Duncan v Associated Newspapers* 1929 SC 14 at 21 per Lord Anderson.
3 On *veritas*, see p 213 below.
4 [1910] AC 20.
5 (1852) 14 D 577.

solvent. The latter successfully sued in defamation, even although the defender was not aware of his existence. Similarly, the unfortunate couple, the birth of whose twins was prematurely announced, sued successfully in spite of the fact that the defender did not know of their existence nor had intended any harm.[1] And Mr Reeves was also able to sue, even although the story concerned another Mr Reeves who lived in America.[2]

While the issue appears to be settled, it is the present writer's view that the solution adopted by the courts is unprincipled. Instead, the courts should have accepted that the defender did not have the intention to insult the pursuers in these cases and accordingly no damages should have been awarded for *solatium*. However, as is clear from the Scottish decisions, there was an element of fault on the part of the defenders in publishing the statements. In *Outram v Reid*,[3] for example, the defender omitted the address of the bankrupt Mr Reid, which had been published in the Official Gazette: if it had been published in the newspaper, the confusion would have been avoided. Again, in *Morrison v Ritchie*,[4] the defender was criticised by the court for failing to check that the facts in the announcement were accurate. Given that it is (at least) arguable that the defenders were at fault in these cases, the pursuers were entitled to damages for patrimonial loss on general principles of *culpa* but not *solatium*. Also they would have to establish patrimonial loss, which would have been difficult in *Morrison*. But until the issue is reconsidered by the Inner House, it must be accepted that the presumption of intention to insult is now irrebuttable and *solatium*, as well as patrimonial loss, can be recovered in these circumstances.

It is unlikely, however, that the matter will be litigated. Section 4 of the Defamation Act 1952 provides a statutory defence which could cover the situations discussed above. Where there has been an innocent publication,[5] the publisher can make an offer of amends. If the offer is accepted, that is the end of the matter. If it is not accepted, then there is a defence that the offer was made as soon as it was practicable to do so and that it has not been withdrawn. If, however, the statement published was not written by the publisher, the defence

---

1 *Morrison v Ritchie* (1902) 4 F 645, discussed at p 210 above.
2 *Wragg v DC Thomson* 1909 2 SLT 315, discussed at p 211, note 1 above.
3 (1852) 14 D 577.
4 (1902) 4 F 645.
5 Ie which the publisher did not intend to refer to the pursuer expressly or by innuendo and in either case took reasonable care in relation to the publication: Defamation Act 1952, s 4(5). The reasonable care provision might not have been satisfied in the cases we have discussed.

is only available if the words written by the original author were
without malice.

(4) Defences

(a) Veritas

As we have seen, if a statement is defamatory, the law presumes that it is
false. This presumption can be rebutted. The onus lies on the defender
to prove that the statement was true. If truth (*veritas*) is established, this
is a complete defence. What is necessary to establish *veritas* will depend
on the nature of the defamatory statement. To allege that someone is a
murderer can be justified by proof of one act of murder; but to say
someone is a thief implies that he is currently dishonest and *veritas* is not
established simply by showing he was twice convicted of petty theft 23
years before.[1] A similar approach is taken in respect of immorality: to
allege that a 50-year-old man is homosexual would not be justified by
establishing that he engaged in homosexual acts with the captain of the
First XV, when he was a schoolboy.[2]

If more than one fact is alleged, *veritas* will operate only if all the
facts which are defamatory are proved true:[3] conversely, if some
non-defamatory facts are admitted to be false, then the defence will
still succeed if the defamatory facts can, nevertheless, be shown to be
true.[4] By section 5 of the Defamation Act 1952 it is provided that

'in an action for defamation in respect of words containing two or more
distinct charges against a pursuer, a defence of *veritas* shall not fail by reason
only that the truth of every charge is not proved if the words not proved to be
true do not materially injure the pursuer's reputation having regard to the
truth of the remaining charges.'

If, however, the allegations are not separable but are part and parcel
of a single defamatory allegation, the section does not apply.

(b) In rixa

Statements made *in rixa*, ie during a quarrel, an argument or a brawl,
do not give rise to an action in defamation unless the pursuer can

---

1 *Fletcher v Wilsons* (1885) 12 R 683.
2 On allegations of immorality, see *Brownlie v Thomson* (1859) 21 D 480 at 483 per Lord
    Murray.
3 *Fairbairn v SNP* 1979 SC 393, 1980 SLT 149.
4 *Sutherland v Stopos* [1925] AC 47.

prove that they were made with intent to injure.[1] The defence is more likely to succeed if the defender has apologised.

(c) Vulgar abuse

If the words used amount to mere vulgar abuse, then no action in defamation lies. To call someone a 'bitch' or a 'dickhead' is not actionable as it is not meant to be taken seriously.

(d) Fair retort

If A makes a statement about B, B is entitled to the opportunity to reply: if B's retort is defamatory it is not actionable unless A can prove that it was said with intent to injure.[2]

(e) Fair comment

Where a defamatory remark takes the form of an opinion, for example that a novel is badly written or an actor gave a bad performance, the defender can plead the defence of fair comment. In order to succeed, the defender must prove (1) that the statement is a comment on fact or facts (2) that the facts upon which the comment is made are true[3] and (3) that the facts concern some matter of public interest. If this can be proved, the onus shifts to the pursuer to show that the comment was made with the intention of harming the pursuer. The comment must be honestly made and relevant to the facts upon which it was based. Thus, a theatre critic who criticises a play, must honestly hold the opinion that the play is bad[4] and must restrict his comments to the play rather than the playwright.[5]

(f) Privilege

A person who makes a defamatory statement may have the defence of privilege. In certain situations, public policy demands that a person

1 *Christie v Robertson* (1899) 1 F 1155.
2 *Gray v Scottish Society for the Prevention of Cruelty to Animals* (1890) 17 R 1185.
3 Where the statement contains facts and opinion, the defence of fair comment is not lost if the facts upon which the opinion is based are true even if other facts are false: Defamation Act 1952, s 6.
4 *Turner v MGM Pictures Ltd* [1950] 1 All ER 449, [1950] WN 83; *Telnikoff v Matusevitch* [1962] 2 AC 343.
5 *Merivale v Carson* (1887) 20 QBD 275.

should be free to speak without fear of litigation on the grounds of defamation. There are two forms of privilege viz absolute privilege and qualified privilege.

(i) **Absolute privilege.** Where a statement is protected by absolute privilege, it cannot form the basis of an action for defamation or verbal injury.[1] It does not matter that the statement is defamatory or was made with the intention to harm the victim (malice). The following situations are covered by absolute privilege:

(a) Statements made in Parliament. Any statement made in Parliament has the protection of absolute privilege. This includes statements made in Parliamentary committees. The statement does not have to be relevant to the proceedings. It is not restricted to statements made by members of either House: it would include, for example, a statement made by a witness giving evidence to a Select Committee. It does not extend to statements made by members of Parliament outside the Houses.

(b) Statements made in judicial proceedings. A statement made by a judge in the course of judicial proceedings is protected by absolute privilege even if it was made maliciously.[2] However, the statement must be made while the judge is acting judicially, ie it must be relevant to the case which is subject to the proceedings.[3] Advocates or solicitors pleading the case also enjoy absolute privilege,[4] provided the statement is relevant to the case. Witnesses giving evidence have absolute privilege as long as the evidence is pertinent to the case.[5] Any findings of fact by a jury is subject to absolute privilege. But parties to a civil action do not enjoy absolute privilege – only qualified privilege.[6] Absolute privilege extends in like way to the participants in quasi-judicial proceedings or tribunals, for example, courts martial, public inquiries, arbitrations, children's hearings, industrial tribunals etc.

(c) Reports authorised by Parliament. Reports of proceedings and papers etc published by or under the authority of either House of Parliament attract absolute privilege.[7]

1 On verbal injury, see pp 218 ff below.
2 *Haggart's Trs v Hope* (1824) 1 Sh App 125; *Primrose v Waterson* (1902) 4 F 783, 10 SLT 37.
3 *Watt v Thomson* (1870) 8 M (HL) 77.
4 *Rome v Watson* (1895) 25 R 733, 5 SLT 377. The privilege extends to written pleadings.
5 *Watson v McEwan* (1905) 7 F (HL) 109. This privilege extends to statements made in precognition: *B v Burns* 1994 SLT 250.
6 See p 217 below.
7 Parliamentary Papers Act 1840.

(d) Miscellaneous. The Lord Advocate is absolutely privileged in respect of what he does in relation to prosecutions on indictment; this protection extends to procurators fiscal and Advocates Depute acting on the Lord Advocate's instructions. Ministers of the Crown are also protected provided the statement is made in the proper exercise of their functions. Reports of the various ombudsmen are also absolutely privileged.

(ii) **Qualified privilege.** When a statement is protected by qualified privilege, the defender is assumed to have acted in good faith and an action of defamation or verbal injury[1] will not succeed unless the pursuer can show that the statement was made with the intention of harming the pursuer (ie with malice). Qualified privilege arises in the following circumstances:

(a) Duty or interest to speak. Where a person has a legal duty to speak, the statement is protected by qualified privilege. The protection extends to situations where there is a moral or social duty to speak, for example, to report a crime or inform a reporter to a children's hearing of child abuse. Complaints to the chief constable about the conduct of police officers attracts protection if an action of defamation is brought against the complainer by the officer who was the subject of the complaint.[2] A person who gives a reference enjoys qualified privilege.[3] Whether a situation involves a duty to speak which attracts qualified privilege is a question of law to be determined by a court. Qualified privilege also arises where a person has an interest to speak, for example, replying to criticism.[4] In these situations, the person who receives the statement must have a reciprocal interest in the information. So, for example, a complaint about the conduct of a police officer is protected by qualified privilege if made to the relevant chief constable but not if made to a newspaper editor.

(b) Reports of proceedings in Parliament in the press or other media attract only qualified privilege. The position is the same in respect of reports of judicial and other quasi-judicial proceedings.[5]

---

1 On verbal injury, see pp 218 ff below.
2 *Fraser v Mirza* 1993 SLT 527.
3 *Farquhar v Neish* (1890) 17 R 716.
4 *Campbell v Cochrane* (1905) 8 F 205.
5 *Richardson v Wilson* (1879) 7 R 237, 17 SLR 122; *Cunningham v Scotsman Publications Ltd* 1987 SCLR 314, 1987 SLT 698.

(c) Parties to a civil action enjoy only qualified privilege in respect of statements made in civil proceedings. If, however, the pursuer can prove that the statement was made with the intention of harming the pursuer (ie maliciously) then an action for defamation or verbal injury may lie.[1] This delict is often called 'judicial slander'.

(d) Under the Defamation Act 1952,[2] certain types of reports published by the media are subject to qualified privilege.

As we have seen, where a statement is subject to qualified privilege, it can be the subject of an action of defamation or verbal injury[3] if the pursuer acted maliciously. In the present writer's view, this simply means that the defender intended to harm or insult the pursuer, although it has been contended that it is sufficient to show that the defender was not motivated by duty or interest. But if that were so, at least in the case of duty or interest to speak, qualified privilege would not attach in the first place. However, as the authorities stand,[4] malice can be established if it could be shown that the defender abused the privileged occasion – as well as proving that he intended to injure the pursuer. Nevertheless, proof of malice is difficult.[5] It may be inferred from extreme language, a previous personal vendetta between the parties or the fact that the defender did not believe that the statement was true.[6] It is not enough simply to establish that the statement was defamatory.[7]

(4) Damages

In an action for defamation and verbal injury,[8] the pursuer is entitled to *solatium* in respect of insult and hurt feelings sustained, and compensation for any patrimonial loss. Where the case is one of defamation, insult is presumed, but any patrimonial loss must be averred and proved. While patrimonial loss, if it has been sustained, is relatively easy to assess, *solatium* is more difficult as it involves no little degree of speculation. In practice, *solatium* is usually a modest sum in Scots law. Everyone is assumed to be of good character, so *solatium* is

1 *Williamson v Umphray and Robertson* (1890) 17 R 905, 27 SLR 742.
2 s 7 and Schedule to the Act. Detailed treatment is outwith the scope of the present text.
3 See pp 218 ff below.
4 See especially *Fraser v Mirza* 1993 SLT 527 at 531 per Lord Keith of Kinkel.
5 For an example of the difficulties, see *Fraser v Mirza* above.
6 *Horrocks v Lowe* [1975] AC 135, [1974] 1 All ER 662.
7 *Adam v Jackson* [1917] AC 309.
8 On verbal injury, see pp 218 ff below.

unlikely to be increased if the pursuer is particularly good; but the more eminent the pursuer, the greater the loss of reputation, and, consequently, more will be awarded by way of *solatium*. In general, the worse the allegation, the greater the sum that will be awarded. However, at the end of the day, *solatium* is intended to compensate loss:[1] a person who brings an action primarily to clear his name will only receive a nominal sum.

An award of *solatium* can be mitigated as a result of a number of factors. First, if the pursuer's character or reputation is already tainted before the defamatory statement, evidence can be led by the defender to show that the pursuer did not therefore suffer as much as an ordinary person.[2] An immediate retraction of the statement and an apology will mitigate the loss.[3] This will also be the case if the pursuer provoked the defender into making the defamatory statement.[4] If the statement has been published by more than one person, the defender can mitigate the damages the pursuer should receive if the pursuer has already received damages in respect of the same words, or words to the same effect, from a third party.[5] So, for example, if A and B defame C using the same words, if C sues A, A can plead mitigation if C has already received damages from B.

C. VERBAL INJURY

Where a statement is made which is not defamatory,[6] the law will not presume that it is false, made with intent to injure, and caused insult to the victim. However, it does not follow that where the non-defamatory statement has undermined a person's character or reputation, that he is without a remedy. Scots law recognises that non-defamatory statements can amount to civil wrongs which are actionable in delict. These are known as verbal injuries.

The most common situation where an action will lie for verbal injury are cases where a non-defamatory statement is made which holds up the pursuer to public hatred, ridicule and contempt. In *Paterson v Welch*[7] the defender stated that the pursuer had made the

1 *Stein v Beaverbrook Newspapers* 1968 SC 272.
2 *C v M* 1923 SC 1, 1922 SLT 634.
3 *Morrison v Ritchie* (1902) 4 F 645.
4 *Paul v Jackson* (1884) 11 R 460.
5 Defamation Act 1952, s 12.
6 On the categories of defamatory statements, see pp 208 ff above.
7 (1893) 20 R 744.

comment that if children from the poorer classes were allowed to attend Madras College, this would 'contaminate the genteel children' currently attending that school. To state that a person holds a controversial opinion is not defamatory, ie it does not lower him in the estimation of right-thinking persons. However, the court was prepared to allow the case to proceed as an action for verbal injury provided the pursuer could aver and prove that (1) the statement was false; (2) the statement was intended to injure the pursuer; and (3) that injury had in fact been sustained by the pursuer.[1] Thus, unlike a case of defamation, where falsity, intention to injure and injury are presumed, in cases of verbal injury, the onus lies on the pursuer to prove these facts.

In *Steele v Scottish Daily Record*[2] the defender made a statement in its newspaper's legal advice and consumer rights page that the pursuer, a car dealer, had acted harshly in refusing to cancel a hire purchase agreement with a customer who had got into financial difficulties. 'Have a heart, that's my message to Motor Dealer, Mr Steele' ran the headline. The statement was not defamatory since it merely suggested that the pursuer was a hard businessman. Nevertheless, the Inner House held that Steele would have an action if he could prove that the statement was false, that it was intended to harm him and had, in fact, caused him harm. The case failed on the basis that the article was not intended to hold Steele up to public hatred, ridicule and contempt, but had been written to persuade him to give his unfortunate customer a better deal. Therefore, before an action can lie for verbal injury on this ground, the effect of the statement, apart from being false, must have been intended to cause the pursuer to be despised or condemned by ordinary members of the public.[3]

An action for verbal injury will also lie if A makes a false statement about the state of B's property, for example, that B's house is falling down[4] (slander of property). Similarly, an action will lie if A falsely alleges that B does not own property which he wishes to sell[5] (slander of title) or if A falsely states that B's business is not run well[6] (slander of business). To succeed in these situations, B must prove that the statement was false, intended to harm B economically and actually caused B patrimonial loss.[7] Because there is no intention to injure the

1 (1893) 20 R 744 at 749 per the Lord President (Robertson).
2 1970 SLT 53.
3 *Steele v Scottish Daily Record* above. See also *Burns v Diamond* (1896) 4 SLT 397.
4 *Argyllshire Weavers Ltd v A Macauley (Tweeds) Ltd* 1965 SLT 21.
5 *Philp v Morton* (1816) Hume 865.
6 *Craig v Inveresk Paper Merchant Ltd* 1970 SLT (Notes) 50.
7 *Argyllshire Weavers Ltd v A Macauley (Tweeds) Ltd* above.

pursuer's character or reputation, *solatium* cannot be recovered;[1] in other words, only patrimonial loss can be recovered. Thus, in order to be actionable as a verbal injury, the statement must have been made to a third party.

Finally, an action for verbal injury may lie if A defames B with the intention of harming C. Because C has not been defamed, ie C's reputation has not been directly attacked, C cannot sue A in defamation. However, if C can prove that A's defamatory statement in respect of B was false, was intended to harm C and did harm C, then in principle, C should have an action for verbal injury against A.[2] So, for example, if a person defames a woman by calling her a prostitute, not only can she sue in defamation but her husband could have an action based on verbal injury if he could prove that the statement was false, that it was made to injure him and in fact did so. Unlike his wife's case of defamation, where these three requisites are presumed in her favour, in his action for verbal injury, the onus lies on the husband to establish these facts.

A defender in an action of verbal injury can rely on the same defences that are available in an action of defamation.[3]

D. CONVICIUM

It is an essential requirement of defamation and verbal injury that the statement is false. However, some writers argue that Scots law recognises another form of verbal injury, *convicium*, where *veritas* is no defence.[4] *Convicium* involves holding the pursuer up to public hatred, ridicule and contempt, and in so far as it ever had an independent existence in Scots law, has, it is submitted, now been overtaken by the genus delict of verbal injury where the statement has to be false before it is actionable.[5]

In the present writer's view, it is too late for the courts to revive this delict, particularly as it could undermine freedom of speech given that

1 Unlike the public hatred, ridicule and contempt cases where, as in defamation, both *solatium* and patrimonial loss are recoverable. Unlike defamation, insult must be proved before *solatium* can be obtained.
2 *North of Scotland Banking Co v Duncan* (1857) 19 D 881 at 887 per Lord Deas. Cf *Broon v Ritchie* (1904) 6 F 942, where the distinction between defamation and verbal injury was not clearly drawn.
3 Discussed at pp 213 ff above.
4 See, in particular, Walker *Delict* (2nd edn) p 736.
5 See pp 218 ff above.

veritas is no defence. Instead, Parliament must give consideration to whether it is desirable to introduce a statutory remedy for unwarranted intrusions into an individual person's privacy.[1] The scope of the remedy – where *veritas* would be no defence – would be determined after balancing an individual's interest in privacy against the public interest in freedom of speech. This is clearly a task for the legislature rather than the judiciary, who would have to develop principles which were, arguably, never part of Scots common law.[2]

1 See *Infringement of Privacy* (Lord Chancellor's Dept, Scottish Office, July 1993).
2 This chapter is strongly influenced by Dr K McK Norrie's seminal article 'Hurts to Character, Honour and Reputation: a Reappraisal' 1984 JR 163. The present writer is also deeply indebted to Dr Norrie for allowing him to have access to his forthcoming article on defamation and verbal injuries to be published in Obligations, 15 *Stair Memorial Encyclopaedia*.

Part IV
DAMAGES

Introduction

The purpose of this last chapter is to give a short account of the law of damages. It begins with a discussion of the difficulties raised by the question of remoteness of damages. There follows a short account of how damages are calculated. Finally, there is an outline of the rules on prescription and limitation which are relevant to delictual liability.

CHAPTER 16

Damages

A. REMOTENESS OF DAMAGES

It will be remembered that Scottish courts once took the view that delictual liability would not be imposed upon a defender if the pursuer's injury was too remote.[1] However, in the present writer's view, these cases should now be analysed as situations where the court was unwilling to impose a duty of care on the defender, ie the duty of care was being used as a threshold device to deny delictual liability. But even where there has been a breach of a duty of care and the defender is liable to make reparation to the pursuer in respect of the pursuer's personal injuries or damage to property, it does not follow that the defender must compensate the pursuer for every loss arising from the delict. Some losses are 'too remote'. Consider the following example:

A, as a result of his careless driving, knocks down a pedestrian, B. B will recover damages for pain and suffering (*solatium*)[2] and derivative economic loss. The latter will include loss of wages between the date of the accident and the date of the action; future loss of earnings from the date of the action, if B is unable to work or can only work at a less well paid job;[3] the cost of medical treatment and nursing up to the date of the action and the cost of such care in the future. However, if as a result of the accident, B was unable to give instructions to his stockbroker to purchase shares which he had intended to buy or if B was unable to post his football coupon, the profits B would have made on the shares or the dividend he would have won if the coupon had been posted are not recoverable, even although they arise from the fact that B was incapacitated as a result of the accident. These losses are too remote and cannot therefore be recovered.

What criteria do the courts use to determine whether or not losses

---

1 See pp 109 ff above.
2 For the calculation of *solatium*, see pp 230 ff below.
3 For the calculation of loss of future earnings, see pp 231 ff below.

are too remote? The classic statement of the rule on remoteness of damages in Scots law was articulated by the Lord Ordinary (Kinloch) in *Allan v Barclay*:[1]

'The grand rule on the subject of damages is, that none can be claimed except such as naturally and directly arise out of the wrong done; and such, therefore, as may reasonably be supposed to have been in the contemplation of the wrongdoer.'

However, there is a potential contradiction inherent in this statement. While many losses which are reasonably foreseeable also directly arise from the wrong done, it is possible to envisage situations where a loss directly arises from the delict but is not reasonably foreseeable and vice versa, ie a loss which is reasonably foreseeable but does not arise directly from the delict.

This problem has been a matter of particular concern in England. In *Re Polemis and Furness, Withy & Co*[2] the Court of Appeal held that the question whether particular damages are recoverable depends only on whether they were the direct consequence of the delictual act; provided some damage was reasonably foreseeable so that there was a breach of a duty of care, the defendant is liable to compensate for all the damage directly resulting from the breach of duty, even if those losses were unforeseeable. In this case, stevedores carelessly allowed a plank to fall into the hold of a ship. The falling plank caused a spark which in its turn ignited petrol vapour in the hold. The vapour caused a fire which destroyed the vessel. The court held that while the fire was not a reasonably foreseeable consequence of allowing the plank to fall, some damage to the vessel was. In the light of these findings, the court was prepared to hold that since it was reasonably foreseeable that some form of damage would result from the negligent act, damages in respect of the fire, albeit not reasonably foreseeable, were nevertheless recoverable as a direct consequence of the foreseeable harm. Although this case is often cited as authority for the proposition that reasonable foreseeability plays no part in determining the extent of recoverable damages, such a conclusion may not be entirely justified. If it had been held that it was not foreseeable that the plank would cause any

---

1 (1864) 2 M 874. The case was concerned with whether an employer could recover damages for the loss of his injured employee's services. In other words, it was concerned with the defender's liability rather than remoteness of damages. Today it would be analysed as an example of non-recoverability of secondary economic loss: see pp 86 ff above. However, the passage has always been regarded as an authoritative statement of remoteness of damages.
2 [1921] 3 KB 560.

damage at all, the court might well have held that the consequences of
the fire were too remote.

However, it may appear illogical to insist that some damage to the
pursuer must be reasonably foreseen as a reasonable and probable
consequence of the defender's act or omission before there is a breach
of a duty of care, ie delictual liability, yet allow the pursuer to recover
losses directly arising from that breach which were not reasonably
foreseeable. In *Overseas Tankship (UK) Ltd v Morts Dock & Engineering
Co (The Wagon Mound No 1)*[1] the Privy Council declined to
follow *Re Polemis*. In this case, a ship was being bunkered when some
oil being loaded on board spilt into the harbour as a result of the
carelessness of the appellant's employees. Morts' employees were
welding nearby when the spillage happened. Some molten metal from
their operations fell onto some debris which caught fire; this in turn
set the oil alight causing substantial fire damage to the wharf owned by
Morts. It was found as a fact that it was not reasonably foreseeable that
the oil could have been ignited in such a way. Although it was reasonably foreseeable that the oil spillage would cause some harm to the
respondent's dock viz fouling the dock, nevertheless the court held
that the appellants were not liable for the damage caused by the
unforeseeable fire. If *Re Polemis* had been applied, it is arguable that
the appellants would have been liable for the damage caused by the
fire: since some damage, ie the fouling of the dock, was foreseeable
and the fire could be regarded as a *direct* result of the breach of duty[2] –
albeit that the fire was unforeseeable. However, since damage by fire
was not reasonably foreseeable as a probable consequence of the spillage, it is submitted that in this case there was no breach of duty of care
ie there was no delictual liability and therefore it is not a remoteness of
damages case at all.[3]

The Scottish courts have not given authoritative guidance on the
matter; instead, reliance is simply placed on Lord Kinloch's 'grand
rule'. In *Kelvin Shipping Co v Canadian Pacific Railway Co ('The
Baron Vernon')*[4] Viscount Haldane LC opined[5] that when

'a collision takes place by the fault of the defendant's ship, the damage is
recoverable, in an action for damages if it is the natural and reasonable result
of the negligent act, and it will assume that character if it can be shown to be

1 [1961] AC 388, [1961] 1 All ER 404.
2 Although in this case it is equally arguable that the fire was *indirectly* caused as a result
   of the molten metal falling on the oil.
3 Cf *Hughes v Lord Advocate* 1963 SC (HL) 31 where injury by fire was reasonably
   foreseeable: only the extent of the injuries was not. For full discussion, see pp 99 ff
   above.
4 1928 SC (HL) 21.
5 1928 SC (HL) 21 at 25.

such a consequence as in the ordinary course of things would flow from the situation which the offending ship created.'[1]

While there are obiter dicta that *Re Polemis* does not reflect the law of Scotland,[2] in *Campbell v F & F Moffat (Transport) Ltd*[3] the Lord Ordinary (Lord Cameron of Lochbroom) held that the test was not whether the loss was reasonably foreseeable but whether it arose naturally and directly out of the wrong. In that case, the pursuer was injured in a road accident and, as a result, his employment was terminated in 1989. Two years later, his former employer closed the mill where the pursuer had worked and gave the employees then working at that date *ex gratia* redundancy payments. In his action for damages, the pursuer sought compensation for the loss of the redundancy payment he would have received if his employment had not been terminated two years earlier as a result of the accident. Lord Cameron took the view that this loss was not so utterly speculative that it could not amount to a natural and direct consequence of the accident.

It is submitted that in Scots law it is too simplistic to see the question of remoteness of damages in terms of reasonable foreseeability on the one hand and direct consequences on the other. The courts use a combination of both tests in assessing whether the loss is a natural consequence of the delictual act. It is only if the loss is utterly speculative[4] that the loss will be too remote and not recoverable in an award of damages. What is clear, however, is that in a case of personal injuries, the defender takes his victim as he finds him. If, for example, A, as a result of his carelessness, burns B, if B has a predisposition to cancer which is triggered by the burn, with the result that B dies, A is liable for B's death even if that was not reasonably foreseeable as a consequence of the burn. In this situation, reasonable foreseeability of death is treated as irrelevant or, alternatively, the defender is deemed to have reasonably foreseen that the pursuer could have been an ill, as opposed to healthy, person.[5]

We have been considering the question of remoteness of damages in the context of delictual liability for unintentional, but careless, conduct. Where the intentional delicts are concerned, the defender is liable to make reparation for all losses suffered by the pursuer which

---

1 However, this case was clearly concerned with the existence of liability, rather than remoteness of damages.
2 See, for example, *Cowan v National Coal Board* 1958 SLT (Notes) 19 per the Lord Ordinary (Cameron).
3 1992 SCLR 551, 1992 SLT 962.
4 As it is submitted is the case in the examples of the loss of profits on the shares and the loss of a football pools' dividend: see p 225 above.
5 *McKillen v Barclay Curle & Co* 1967 SLT 41.

directly arise from the delict – whether or not these losses are reasonably foreseeable. The intention to injure the pursuer, which is an essential requisite of these delicts, disposes of any question of remoteness of damages.

B. CALCULATION OF DAMAGES

(1) Introduction

The purpose of an award of damages is to compensate the pursuer for those losses which arose as a result of the delict. It is, so far as money can, to place the pursuer in the financial position he would have been in if the delict had not occurred.[1] Where the claim is in respect of damage to property, damages are relatively simple to assess viz the cost of repair or replacement of the property. Where delictual liability for pure economic loss is recognised,[2] again the loss should be relatively easy to quantify; for example, where there has been a negligent survey of a house, the damages will be either the cost of repair or the difference between the value of the property if there were no structural faults and the value of the property with the structural faults which should have been discovered if the surveyor had taken reasonable care. As we have seen,[3] in wrongful birth actions, damages include the anticipated costs of bringing up a child. Greater difficulties arise in calculating damages in personal injury cases and these deserve fuller treatment.

(2) Personal injury claims

Where a party suffers personal injuries as a result of the delictual conduct of the defender, he is entitled to obtain reparation in respect of the physical injury and for any derivative economic loss which he has sustained as a result. Compensation for the pain and suffering arising as a result of physical injury is known as *solatium*; while compensation in respect of pecuniary claims is known as patrimonial loss. Again,

---

1 See, for example, *O'Brien's Curator Bonis v British Steel plc* 1991 SCLR 931, 1991 SLT 477 at 480 per the Lord President (Hope).
2 For discussion, see pp 67 ff above. Of course, economic loss will most often arise in the context of the economic delicts and fraud.
3 Pages 67 ff above.

'the objective' is, so far as money can, to compensate the injured party for the consequences of the wrongful act.[1]

(a) Solatium

It is, of course, clear that no money sum can in effect compensate for physical injury. In *Wright v British Railways Board*[2] Lord Diplock said of the English equivalent of *solatium* that

'such loss is not susceptible of *measurement* in money. Any figure at which the assessor of damages arrives cannot be other than artificial and, if the aim is that justice meted out to all litigants should be even handed instead of depending on idiosyncrasies of the assessor, whether jury or judge, the figure must be "basically a conventional figure derived from an experience of awards in comparable cases".'[3]

In *McMillan v McDowell*[4] the judge opined that 'While the assessment of *solatium* is not a precise science and has frequently been called a jury question, the view of [a Lord Ordinary] in a similar case must be treated with respect'.[5]

The court therefore approaches the question of *solatium* on the basis of comparing one case with another and making a determination taking into account the severity and nature of the injuries sustained by the pursuer. The court assesses *solatium* as at the date of the proof and does not attempt to assess *solatium* as it would have been at the date of the injury itself.

In making an award for *solatium* the court takes into account not only the extent of the injury but also the pursuer's awareness of pain.[6] No award can be made under this head therefore if, as a result of his injuries, the pursuer has been rendered permanently unconscious. Such awards are made not only in respect of physical injury. A person who, for example, suffers from an identifiable psychological condition (nervous shock) can be awarded damages where the condition arises as a consequence of a delict.[7] In making its assessment of *solatium*, the court takes into account not only the pain and suffering which has

---

1 *Admiralty Commissioners v SS Susquehanna* [1926] AC 55.
2 [1983] 2 AC 733, [1983] 2 All ER 698, HL.
3 [1983] 2 All ER 698 at 699 (Lord Diplock's emphasis). It is submitted that the position is the same in Scots law.
4 1993 SLT 311.
5 1993 SLT 311 at 312 per T G Coutts QC.
6 *Lim Poh Choo v Camden and Islington Area Health Authority* [1980] AC 174, [1979] 2 All ER 910, HL.
7 *Alcock v Chief Constable of South Yorkshire Police* [1992] 1 AC 310, [1991] 4 All ER 907. On liability for nervous shock, see pp 62 ff above.

been experienced by the pursuer but also the pain and suffering which he is likely to experience in the future. A global award is made. The award also takes into account the pursuer's loss of amenity. Everything which reduces the pursuer's enjoyment of life, which has been sustained as a result of the accident, will be reflected in a claim for *solatium*. It has been held in England that the important element in such a claim is the fact of deprivation of amenity and not whether the injured person is aware of such deprivation.[1] Also included in an award of *solatium* is the pain and suffering occasioned when the pursuer is, was, or at any time will be, likely to become aware that his expectancy of life has been shortened by his injuries.[2]

(b) Patrimonial loss

Having assessed damages in respect of *solatium* the court must then turn to the question of patrimonial loss. The court first of all assesses damages in respect of past loss, that is loss incurred between the date of the accident and the date of the proof: it then attempts to assess the pursuer's future loss.

(i) **Damages for patrimonial loss to the date of proof.** If the pursuer has been out of work since the date of his accident, he will be entitled to be compensated for his loss of wages. Apart from being compensated for loss of wages, the pursuer will frequently also have a claim for expenses. The general rule is that reasonable expenses are recoverable. Consequently, reasonable medical expenses can be recovered even if it is shown at a later stage that they are unnecessary.[3] Expenses need not be confined to medical or nursing services. By section 8 of the Administration of Justice Act 1982,[4] when a person has sustained personal injuries or has died in consequence of personal injuries sustained, the defender is liable to pay damages in respect of necessary services which have been, or will be, rendered to the injured person by a relative in consequence of the injuries in question. Section 9 of the Act[5] also imposes an obligation upon the wrongdoer to pay to the

---

1 *Lim Poh Choo v Camden and Islington Health Authority* above. Of course, if the person has been rendered unconscious, he will not obtain compensation for pain and suffering.
2 Damages (Scotland) Act 1976, s 9A as added by s 5 of the Damages (Scotland) Act 1993.
3 *Clippens Oil Co Ltd v Edinburgh and District Water Trustees* 1907 SC (HL) 9, 15 SLT 92; *Rubins v Walker* 1946 SC 215.
4 Discussed at p 192 above.
5 Discussed at pp 192 ff above.

injured person a reasonable sum by way of damages when he is unable, as a result of the accident, to render gratuitous personal services to his family.

In calculating loss of earnings, the pursuer's income tax must be taken into account and his liability to pay national insurance contributions.[1] Accordingly, in so far as past patrimonial loss is concerned, the wages which form the basis of the calculation are the pursuer's net earnings.

(ii) **Damages for future patrimonial loss.** This head of claim is by far the most important in assessing damages in respect of personal injury. The first stage is to assess damages in respect of future loss of earnings. This is done by taking the loss of the pursuer's net earnings at the date of proof and calculating that on an annual basis; the courts do not attempt to speculate on future rates of taxes and national insurance contributions, but base their calculation on the rates current at the date of proof.[2] No allowance is made for possible increases in the pursuer's earnings if he had not been injured. The figure produced is known as the multiplicand. The second stage is to find a multiplier. It might be thought that this should simply be based on the pursuer's life expectancy. However, the court has to take into account several variables: for example, if the pursuer had not been injured he might, nevertheless, in the future lose his job through redundancy,[3] marry and voluntarily leave work or die or be killed. Moreover, account is also taken of the fact that normally damages[4] are paid in a lump sum which if invested, provides the pursuer with an accelerated income. The multiplier is therefore always less than the actual number of years over which wages in the ordinary course of events would be earned. The third stage is for the court to multiply the multiplicand by the multiplier to give a lump sum: so, for example, if the multiplicand is £20,000 and the multiplier is 10, then the total sum awarded is £200,000. The court can also take into account lost wages which the pursuer would have earned if his life expectancy had not been reduced as a result of the accident.[5]

Where a pursuer is severely injured, damages can be awarded for the cost of his maintenance, nursing and medical care in the future.

---

1 *British Transport Commission v Gourlay* [1956] AC 185, [1955] 3 All ER 796, HL; *Cooper v Firth Brown* [1963] 2 All ER 31, [1963] 1 WLR 148.
2 *British Transport Commission v Gourlay* above.
3 *O'Neil v British Coal Corporation* 1990 SCLR 569, 1991 SLT 367 (loss of pension rights – uncertainty of continuing in employment in the coal industry taken into account).
4 On provisional damages, see pp 237 ff below.
5 Damages (Scotland) Act 1976, s 9(1) and (2).

Again, the multiplicand/multiplier method is adopted. The court assesses the cost of maintenance and care on an annual basis and then applies a multiplier based on the number of years such maintenance and care is required. Because the variables are less speculative than in the case of loss of future earnings, the multiplier will be closer to – though still less than – the pursuer's expectation of life.[1] However, in relation to both loss of future earnings and cost of maintenance and medical care, the courts will use the Ogden actuarial tables as a check on the multiplier which has been arrived at by the conventional method.[2] It should be noted that in a personal injuries' case, the multiplier is applied at the date of proof: if, however, the pursuer died of his injuries between the date of the accident and the proof, the multiplier is applied at the date of death.[3]

Loss of pension rights can also be taken into account in assessing future patrimonial loss[4] as can the pursuer's general loss of value in the labour market. In some cases, the court will abandon the multiplicand/multiplier method of calculating future patrimonial loss. This would arise where, for example, the pursuer has been able to continue working albeit on light work at a reduced wage, or there is evidence that the pursuer will be able to resume employment in the very near future, even although the job may be less well paid than previously.[5]

(3) Interest

Having assessed the quantity of damages the court is then obliged to consider the question of interest. Interest is payable under the Interest and Damages (Scotland) Act 1958 and the Interest and Damages (Scotland) Act 1971.

While *solatium* is awarded as a lump sum, it is important for the purpose of awards of interest to distinguish past and future *solatium*. Past *solatium* is a sum awarded for the pursuer's pain and suffering until the date of proof. But if the pursuer is experiencing pain and suffering and loss of amenities at the date of the proof, the court will estimate

---

1 *O'Brien's Curator Bonis v British Steel plc* 1991 SLT 477.
2 Ibid. The Ogden tables provided actuarial calculations of lump sums which are required to provide income for injured persons at different ages: see C N McEarchran *'O'Brien's CB v British Steel'* 1992 SLT (News) 139.
3 On death from personal injuries, see pp 193 ff above.
4 *Mitchell v Glenrothes Development Corporation* 1991 SLT 284 (conventional multiplicand/multiplier method used).
5 *Stevenson v British Coal Corporation* 1989 SLT 136.

damages to compensate the pursuer for the fact that these may continue in the future. So, for example, a court might award a total sum of £10,000 by way of *solatium*, made up of £6,000 for past *solatium* and £4,000 for future *solatium*. Interest on past *solatium* is paid at the average court rate for the period between the date of the accident and when the 'pain' diminished: this could, of course, have occurred before the date of the proof. Interest on future *solatium* is paid at one half of the average court rate for the period from the date of the proof until the date when the court estimates that the 'pain' will have diminished. This therefore requires an apportionment to be made between past and future *solatium*.[1]

Subject to the court's discretion, interest on patrimonial loss runs from the date of the accident.[2] Again, while a global sum is awarded, damages are divided between past and future loss. In the case of past losses, interest is awarded at one half of the average court rate from the date of the accident to the date of proof. There is no interest payable on awards in respect of future patrimonial loss. The rules applicable to interest in respect of personal injuries operate without prejudice to the general rule which awards interest at the court rate from the date of decree until the date of payment by the defender.

(4) Deductions from awards

Deductions may have to be made from an award of damages for patrimonial loss. Section 10 of the Administration of Justice Act 1982 prohibits the taking into account for the purposes of reduction of damages any benefit the pursuer received in respect of: (a) any contractual pension; (b) any pension or retirement benefit to which section 2(1) of the Law Reform (Personal Injuries) Act 1948 applied; (c) any benefit payable from public funds in respect of any period after the date of the award of damages which is designed to secure to the injured person or any relative of his a minimum level of subsistence; (d) any statutory redundancy payment;[3] (e) any payment made to the injured person or to any relative of his by the injured person's employer following upon the injuries in question where the recipient is under an obligation to reimburse the employer in the event of damages being

---

1 *Keicher v National Coal Board* 1988 SLT 318; *Preston v Grampian Health Board* 1988 SLT 435.
2 *McRae v Reid & Mallick Ltd* 1961 SLT 96.
3 Reversing *Wilson v National Coal Board* 1981 SC (HL) 9, 1981 SLT 67. An *ex gratia* non-statutory payment falls to be deducted: *Duncan v Glacier Metal Co Ltd* 1988 SCLR 320, 1988 SLT 479.

recovered in respect of his injuries; and (f) any payment of a benevolent character made to the injured person or to any relative by any person following upon the injuries in question. The section directs, however, that any remuneration or earnings from unemployment, any unemployment benefit payable from public funds payable prior to the date of the award of damages, or any payment of a benevolent character made by the person responsible for the accident to the injured person, shall be taken into account. Any savings to the pursuer as a result of being maintained in hospital is deducted.[1]

Prior to the introduction of the Social Security Act 1989, in assessing damages for patrimonial loss, a deduction was made of only one half of the value of certain specified benefits viz sickness, invalidity or disablement benefit, which the pursuer had received during a period of five years from the date of the accident; but in *Hodgson v Trapp*[2] the House of Lords held that the full value of other benefits, such as attendance and mobility allowances, was to be deducted. However, the Social Security Act 1989 section 22 and Schedule 4, which came into effect on 30 September, 1990, made major changes in the way in which benefit deductions are dealt with. The provisions of the 1989 Act are now consolidated in the Social Security Administration Act 1992, Part VI, the relevant provisions of which came into force on 1 July 1992.

The new rules apply to an accident or injury occurring on or after 1 January 1989 or if the claim is made in respect of disease, where the pursuer's first claim for benefit in consequence of the disease was made after that date. Section 82(1) of the 1992 Act provides that a person, known as the 'compensator', who makes a compensation payment (ie pays an award of damages) to a pursuer will deduct from any such payment the amount certified by the Secretary of State for Social Security as the 'total benefit' paid by the Department. The Act provides that the deduction so made will then be paid to the Secretary of State. A benefit is defined as any benefit under the Social Security Contributions and Benefits Act 1992 with the exception of child benefit. The following benefits are therefore taken into account: (a) attendance allowance; (b) disablement benefit; (c) family credit; (d) income support; (e) invalidity benefit allowance; (f) mobility allowance; (g) benefits payable under schemes made under the Old Cases Act; (h) reduced earnings allowance; (i) retirement allowance; (j) severe disablement allowance; (k) sickness benefit; (l) statutory sick pay; (m) unemployment benefit; (n) any increase in any of the benefits mentioned above, payable in accordance with the Social Security Acts

1 Administration of Justice Act 1982, s 11.
2 [1989] AC 807, [1988] 3 All ER 870, HL.

1975 to 1989 or the Old Cases Act or any regulation Council Order or Scheme made thereunder. It is only those benefits which have been paid during the relevant period which have to be deducted. The relevant periods are (a) in the case of disease, the period of five years beginning with the date from which the victim first claims the relevant benefit or (b) in any other case, the five years immediately following the date on which the accident or injury in question occurred.[1] However, it is further provided that, in the assessment of damages in respect of an accident, injury or disease, the amount of any relevant benefits paid or likely to be paid are to be disregarded. What this means is that any benefits paid *after* the relevant period are not to be deducted in quantifying the pursuer's loss.[2]

The major effect of the 1992 Act is therefore to abolish the provision that only one half of the specified benefits should be taken into account in assessing damages.[3] Under the new law *all* the benefits received by the pursuer during the relevant period are fully to be taken into account. Benefits received after the five-year period are not affected and are not to be taken into account. The position is therefore that both pursuers and defenders are worse off under the new legislation. As far as the pursuer is concerned, he is worse off by not keeping half the value of any sickness, invalidity or disablement benefit received during the relevant period and because the deduction is made from the total award of damages including *solatium* and not simply damages for patrimonial loss. However, he is better off in that after the relevant period, those benefits which would have previously been deducted in full when assessing damages under the rule in *Hodgson v Trapp*,[4] for example, attendance and mobility allowances, are no longer taken into account. The defender is worse off in that (i) he now pays the specified benefits in full during the relevant period whereas before he paid only half their value to the pursuer as damages and (ii) he can no longer take the advantage of the rule in *Hodgson v Trapp*, ie that the full value of other benefits paid to the pursuer would be deducted when assessing the damages. The only party who wins under the new regime is the Secretary of State for Social Security! However, where the total value of the compensation is less than £2,500, no deduction in respect of benefits paid during the relevant period is made.

1 Social Security Administration Act 1992, s 88(1).
2 Ie *Hodgson v Trapp* [1989] AC 807 is overruled.
3 See p 235 above.
4 Above.

C. PROVISIONAL AND INTERIM DAMAGES

The normal rule in actions of damages for personal injuries is that the damages are assessed once and for all at the date of proof. As a consequence, pursuers, hitherto, frequently delayed bringing proceedings for a considerable period until they could ascertain the full extent of their loss. Pursuers often therefore suffered hardship during the period between the accident and the date of proof. The situation was particularly unfair if the pursuer's physical condition was likely to deteriorate as a result of the injuries at some time in the future after the date of the proof. In *Stevenson v Pontifex and Wood*[1] the Lord President (Inglis) observed:[2]

'I hold the true rule of practice based on sound principle to be, that though the delict . . . be of such a nature that it will necessarily be followed by injurious consequences in the future, or though it may for this reason be impossible to ascertain with precise accuracy at the date of the action . . . the amount of loss which will result, yet the whole damage must be recovered in one action.'[3]

A pursuer's position in these circumstances has, to some extent, been alleviated by section 12 of the Administration of Justice Act 1982, which provides that the court is entitled to make an award of provisional damages in respect of personal injuries. Such an award can be made when it is proved, or admitted, that there is a risk that at some definite or indefinite time in the future, the pursuer will, as a result of the act or omission of the defender, which gave rise to the cause of the action, develop some serious disease or some serious deterioration in his physical or mental condition.[4] Provisional damages can only be awarded where the defender was, at the time of the accident giving rise to the cause of action, either a public authority or an insured person.[5] The purpose of this provision is therefore to give the pursuer an opportunity to claim damages in circumstances where his position is likely to worsen but where he cannot assess the full extent of his loss because the condition will take some time to deteriorate.

Before an award of provisional damages can be made, the pursuer

---

1 (1887) 15 R 125.
2 (1887) 15 R 125 at 129.
3 See also *Dunlop v McGowans* 1979 SC 22, 1979 SLT 34 at 39 per the Lord Justice-Clerk (Wheatley).
4 Administration of Justice Act 1982, s 12(1)(a).
5 Ibid, s 12(1)(b).

must establish that there is a risk[1] that at some time in the future he will develop some serious disease or some serious deterioration in his physical or mental condition. While assessment of the risk may be difficult,[2] nevertheless it is clear that the risk must be more than *de minimis*.[3] There must be evidence that there is the possibility of a *serious* deterioration in the pursuer's condition.[4] If, for example, the pursuer's health or disability will incrementally become worse, there is no grounds for an award of provisional damages, because there is no 'clear cut and severable threshold'[4] when the pursuer could apply for damages in the future on the basis that a serious deterioration had in fact taken place.[5] While the deterioration must be as a consequence of the delictual act or omission of the defender that led to the pursuer's personal injuries in the first place, nevertheless in deciding whether or not the deterioration is serious, account must be taken of the effect of such deterioration upon the pursuer's physical abilities in the context of his ordinary life: 'Seriousness cannot be assessed in a vacuum'.[6] Damages can only be deferred in respect of the serious deterioration in the pursuer's condition.[7]

Even if the pursuer satisfies the statutory criteria, the court is not obliged to defer the award of damages. The interests of the defender in not being called upon to pay further damages at some indefinite time in the future must also be considered.[8] Accordingly, an application for provisional damages is unlikely to be successful, unless the medical evidence establishes that the deterioration is likely to take place in, say, a period of not more than ten years. Moreover, the court has the discretion to stipulate a time limit after which the pursuer is unable to claim further damages for a deterioration in his condition.[9] In *McColl v Barnes*,[10] for example, where it was established that there was a risk

---

1 Cf the approach of the Lord Ordinary (Devaird) who suggested (obiter) that if there was no risk but a certainty that there would be a deterioration, this would *not* be a suitable case for provisional damages: *Prentice v William Thyne Ltd* 1989 SLT 336 at 337.
2 *Potter v McCulloch* 1987 SLT 308, OH at 310 per the Lord Ordinary (Weir)
3 *White v Inveresk Paper Co Ltd (No.2)* 1988 SLT 2 at 6 per the Lord Ordinary (Murray).
4 1988 SLT 2 at 5. See also *Potter v McCulloch* 1987 SLT 308 at 310 per the Lord Ordinary (Weir); *Meek v Burton's Gold Medal (Biscuits) Ltd* 1989 SLT 338 at 339 per the Lord Ordinary (Prosser).
5 See also *Prentice v William Thyne Ltd* 1989 SLT 336 ('clear and sensible threshold'); *Robertson v British Bakeries Ltd* 1991 SLT 434 ('recognisable threshold').
6 *Robertson v British Bakeries Ltd* 1991 SLT 434 at 439 per the Lord Ordinary (Osborne).
7 *Meek v Burton's Gold Medal Biscuits Ltd* 1989 SLT 338.
8 *Paterson v Costain Mining Ltd* 1988 SCLR 70, 1988 SLT 413.
9 Administration of Justice Act 1982, s 12(2).
10 1991 SCLR 907, 1992 SLT 1188; see also *Lappin v Britannia Airways Ltd* 1989 SLT 181 (five years).

that post-traumatic epilepsy might occur within seven years of the date of the accident, the pursuer was allowed to apply within that period for a further award of damages if the risk should in fact materialise. In the course of his judgment, the Lord Ordinary (Morrison) said:[1]

'In my opinion this is a most appropriate case for such an order to be made. An assessment made to reflect the possibility of the condition occurring would be unrealistic and impracticable. If no assessment were made and the risk were to materialise, the pursuer would be unjustly deprived of compensation for a serious injury which would be a result of the accident. Since the additional risk becomes negligible after a period of seven years from the date of the accident I shall restrict the order . . . to that period. . .'

The court is also entitled to award interim damages. Interim damages are to be distinguished from provisional damages in so far as they do not depend upon a pursuer suffering from a continuing disability, the eventual seriousness of which cannot be ascertained. Interim payments can be made in the Court of Session in terms of Rule of Court 89A(1) and will be awarded if the court is satisfied that the defender or defenders have admitted liability or that if the action proceeded to proof the pursuer would succeed in a question of liability without any substantial finding of contributory negligence on his part.[2] An interim award is taken into account in making the final award and will not be made against the defender unless that defender is either a person who is insured in respect of the pursuer's claim or is a public authority or 'is a person whose means and resources are such as to enable him to make interim payment'.

Any award of damages can be reduced on the grounds of contributory negligence.[3] Damages in respect of death[4] and defamation and verbal injury[5] have already been discussed.

D. PRESCRIPTION AND LIMITATION[6]

A pursuer may lose his right to obtain reparation if he does not begin proceedings against the defender within certain prescribed periods.

---

1 1992 SLT 1188 at 1190.
2 See, for example, *Hutcheson v Ascosmit Co* 1992 SLT 1115.
3 See pp 125 ff above.
4 See pp 191 ff above.
5 See Chapter 15.
6 See generally D M Walker *The Law of Prescription and Limitation of Actions in Scotland* (4th edn, 1990, Greens).

By section 6 of the Prescription and Limitation (Scotland) Act 1973[1] the obligation to make reparation for a delictual act[2] is extinguished after five years. The five year prescriptive runs from the date on which the delict is complete, ie when the pursuer suffers *damnum*.

'The right to raise such an action acrues when *injuria* concurs with *damnum*. Some interval of time may elapse between the two . . . and . . . in such circumstances time is to run from the date when *damnum* results, not from the earlier date of *injuria*.'[3]

This can nevertheless cause injustice in cases where the damage suffered is latent and the pursuer does not discover that, for example, his house is unstable as a result of defective foundations until five or more years after the damage was in fact sustained.

There are, however, important exceptions to the general rule. First, liability for defective products under Part I of the Consumer Protection Act 1987[4] is extinguished after 10 years.[5] Delictual liability in respect of personal injuries or death[6] and liability for defamation or verbal injury[7] prescribe after 20 years.[8] However, while these obligations are not extinguished until after 10 and 20 years respectively, the pursuer must bring a claim for reparation within a period of three years. This is known as a limitation period. If the action is not commenced within the three year period, the pursuer cannot enforce his rights unless the defender waives his right to defend the action on the ground that the limitation period has expired.

In the case of personal injuries or property damage as a result of a defective product, the action is not competent if it is brought after a period of three years from the date when the pursuer knew that it was reasonably practicable for him to be aware that there was a defect in the product, that the injury or damage was caused by the product, that the injury or damage was sufficiently serious to bring an action for reparation and that the defender was liable under section 2 of the Consumer Protection Act 1987.[9] A similar limitation period applies to actions brought in relation to death caused by a defective product.[10]

---

1 In this section references are to the 1973 Act unless otherwise stated.
2 Sch 1 (1)(d).
3 *Dunlop v McGowans* 1980 SLT 129 at 132–133 per Lord Keith of Kinkel; see also *Renfrew Golf Club v Ravenstone Securities Ltd* 1984 SLT 170.
4 See Chapter 8.
5 s 22A; Sch 1(2) (ggg). In this case the 10 years run from the date the product is first put on the market, not the date when the *damnum* occurs.
6 Sch 1(2) (g).
7 Sch 1(2) (gg).
8 s 7.
9 s 22 B.
10 s 22A.

In respect of defamation actions, it is simply stated that the three-year limitation period runs from the date when the right of action accrued.[1]

An action for damages for personal injuries must commence within three years from the date on which the injuries were sustained.[2] However, the three-year period does not begin to run from the date when the injuries were sustained unless it was reasonably practicable for the pursuer to be aware of all the following facts viz that the injuries were sufficiently serious to bring an action of damages; that the injuries were caused by an act or omission; and that the defender was responsible for the act or omission. So, for example, where a pursuer sustained personal injury as a result of the defender's delictual conduct, but the pursuer did not know that he was injured, as in the case of an insidious disease, the three-year period only begins to run when it was reasonably practicable for him to realise that the illness was attributable to the defender's acts or omissions ie when he knows he is ill. Similarly, the three-year period will only begin when the pursuer knows that the defender is responsible for the delictual conduct; if this knowledge arises after the date when the injuries were sustained, the three-year period only begins to run from the later date. A similar limitation period applies to actions for damages brought in relation to death which has resulted from personal injuries.[3] In all these limitation periods, time does not run against a pursuer who is or was under legal disability by reason of non-age or unsoundness of mind.[4]

However, in the case of the limitation periods in respect of actions for damages in respect of personal injuries or death from personal injuries *and* actions for defamation or verbal injury, the court has a discretion to allow the action to proceed outwith the three-year period if 'it seems equitable to do so'.[5] All the circumstances of the case are taken into consideration, including the length of time in bringing the action, whether the pursuer was responsible for the delay, whether there is an action available against the pursuer's solicitor if the solicitor was responsible for the delay, the inconvenience to the defender etc.[6] The issue is entirely a matter for the discretion of the presiding judge. In

---

1 s 18A(1).
2 s 17(1) and (2). If the act or omission which caused the injuries was continuing, the three-year period runs from the date when the injuries were sustained or the date when the act or omission ceased, whichever is later.
3 s 18.
4 ss 17(3), 18(3), 18A(2), 22B(4), 22C(3).
5 s 19A.
6 For examples, see *McCullough v Norwest Socea* 1981 SLT 201; *Carson v Howard Doris* 1981 SC 278, 1981 SLT 273; *Donald v Rutherford* 1983 SLT 253, 1984 SLT 70; *Whyte v Walker* 1983 SLT 441.

practice, the power is used sparingly in claims for personal injuries or death from personal injuries as a result of the knowledge provisions which have to be satisfied before the three-year limitation period begins to run.[1]

1 See p 241 above.

Appendix

Damages (Scotland) Act 1976 (c13)

ARRANGEMENT OF SECTIONS

1. Rights of relatives of a deceased person

(1) Where a person dies in consequence of personal injuries sustained by him as a result of an act or omission of another person, being an act or omission giving rise to liability to pay damages to the

injured person or his executor, then, subject to the following provisions of this Act, the person liable to pay those damages (in this section referred to as 'the responsible person') shall also be liable to pay damages in accordance with this section to any relative of the deceased, being a relative within the meaning of Schedule 1 to this Act.

(2) No liability shall arise under this section if the liability to the deceased or his executor in respect of the act or omission has been excluded or discharged (whether by antecedent agreement or otherwise) by the deceased before his death, or is excluded by virtue of any enactment.

(3) The damages which the responsible person shall be liable to pay to a relative of a deceased under this section shall (subject to the provisions of this Act) be such as will compensate the relative for any loss of support suffered by him since the date of the deceased's death or likely to be suffered by him as a result of the act or omission in question, together with any reasonable expense incurred by him in connection with the deceased's funeral.

(4) If the relative is a member of the deceased's immediate family (within the meaning of section 10(2) of this Act) there shall be awarded, without prejudice to any claim under subsection (3) above, such sum of damages, if any, as the court thinks just by way of compensation for the loss of [all or any of the following—
  (a) distress and anxiety endured by the relative in contemplation of the suffering of the deceased before his death;
  (b) grief and sorrow of the relative caused by the deceased's death;
  (c) the loss of such non-patrimonial benefit as the relative might have been expected to derive from the deceased's society and guidance if the deceased had not died,
and the court in making an award under this subsection shall not be required to ascribe specifically any part of the award to any of paragraphs (a), (b) and (c) above.]

(5) [Subject to subsection (5A) below] in assessing for the purposes of this section the amount of any loss of support suffered by a relative of a deceased no account shall be taken of—
  (a) any patrimonial gain or advantage which has accrued or will or may accrue to the relative from the deceased or from any other person by way of succession or settlement;
  (b) any insurance money, benefit, pension or gratuity which has been, or will be or may be, paid as a result of the deceased's death;
and in this subsection—

'benefit' means benefit under the Social Security Act 1975 or the Social Security (Northern Ireland) Act 1975, and any payment by a friendly society or trade union for the relief or maintenance of a member's dependants;
'insurance money' includes a return of premiums; and
'pension' includes a return of contributions and any payment of a lump sum in respect of a person's employment.

[(5A) Where a deceased has been awarded a provisional award of damages under section 12(2) of the Administration of Justice Act 1982, the making of that award does not prevent liability from arising under this section but in assessing for the purposes of this section the amount of any loss of support suffered by a relative of the deceased the court shall take into account such part of the provisional award relating to future patrimonial loss as was intended to compensate the deceased for a period beyond the date on which he died.]

(6) In order to establish loss of support for the purposes of this section it shall not be essential for a claimant to show that the deceased was, or might have become, subject to a duty in law to provide or contribute to the support of the claimant; but if any such fact is established it may be taken into account in determining whether, and if so to what extent, the deceased, if he had not died, would have been likely to provide or contribute to such support.

(7) Except as provided in this section [or in Part II of the Administration of Justice Act 1982] [or under section 1 of the International Transport Conventions Act 1983] no person shall be entitled by reason of relationship to damages (including damages by way of solatium) in respect of the death of another person.

NOTES to section 1
Sub-s (3): See the Administration of Justice Act 1982 (c 53), s 9(2).
Sub-s (4): Words substituted by the Damages (Scotland) Act 1993 (c 5), s 1(1).
Sub-s (5): Words added by the Damages (Scotland) Act 1993 (c 5), s 1(2).
Sub-s (5A): Sub-s added by the Damages (Scotland) Act 1993 (c 5), s 1(3).
Sub-s (7): Words added by the Administration of Justice Act 1982 (c 53), s 14(1); and the International Transport Conventions Act 1983 (c 14), Sch 1, para 4(a).

[1A. Transmissibility to executor of rights of deceased relative

Any right to damages under any provision of section 1 of this Act which is vested in the relative concerned immediately before his death shall be transmitted to the relative's executor; but, in determining the amount of damages payable to an executor by virtue of this section, the court shall have regard only to the period ending immediately before the relative's death.]

NOTES to section 1A
Section added by the Damages (Scotland) Act 1993 (c 5), s 2.

[2. Rights transmitted to executor in respect of deceased person's injuries

(1) Subject to the following provisions of this section, there shall be transmitted to the executor of a deceased person the like rights to damages in respect of personal injuries (including a right to damages by way of solatium) sustained by the deceased as were vested in him immediately before his death.

(2) There shall not be transmitted to the executor under this section a right to damages by way of compensation for patrimonial loss attributable to any period after the deceased's death.

(3) In determining the amount of damages by way of solatium payable to an executor by virtue of this section, the court shall have regard only to the period ending immediately before the deceased's death.

(4) In so far as a right to damages vested in the deceased comprised a right to damages (other than for patrimonial loss) in respect of injury resulting from defamation or any other verbal injury or other injury to reputation sustained by the deceased, that right shall be transmitted to the deceased's executor only if an action to enforce that right had been brought by the deceased before his death and had not been concluded by then within the meaning of section 2A(2) of this Act.]

NOTES to section 2
Section substituted by the Damages (Scotland) Act 1993 (c 5), s 3.

[2A. Enforcement by executor of rights transmitted to him

(1) For the purpose of enforcing any right transmitted to an executor under section 1A or 2 of this Act the executor shall be entitled—
  (a) to bring an action; or
  (b) if an action for that purpose had been brought by the deceased but had not been concluded before his death, to be sisted as pursuer in that action.

(2) For the purpose of subsection (1) above, an action shall not be taken to be concluded while any appeal is competent or before any appeal taken has been disposed of.]

NOTES to section 2A
Section added by the Damages (Scotland) Act 1993 (c 5), s 4.

3. . . .

NOTES to section 3
Section repealed by the Damages (Scotland) Act 1993 (c 5), s 7(3).

4. Executor's claim not to be excluded by relatives' claim: and vice versa

A claim by the executor of a deceased person for damages under secvtion 2 of this Act is not excluded by the making of a claim by a relative of the deceased for damages under section 1 of this Act; [or by a deceased relative's executor under section 1A of this Act; nor is a claim by a relative of a deceased person or by a deceased relative's executor for damages under the said section 1 or (as the case may be) the said section 1A] excluded by the making of a claim by the deceased's executor for damages under the said section 2. . . .

NOTES to section 4
Words added by the Damages (Scotland) Act 1993 (c 5), s 7(2), Sch, para 1.
Words repealed by the Administration of Justice Act 1982 (c 53), s 14(2)(a).

5. . . .

NOTES to section 5
Section repealed by the Administration of Justice Act 1982 (c 53), Sch 9, Pt 1.

6. Limitation of total amount of liability

(1) Where in any action to which [this section] applies, so far as directed against any defender, it is shown that by antecedent agreement, compromise or otherwise, the liability arising in relation to that defender from the personal injuries in question had, before the deceased's death, been limited to damages of a specified or ascertainable amount, or where that liability is so limited by virtue of any enactment nothing in this Act shall make the defender liable to pay damages exceeding that amount; and accordingly where in such an action there are two or more pursuers any damages to which they would respectively be entitled under this Act apart from the said limitation shall, if necessary, be reduced *pro rata*.

(2) Where two or more such actions are conjoined, the conjoined actions shall be treated for the purposes of this section as if they were a single action.

[(3) This section applies an any action in which, following the death of any person from personal injuries, damages are claimed—
  (a) by the executor of the deceased, in respect of the injuries from which the deceased died;
  (b) in respect of the death of the deceased, by any relative of his] [or, if the relative has died, by the relative's executor.]

NOTES to section 6
Sub-s (1): Words substituted by the Administration of Justice Act 1982 (c 53), s 14(2)(b)(i).
Sub-s (3): Sub-s added by the Administration of Justice Act 1982 (c 53), s 14(2)(b)(ii).
Sub-s (3)(b): Words added by the Damages (Scotland) Act 1993 (c 13), s 7(2), Sch, para 3.

---

7. Amendment of references in other Acts

In any Act passed before this Act, unless the context otherwise requires, any reference to solatium in respect of the death of any person (however expressed) shall be construed as a reference to a loss of society award within the meaning of section 1 of this Act; and any reference to a dependant of a deceased person, in relation to an action claiming damages in respect of the deceased person's death, shall be construed as including a reference to a relative of the deceased person within the meaning of this Act.

8. Abolition of right to assythment

After the commencement of this Act no person shall in any circumstances have a right to assythment, and accordingly any action claiming that remedy shall (to the extent that it does so) be incompetent.

9. Damages due to injured person for patrimonial loss caused by personal injuries whereby expectation of life is diminished

(1) This section applies to any action for damages in respect of personal injuries sustained by the pursuer where his expected date of death is earlier than it would have been if he had not sustained the injuries.

(2) In assessing, in any action to which this section applies, the amount of any patrimonial loss in respect of the period after the date of decree—

(a) it shall be assumed that the pursuer will live until the date when he would have been expected to die if he had not sustained the injuries (hereinafter referred to as the 'notional date of death');

(b) the court may have regard to any amount, whether or not it is an amount related to earnings by the pursuer's own labour or other gainful activity, which in its opinion the pursuer, if he had not sustained the injuries in question, would have received in the period up to his notional date of death by way of benefits in money or money's worth, being benefits derived from sources other than the pursuer's own estate;

(c) the court shall have regard to any diminution of any such amount as aforesaid by virtue of expenses which in the opinion of the court the pursuer, if he had not sustained the injuries in question, would reasonably have incurred in the said period by way of living expenses.

[9A. Solatium for loss of expectation of life

(1) In assessing, in an action for damages in respect of personal injuries, the amount of damages by way of solatium, the court shall, if—

(a) the injured person's expectation of life has been reduced by the injuries; and

(b) the injured person is, was at any time or is likely to become, aware of that reduction, have regard to the extent that, in consequence of that awareness, he has suffered or is likely to suffer.

(2) Subject to subsection (1) above, no damages by way of solatium shall be recoverable in respect of loss of expectation of life.

(3) The court in making an award of damages by way of solatium shall not be required to ascribe specifically any part of the award to loss of expectation of life.]

NOTES to section 9A
Section added by the Damages (Scotland) Act 1993 (c 5), s 5.

---

10. Interpretation

(1) In this Act, unless the context otherwise requires—

. . .

'personal injuries' includes any disease or any impairment of a person's physical or mental condition [and injury resulting from defamation or any other verbal injury or other injury to reputation]; 'relative', in relation to a deceased person, has the meaning assigned to it by Schedule 1 to this Act.

(2) References in this Act to a member of a deceased person's immediate family are references to any relative of his who falls within subparagraph (a), [(aa),] (b) or (c) of paragraph 1 of Schedule 1 to this Act.

(3) References in this Act to any other Act are references to that Act as amended, extended or applied by any other enactment, including this Act.

NOTES to section 10
Sub-s (1): Words repealed by the Damages (Scotland) Act 1993 (c 5), s 7(3); and words added by the Damages (Scotland) Act 1993 (c 13), s 7(2), Sch, para 3.
Sub-s (2): Word added by the Administration of Justice Act 1982 (c 53), s 14(4).

11. . . .

NOTES to section 11
Section repealed by the Damages (Scotland) Act 1993 (c 5), s 7(3).

12. Citation, application to Crown, commencement and extent

(1) This Act may be cited as the Damages (Scotland) Act 1976.

(2) This Act binds the Crown.

(3) . . .

(4) . . .

(5) This Act extends to Scotland only.

NOTES to section 12
Sub-ss (3), (4): Sub-ss repealed by the Damages (Scotland) Act 1993 (c 5), s 7(3).

SCHEDULES

SCHEDULE 1

DEFINITION OF 'RELATIVE'

1. In this Act 'relative' in relation to a deceased person includes—

(a) any person who immediately before the deceased's death was the spouse of the deceased;

[(aa) any person, not being the spouse of the deceased, who was, immediately before the deceased's death, living with the deceased as husband or wife;]

(b) any person who was a parent or child of the deceased;

(c) any person not falling within paragraph (b) above who was accepted by the deceased as a child of his family;

(d) any person who was an ascendant or descendant (other than a parent or child) of the deceased;

(e) any person who was, or was the issue of, a brother, sister, uncle or aunt of the deceased; and

(f) any person who, having been a spouse of the deceased, had ceased to be so by virtue of a divorce;

but does not include any other person.

2. In deducing any relationship for the purposes of the foregoing paragraph—

(a) any relationship by affinity shall be treated as a relationship by consanguinity; any relationship of the half blood shall be treated as a relationship of the whole blood; and the step-child of any person shall be treated as his child; and

[(b) section 1(1) of the Law Reform (Parent and Child) (Scotland) Act 1986 shall apply; and any reference (however expressed) in this Act to a relative shall be construed accordingly.]

NOTES to Schedule 1
Para 1(aa): Sub-para added by the Administration of Justice Act 1982 (c 53), s 14(4).
Para 2(b): Sub-para substituted by the Law Reform (Parent and Child) (Scotland) Act 1986 (c 9), Sch 1, para 15.

SCHEDULE 2

***

NOTES to Schedule 2
Schedule repealed by the Damages (Scotland) Act 1993 (c 5), s 7(3).

Index